Mac OS X 10.6 Snow Leopard

Peachpit Learning Series

Mac OS X 10.6 Snow Leopard

Robin Williams with John Tollett

 **Peachpit Press**

Mac OS X 10.6 Snow Leopard: Peachpit Learning Series

ROBIN WILLIAMS WITH JOHN TOLLETT

Copyright ©2010 Robin Williams and John Tollett

Peachpit Press
1249 Eighth Street
Berkeley, CA 94710
510.524.2178   voice
510.524.2221   fax

Find us on the web at www.peachpit.com
To report errors, please send a note to errata@peachpit.com
Peachpit Press is a division of Pearson Education

Editor: Nikki McDonald
Interior layout design: Kim Scott and Robin Williams
Production: John Tollett
Compositor: John Tollett

ISBN 13: 978-0-321-63538-9
ISBN 10:   0-321-63538-8
10 9 8 7 6 5 4 3 2 1
Printed and bound in the United States of America

It's great to be Mac users.

Robin and John

Contents at a Glance

Contents

Contents

MAC OS X APPLICATIONS IN SNOW LEOPARD

Contents

MAKE IT **YOUR OWN MAC**

TECH STUFF

THE END **MATTERS**

Mac OS X Basics for New Mac Users

1

GOALS

Become familiar and
comfortable with the
Desktop and Finder

Get to know the Finder
windows and how
to use them

Create your own folders

Understand the Dock

Use the Trash basket

Know how and when to
use keyboard shortcuts

Learn to watch for tool tips
and other visual clues

Know where to go for
more information

Introduction to the Mac OS X Desktop

If you have a Mac running Snow Leopard (Mac OS X version 10.6), you're ready to jump right in! In this lesson you'll become familiar with using the basic features of your Mac and its Desktop/Finder.

This book assumes you are familiar with how to operate a computer—how to use a mouse, select items from menus, distinguish one icon from another, move files and folders and windows around, how and why to save the documents you create, etc. If you're brand new to computers in general, we strongly suggest you use *The Little Mac Book, Snow Leopard Edition* before you read this book—*The Little Mac Book* introduces you to using a computer in much more detail and at a much slower pace than this book.

Get to Know your Desktop and Finder

When you turn on your Mac, you'll always see your **Desktop,** shown below. This is also called the **Finder,** although technically the Finder is the application that runs the Desktop. Whenever you see a direction that tells you to go to the Desktop or to the Finder, this is where you need to go.

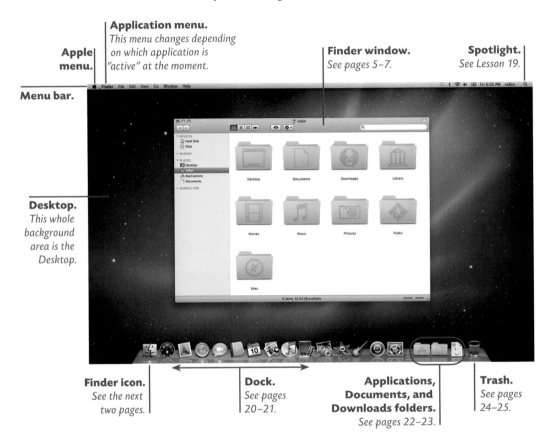

Apple menu.

Application menu.
This menu changes depending on which application is "active" at the moment.

Finder window.
See pages 5–7.

Spotlight.
See Lesson 19.

Menu bar.

Desktop.
This whole background area is the Desktop.

Finder icon.
See the next two pages.

Dock.
See pages 20–21.

Applications, Documents, and Downloads folders.
See pages 22–23.

Trash.
See pages 24–25.

> **TIP** —— Because of the way the computer works, you might see the Desktop but not actually be in the Finder. Get in the habit of checking the application menu (shown top-left and on the opposite page). When you are really in the Finder or at the Desktop, the application menu will show "Finder."

> **TIP** —— To enable an uncluttered Desktop appearance, the "Hard Disk" icon (shown in the top-right corner) is not visible by default in Snow Leopard. If you're used to seeing it there and want to bring it back, see page 274.

Make sure you can get to the Desktop or Finder whenever necessary

As you work on your Mac, you will be using a number of applications in which you'll create your documents, but you'll often want to go back to the Finder, which is like home base. The name of the *active* application, the one that's currently open and available to use (including the Finder), will always be displayed in the application menu. Keep an eye on that menu.

To go to the Finder at any time, do one of these things:

- Single-click on any blank area of the Desktop.

- Single-click on any Finder window (shown below) that you see.

- Single-click the Finder icon in the Dock (shown on the opposite page).

Check to make sure the **application menu** says "Finder," as shown circled below.

Get to Know your Home and its Folders

When you open a Finder window, it usually opens to the Home window, as shown below. You can tell it's Home because your user name and the little house icon are in the title bar. It can be confusing that the Home icon isn't labeled "Home"—it's labeled with the "short name" that was chosen when the computer was first turned on and set up. In the example below, the Home icon is named "robin."

- **To open a Finder window,** single-click on the Finder icon (shown to the left) in the Dock (the Dock is that row of icons that is usually found across the bottom of your screen).

  If the window that opens doesn't display your Home folders, as shown below, single-click the Home icon you see in the Sidebar.

Your Home window displays a number of special folders. Do not change the names of these folders or throw them away unless you are very clear on what you're doing and why you're making that choice! For now, just let them be.

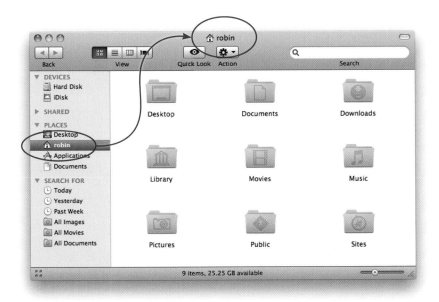

TIP ——— If several people use your Mac, or if you occasionally have a guest who wants to use it, you can create individual Homes for each user; everyone's files will be perfectly safe from any other user. See Lesson 18 for information about multiple users.

What each folder in your Home window is for

Desktop This folder holds any files that might be sitting directly on the Desktop (see page 4). Putting files on the Desktop is like keeping them on your office desk instead of putting them in a filing cabinet. Having this folder to hold the same files means you can get to them when you're not actually at the Desktop, as when you want to open a file from within an application.

Documents At first, your Mac makes sure every document you create is safely tucked into this Documents folder. Later, you can create your own folders (see pages 10–11) and store your documents in them.

Downloads This folder holds most of the files that you download through Bonjour, iChat, or the Internet. Files that come to you through email will also end up here if you click the "Save" button in an email message. The Downloads folder in the Dock holds the exact same files.

Library This folder is used by the operating system. *Do not rename this folder, do not throw it away, do not take anything out of it, and do not put anything in it* unless you know exactly what you are doing. Just ignore it for now. For details, see page 39.

Movies The iMovie application uses this folder to automatically store the files necessary for creating the movies you make.

Music The iTunes application uses this folder to automatically keep track of all the music files you buy and all of your playlists.

Pictures The iPhoto application uses this folder to automatically keep track of all your photos and albums.

Public You'll use this folder to share files with other people who also use (or access) your Mac, as explained in Lesson 18.

Sites You can create a web site, store it in this folder, and share it with anyone on the Internet. (Directions for that process are not in this book!)

TIP —— You can have as many Finder windows open as you like. This makes it easier to move files from one window to another. **To open another window,** make sure you are at the Finder (see pages 4–5), then go to the File menu and choose "New Finder Window."

Get to Know your Finder Window

Below, you see a typical **Finder window.** This is called a *Finder* window to distinguish it from similar (but different) windows you will use in your applications. The following pages go into further detail about this very important window.

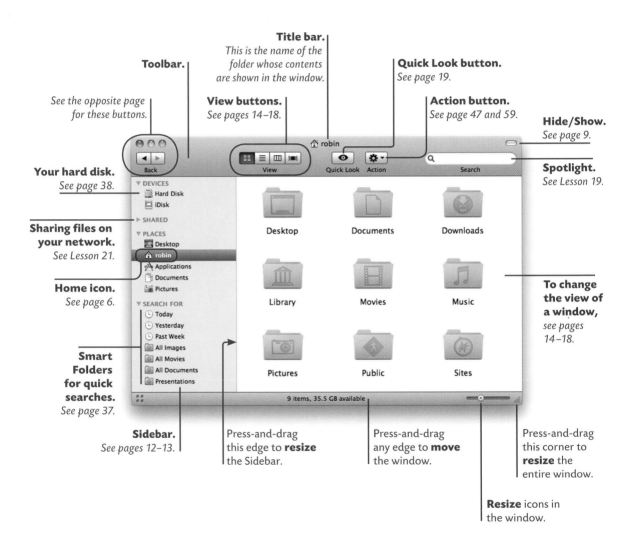

Title bar.
This is the name of the folder whose contents are shown in the window.

Quick Look button.
See page 19.

Toolbar.

See the opposite page for these buttons.

View buttons.
See pages 14–18.

Action button.
See page 47 and 59.

Hide/Show.
See page 9.

Your hard disk.
See page 38.

Sharing files on your network.
See Lesson 21.

Home icon.
See page 6.

Smart Folders for quick searches.
See page 37.

Spotlight.
See Lesson 19.

To change the view of a window,
see pages 14–18.

Sidebar.
See pages 12–13.

Press-and-drag this edge to **resize** the Sidebar.

Press-and-drag any edge to **move** the window.

Press-and-drag this corner to **resize** the entire window.

Resize icons in the window.

Use the buttons in the Finder Window

There are several buttons in the Toolbar of every Finder window.

Red, yellow, and green buttons

● Single-click the **red button to *close*** the window.

● Single-click the **yellow button to *minimize*** the window, which sends a tiny icon down into the Dock, on the right side. Try it.

To open that window again, single-click its icon in the Dock.

● Single-click the **green button to *resize*** the window bigger or smaller.

Back and Forward buttons

These buttons go back and forward through the contents of windows you have viewed (just like the back and forward buttons on web pages). Every time you open a new window, these buttons start over.

Hide/Show the Toolbar and Sidebar

In the upper-right corner of every Finder window is a small gray button. Single-click this button to hide the Toolbar and the Sidebar, as shown below. When you double-click on a folder while the Toolbar and Sidebar are hidden, a new and separate window will open. Try it. **To show the Toolbar and Sidebar again,** click the small gray button again.

Hide/show the Toolbar and Sidebar.

Resize the icons in the window.

TIP — If you *always* want a new and separate window to open, change your Finder preferences; see pages 274–277.

Create your Own Folders

At any time, you can create your own **folders** where you can **store** your documents and **organize** your files. For instance, you might want a folder in which to store all your financial documents. And another folder for all your newsletter files. And yet another for the screenplays you're writing. All of these documents *could* go inside the Documents folder, but that's like putting every document in your office in one big manila folder.

Use digital folders on your Mac as you would use manila folders in a metal filing cabinet. See pages 48–49 for tips on how to save files directly into your custom folders.

■ **To make a new folder,** go to the File menu and choose "New Folder." The new folder appears *inside the window whose name is in the title bar* (shown circled, below). That is, if you want to put the new folder into the Documents folder, first open the Documents folder before you make a new one.

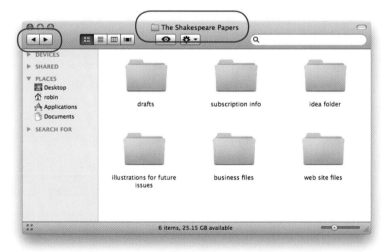

In my Documents folder, I made a new folder called "The Shakespeare Papers." Inside that folder, I made these six new folders.

■ **To rename a folder:**

1 Single-click the folder to select it.

untitled folder

This is a new, untitled folder.

This folder is highlighted, or selected.

2 Then single-click directly on the name to highlight the name (you'll see a blue outline around the name).

This folder is ready for a new name.

3 Type to replace the existing name. (You don't need to delete the original name first.)

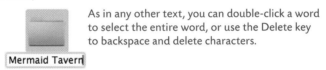

Mermaid Tavern

As in any other text, you can double-click a word to select the entire word, or use the Delete key to backspace and delete characters.

4 Hit Return or Enter to set the name.

Mermaid Tavern

Mermaid Tavern

Click on any blank spot in the Finder window to unhighlight the folder.

■ **To open a folder,** double-click it.

■ **To go back** to the contents of the previous folder, single-click the left-pointing triangle, called the Back button (circled on the opposite page).

■ **To move a folder,** just drag it to another window or another folder.

Take Advantage of the Sidebar

The **Sidebar** of every Finder window is customizable—you can add or remove any folder or document as often as you like. Items in the Sidebar are always *aliases,* or icons that merely *represent* the real file. This means you can delete an icon from the Sidebar and it does not delete the actual file that it represents.

As shown below, each of the current icons in the Sidebar actually represents a file or folder somewhere else on your hard disk.

Because a folder or document in the Sidebar is a *picture* (alias) of the real thing, you can put files into the icon in the Sidebar (just drag them in and drop them) *or* into the original folder and they go to the same place. **Try it:** Drop a file into the Documents folder in the Sidebar, then open the Documents folder in the Home window and you'll see the new document.

Add a folder or document to the Sidebar. This makes it easier to put other files into that folder, and it makes a document easier to open (just single-click it). It's easier also when you are working in an application and want to save a file, because the folder shows in the sidebar of Open and Save dialogs (see pages 48–49).

- **To add a folder or document to the Sidebar,** simply drag the icon from any window or from the Desktop and drop it into the Sidebar.

- Use the Finder preferences to add hard disk icons and more; see page 266.

Remove folder or document icons from the Sidebar that you don't use. Don't worry—removing the picture of a folder from the Sidebar does not throw away the original folder nor anything in it!

- **To remove an item from the Sidebar,** simply press on it with the mouse and drag it out of the Sidebar. Let go when the mouse pointer is on the Desktop. As you can see below, the icon disappears in a puff of smoke. Notice that although I removed the Pictures folder from the Sidebar, the original Pictures folder is still safe and sound in the Home window.

Customize the Sidebar to contain just the items you want to see. Click on the Desktop to make the Finder the current active application, then from the Finder menu (next to the Apple icon), choose "Preferences…." Click the "Sidebar" icon in the toolbar (circled, above-right), then checkmark the items you want to show in the Sidebar, and uncheck items that you don't want. If you uncheck all items in a category, such as "Search For," the entire category, including the header, disappears from the Finder window sidebar.

Change the View of the Finder Window

You can change how the items inside any window are displayed. That is, you can show them as icons, as a list of items, in columns of information, or in a slideshow-like view. You might prefer one view for certain things and a different view for others—with the click of a button, you can switch from one to the other. Experiment with the **four different views** and decide for yourself how you like to work.

- ▪ **To change views,** single-click one of the four little View buttons.

 From left to right, the View buttons display Icon View, List View, Column View, Cover Flow view.

The Icon View

Obviously, this displays every file as an **icon,** or small picture. Double-click an icon to open it.

Icon View button

These folders are in my Home folder ("Robin," highlighted in the Sidebar).

Sidebar

Drag this slider to resize icons, up to 512 x 512 pixels.

Enhanced icon view: Enlarge the icons with the size slider for easy viewing. Multi-page documents and movies can be previewed right in the icon.

 Hover the pointer over the icon of a multi-page document. To browse through the pages, click the left and right arrows that appear at the bottom of the icon.

 Hover the pointer over the icon of a movie, then click the Play button that appears.

The List View

In the **List View,** you can organize the list of files alphabetically by names, by the dates the files were last modified, by what kind of items they are, and other options. You can also see the contents of more than one folder at once.

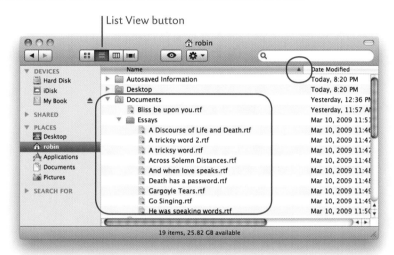

The **blue column heading** is a *visual clue* that the contents are organized, or "sorted," by that heading. You can see, above, that the files in this window are sorted by "Name." To organize the contents by the dates they were modified, their size or kind, single-click that column heading (you might have to open the window wider or drag the blue scroll bar to the right to see the other columns and headings).

The **tiny triangle** in the column heading (circled above) is a *visual clue* that tells you whether the information is sorted from first to last or last to first. Single-click the triangle to reverse the order. Try it.

In the List View, single-click vs. double-click:

 Folder icon: Single-click the **disclosure triangle** to the left of a folder to display its contents as a sublist, as shown circled above. You can view the contents of more than one folder at once.

 Double-click the **folder icon** to display its contents in the window, which will *replace* the contents you currently see in the window.

 Document icon: Double-click a document to open not only that document, but also the application it was created in.

Application icon: Double-click an application icon to open the application.

15

The Column View

Viewing a Finder window in **columns** allows you to see the contents of a selected folder or hard disk, and easily keep track of where each file is located. You can also view the contents of another folder without losing sight of the first one. This view helps you understand where everything is kept in your computer.

If you have photographs, graphic images, movies or PDFs in your folders, the last column displays **previews** of the items. You can even play a small movie in this preview column. Some documents can display previews as well.

Column View button

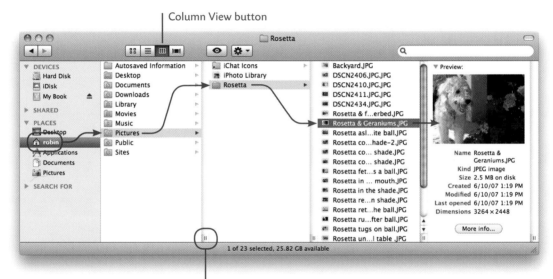

To resize an individual column, drag one of these "thumbs." Or double-click the thumb to atuomatically expand the column.

To resize all columns, Option-drag a thumb (hold down the Option key while you drag with the mouse).

You won't see a column to the right until you **single-click** a folder or a file—then a new column to the right appears to display the contents of that folder or a preview of the file. A triangle indicates that file is a folder that can contain other files.

In the example above, you can see that the "top level" folder is my Home folder, "robin." In "robin," I selected the folder "Pictures" (I clicked once on it) and in that folder I selected "Rosetta," and in that folder I selected "Rosetta & Geraniums.JPG," and the last column displays a preview of the selected file and information about it. (That's my dog.)

In the Column View, single-click files to display columns:

Documents ▶ **Folder icon:** Single-click a folder to display its contents in the column to the right. If there is no column to the right, one will appear.

Mabel.rtf **Document icon:** Single-click a document to see a preview in the column to the right. Not all documents can provide content previews, but the preview will at least give you information about that file.

Double-click a document to open not only that document, but also the application it was created in.

TextEdit.app **Application icon:** Single-click an application icon to preview information about it, such as its version and date of modification.

Double-click an application icon to open that application.

TIP —— You can customize many features about the Finder windows, such as the font size, the icon size, even the color inside the window. You can organize the List View by different columns of information, choose to turn off the preview in Column View, and more. See Lesson 15, Personalize Your Mac.

TIP —— No matter which view you are in, you can always open a folder into a **new, separate window:** Hold down the Command key and double-click any folder in any view.

The Cover Flow View

The Cover Flow View displays your files graphically in a slideshow-like format at the top of the window. You can click on the icons on either side of the center image to flip through them, drag the slider bar, click the triangles on the left or right side of the slider bar, or click the items in the list below the Cover Flow pane. You can even use the Arrow keys on your keyboard to move through the Cover Flow view.

For the columns below the Cover Flow pane, organize and use them just as you would in List View, as described on the previous pages.

Cover Flow View button.

Double-click an icon here to open that document or application.

While in Cover Flow view, single-click any item in the Sidebar to display it or its contents in the window.

Single-click an icon here to display it in the Cover Flow view window above.

Double-click an icon here to open that document or application.

Click the end triangles to navigate through the Cover Flow files, or drag the center slider bar.

Drag this "thumb grip" to enlarge the Cover Flow area of the window.

Quick Look/Slideshow button

The button in the toolbar with an eyeball on it is the **Quick Look/Slideshow** button. This is a terrific feature that lets you preview any file, photograph, graphic, PDF, or whatever. An image appears immediately in front of you and no application opens. With the click of the mouse, the preview disappears.

If you preview a text file, you can actually scroll through the document. If you preview a Keynote presentation, you'll see your slides and your notes. If you preview a PDF with lots of pages, you can scroll through the pages.

Once you have a Quick Look preview open, you can click on other files in the Finder and they will appear in that preview.

Select more than one file and your Quick Look automatically becomes a Slideshow with back and forward buttons.

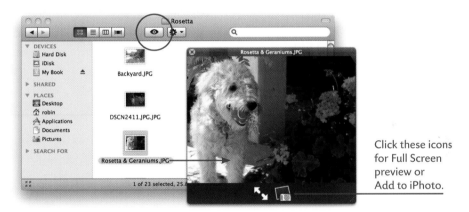

Click these icons for Full Screen preview or Add to iPhoto.

There are three other ways to open a Quick Look:

- Select files and hit the Spacebar *or* press Command Y.
- Select one or more items, go to the File menu, and choose "Quick Look *filename.*"
- Control-click (or right-click) and choose "Quick Look *filename.*"

Ways to put away a Quick Look:

- Hit the Spacebar *or* press Command Y.
- Click the **X** in the upper-left corner of the Quick Look window.
- Go to the File menu and choose "Close Quick Look."

Use the Dock

The **Dock** is that strip of icons across the bottom of the screen*. The specific icons that appear in the Dock will change as you open and close applications, view photos, or customize what's in the Dock. "Hover" your mouse over an icon (just position the pointer and hold it there, but don't click) to see a label appear that tells you the name of the application or file.

■ **To open an application or document** from the Dock, single-click its icon.

The **tiny blue light** underneath an icon indicates that particular application is open and available. Even if you don't see that application on your screen, you can single-click the Dock icon and that application comes forward, ready for you to work in. Keep an eye on the application menu (as explained on pages 4–5) to verify which application is "active" at any moment.

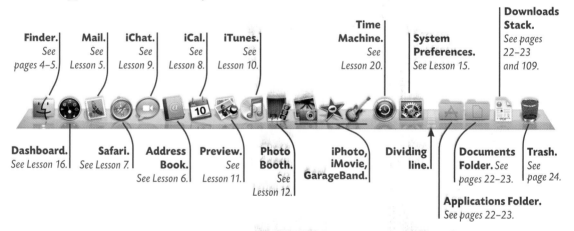

Finder. *See pages 4–5.* **Mail.** *See Lesson 5.* **iChat.** *See Lesson 9.* **iCal.** *See Lesson 8.* **iTunes.** *See Lesson 10.* **Time Machine.** *See Lesson 20.* **System Preferences.** *See Lesson 15.* **Downloads Stack.** *See pages 22–23 and 109.*

Dashboard. *See Lesson 16.* **Safari.** *See Lesson 7.* **Address Book.** *See Lesson 6.* **Preview.** *See Lesson 11.* **Photo Booth.** *See Lesson 12.* **iPhoto, iMovie, GarageBand.** **Dividing line.** **Documents Folder.** *See pages 22–23.* **Trash.** *See page 24.*

Applications Folder. *See pages 22–23.*

You can **rearrange** any of the icons. You can **add** or **remove** applications from the *left* side of the dividing line (see callout, above), and you can **add** or **remove** folders, documents, and web page locations from the *right* side of the dividing line. Do all this by dragging:

■ **To rearrange an icon,** press the mouse on it and drag it left or right. The other icons will move over to make room.

■ **To add an application,** first open the Applications folder: single-click the Applications icon in the Sidebar of any Finder window. Then drag an application icon down to the Dock, to the *left* side of the dividing line. Also, if you double-click an application in a Finder window, its icon is automatically put in the Dock.

- **To add a folder or a document,** drag it to the *right* side of the dividing line.

- **To remove any icon from the Dock,** press it with the mouse and drag it upwards, off the Dock. Let go of the mouse and the icon will disappear in a poof of smoke. This doesn't hurt anything! *Never* will you delete any original item by removing its icon from the Dock. You can also Control-click (or right-click) a Dock item, then choose "Remove from Dock."

- **To add a web page,** open your browser application, Safari (see Lesson 7 about Safari). Go to the web page that you want to have easy access to in your Dock. Drag the tiny icon that you see on the left of the web page address in the location field (circled, below) and drop it in the Dock—on the *right* side of the dividing line.

- The advantage of putting a web page icon in your Dock is that you can be using any application on your Mac, and if you click that icon, your web browser opens to that page—you don't have to go find your browser first and then find the bookmark.

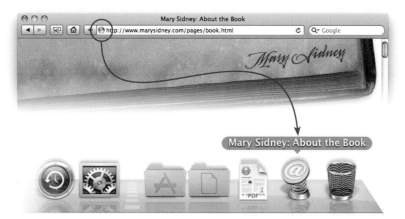

*Is the Dock missing?

The Dock can be customized in many ways. It might be along either side of the screen instead of at the bottom, or it might even be hidden. If you don't see the Dock anywhere, push your mouse to the far left, the far right, or the deep bottom of the screen and the hidden Dock will appear from one of those edges. See Lesson 15 for details about how to customize the Dock to fit your needs.

Documents and Downloads folders in the Dock

The right side of the Dock contains an Applications folder, a Documents folder, and a Downloads folder to provide convenient access to applications that are not in the Dock, or files that you've created, or downloaded to your Mac through Bonjour, iChat, or the Internet. Files that come to you attached to email will also end up in this Downloads folder if you click the "Save" button in an email message.

Documents folder.

Applications folder.   Downloads folder, shown as a Stack (of icons).

You can choose between two different ways to show these folders in the Dock: as a **Stack** (as shown above) or as a **Folder.** Control-click one of the folders to get the pop-up menu shown below. In the "Display as" section of the pop-up menu, choose "Folder" or "Stack." If you choose the "Folder" option, a folder replaces the stack of icons that represent the files and folders that are actually in the Downloads folder. If you choose "Stack," the icon on top of the Stack is the most recent file added to the folder (shown above). Dazzling, but not very useful. I prefer the Folder display.

To remove a folder or file from the Dock, Control-click it. From the pop-up menu (below), choose "Options," then choose "Remove from Dock." Or, you can drag a folder or file to the Desktop to remove it from the Dock.

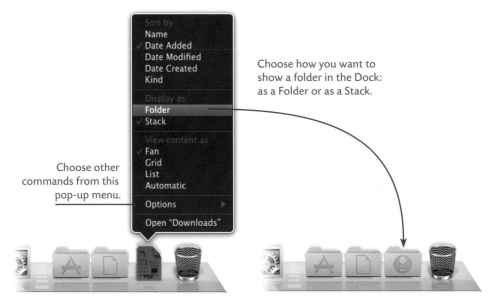

Choose how you want to show a folder in the Dock: as a Folder or as a Stack.

Choose other commands from this pop-up menu.

When you click one of the folders to view its contents, you can choose how to show the contents: press the Folder or Stack to get the pop-up menu shown on the previous page, then, from the "View content as" section, choose "Fan," "Grid," or "List." If you choose "View contents as Automatic," the Stack opens in Fan view when ten or fewer items are present. More than ten items opens in Grid view. Single-click a file or folder to open it. Each view includes an "Open in Finder" command.

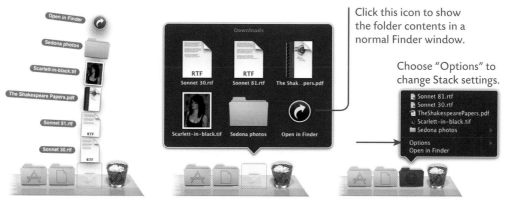

Click this icon to show the folder contents in a normal Finder window.

Choose "Options" to change Stack settings.

View contents as a Fan.   View contents as a Grid.   View contents as a List.

The Grid view of Stack contents makes navigation of folders easy. Click a folder in Grid view (below, left) to see its contents (below, right). To return to the previous folder, click the return path button (to the previous folder) that's in the top-left corner of the Grid view.

When necessary (when too many items are present), Grid view puts a dark gray scroll bar on the right side of the window.

To previous folder.   Current folder.

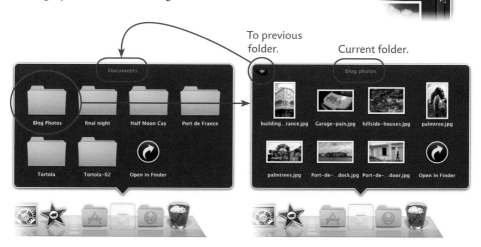

Use the Trash

The **Trash basket** in the Dock is where you throw away any files you don't want.

- ■ **To put a file in the Trash,** press on any file and drag it to the Trash basket. When the *tip of the pointer* touches the basket, the basket changes color— this means you're in the right place. Let go of the mouse button and that file is in the Trash. Remember, it's the *tip of the pointer,* not the icon image, that selects the Trash basket.

- ■ **To empty the Trash,** press *(don't click)* on the Trash icon and a little menu pops up with an option that says, "Empty Trash." Choose that option, or go to the Finder menu and choose "Empty Trash."

- ■ If you want to browse the files in the Trash before deciding which ones to delete, open the Trash window, select the files you don't want, then click the "Empty" button in the top-right corner (shown at the bottom of the next page).

When you empty the Trash, you'll get a warning asking if that's what you really want to do. Some people like to have this reminder; others hate it. You can tell your Mac to stop reminding you about emptying the Trash (next page).

■ **To turn off (or on) the Trash warning:**

1 From the Finder menu, choose "Preferences...."

2 Click the "Advanced" icon in the toolbar at the top.

3 Uncheck (or check) the box to "Show warning before emptying the Trash."

4 Click the red button in the upper-left of the preferences pane to put it away.

■ **To take an item out of the Trash,** click once on the Trash icon in the Dock to open its window. Assuming you have not yet emptied the Trash, you can drag the item you want to retrieve out of the window and put it back where you want it.

■ Or you can select one or more items in the Trash window, Control-click (or right-click) the item, then choose "Put Back." The item will automatically be placed in its original location. You can also access the "Put Back" command from the File menu.

Take Advantage of Keyboard Shortcuts

Most actions that you can do with the mouse and menus can also be done with **keyboard shortcuts.** Often this is not only faster, but more convenient because you don't have to take your hands off the keyboard to pick up and maneuver the mouse. You will see lots of keyboard shortcuts in the menus across the top of the screen, such as the ones shown below in the Edit menu. Use a keyboard shortcut *instead* of going to the menu.

Take careful notice of which modifier keys are used and which character keys are used.

Recognize the common modifier keys

Keyboard shortcuts work with **modifier keys,** which are those keys that don't do anything by themselves. For instance, the Shift key doesn't do anything when you press it down by itself, *but it modifies the behavior of other keys.*

Each key has a **symbol** by which it is known. These are the key symbols you will see in menus and charts:

⇧	**Shift**	↻	**Escape (esc)**
⌘	**Command**	⇞ ⇟	**PageUp or PageDown**
⌥	**Option**	⌫	**Delete**
^	**Control**	↑↓←→	**Arrow keys**
↵	**Return**	⌤	**Enter**

Fkeys are those keys across the top of the keyboard that are labeled with the letter F and a number, such as F2 or F13.

The **fn** key (function key) enables individual keys do more than one function.

Keyboard shortcuts typically use one or more modifier key(s), plus one number, character, or Fkey, as you can see in the example of the Edit menu above: the keyboard shortcut to copy *selected* text is Command C, or ⌘C.

Use a keyboard shortcut

The trick to using a keyboard shortcut is this: *Hold down* the modifier keys all together and keep them held down, then *tap* the associated letter, number, or Fkey *just once* for each time you want to perform an action.

For instance, the keyboard shortcut to close a window is Command W, so hold the Command key down and tap the letter W just once. If there are three windows open on your Desktop, you can hold the Command key down and tap the letter W three times and it will close three windows.

Notice gray vs. black commands

When commands in a menu are gray instead of black, the Mac is giving you an important visual clue. Here's a short exercise to demonstrate.

1   Click an empty spot on the Desktop.

2   Now take a look through the Finder menus and notice the shortcuts for different actions, or commands. Notice how many commands are gray.

If a command is **gray,** that means you cannot use that command at the moment. Often this is because you have not *selected* an item first, an item to which the command should apply. For instance, you can't use the command to close a window unless an open window is *selected.*

3   Now open a Finder window (if there isn't one already) and *select* a folder icon (click *once* on it).

4   Look at the File menu again, and notice how many more commands are available (they're in **black,** not gray).

5   In the File menu, find the keyboard shortcut to "Open," but don't choose the command—just remember the shortcut (Command O). Click somewhere off the menu to make the menu go away.

6   Make sure a folder is selected. Now use the keyboard shortcut, Command O, to open it.

Learn More About Mac OS X

There are a number of ways to learn more about your Mac and how to use it, all available right from your Desktop. Keep these tips in mind as you spend time on your Mac—you will learn a lot from them.

Tool tips

Most applications and dialog boxes provide little **tool tips** that pop up when you "hover" your mouse over an item. They tell you what the items do. Just hold the mouse still over a button or icon for about three seconds and if there is a tool tip, it will appear, as shown in the examples below.

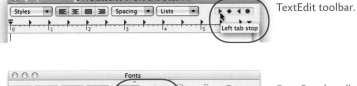

TextEdit toolbar.

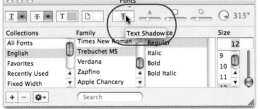

Font Panel toolbar.

Preview's toolbar.

Hover tips

As mentioned in the previous paragraph, tool tips appear when you hover your mouse. For instance, you've probably already noticed that when you hover over an item in the Dock, the name of that item appears. Actually, all kinds of things appear when you hover—try it on everything! Below are some examples. Remember, "hover" means to hold your mouse still while pointing to an item—don't click or press the button.

In iChat, hover over a name in your Buddy List or Bonjour List to see that person's information.

In Mail, hover over a name in an email to see what address it came from.

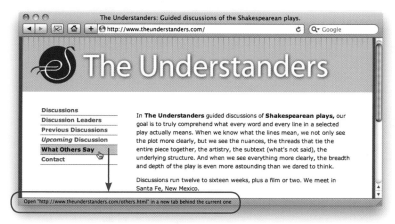

In Safari (your web browser), hover over a link name to see exactly where it goes—the destination will appear in the Status Bar at the bottom of the window. (If you don't see this Status Bar, go to the View menu in Safari and choose "Show Status Bar.")

Visual clues

Keep a constant eye out for the **visual clues** that the Mac is always providing. Every little visual extra means something! When the pointer turns into a double-headed arrow, that's a clue. When you see a little dot in a divider bar, that's a clue. When you see a triangle anywhere, that's a clue.

You are probably already aware of visual clues such as the underline beneath text on a web page to indicate a link, or the line of little colored dots in your word processor that indicates a word is misspelled. Here are a few others that will help you start noticing what your Mac is telling you.

This flashing insertion point is a clue that if you type, the text will appear at that point.

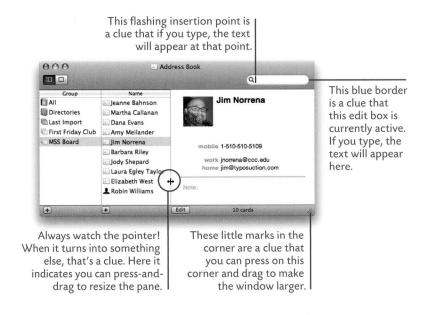

This blue border is a clue that this edit box is currently active. If you type, the text will appear here.

Always watch the pointer! When it turns into something else, that's a clue. Here it indicates you can press-and-drag to resize the pane.

These little marks in the corner are a clue that you can press on this corner and drag to make the window larger.

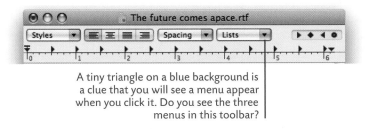

A tiny triangle on a blue background is a clue that you will see a menu appear when you click it. Do you see the three menus in this toolbar?

Sometimes our eyes glaze over because there is so much visual stimulation on the Mac screen. Just keep in mind that everything means something, and slowly get to know the visual clues.

Below you see a typical title bar of a document. There are two visual clues in this title bar: the **red button** has a dark dot in it, and the **tiny icon** next to the title is gray. Both of these visual clues mean the same thing: this file has unsaved changes. Once you save the document, the dark dot goes away and the tiny icon is no longer gray.

You might see a **dot** next to a document name in an application's Window menu—that's another visual clue that the document has not been saved recently. The **checkmark** indicates the active document, or the one that is in front of all the others and that you're currently working on.

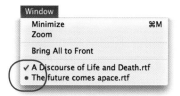

Everywhere on your Mac you will see buttons to save a document, to not save, to cancel a process, etc. One of these buttons is always **blue.** The blue is a visual clue that you can hit the Return or Enter key to activate that button instead of picking up the mouse to click on it.

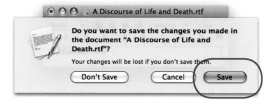

Help files

No matter where you are on the Mac or what application you are working in, you'll always find **Help** just a click away. At the Finder, go to the Help menu to look up tips and techniques on just about anything.

Every application has a Help menu, and it's always at the far end of the menu choices, as shown below. Choose the Help option for that particular application, then type in a word or two that you want to look up. You see two different kinds of options available, "Menu Items" and "Help Topics."

Menu Items This tells you where the item you're looking for can be found in the menus. It doesn't explain anything about that item. When you select an option in the "Menu Items" list, a menu drops down and a big moving arrow points to the item you're looking for.

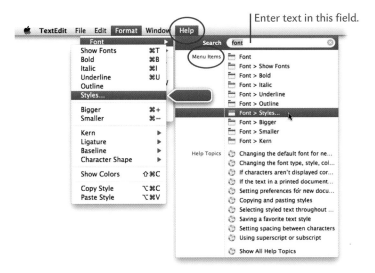

Help Topics If Apple has written information in the Help file, you will see a list of the possible topics. Choose one and the Help file opens to that piece of information.

Support pages

The Apple web site has a huge number of **support pages.** Here you can find manuals that you can view on screen or download (copy) to your computer. There are discussion pages where users talk about different products and software packages on the Mac, ask questions, and answer questions. You can sign up for training at a local Apple store, read the product question-and-answer pages for hardware and software, and more. Go to www.Apple.com/support.

Mac video tutorials

Apple provides hundreds of video tutorials about Mac basics, Mac applications (such as iPhoto, iMovie, iWeb, GarageBand, iWork, and MobileMe) on their web site. Visit www.Apple.com/startpage and look for **Mac Video Tutorials.** Or just use Safari to do a Google search for "Mac video tutorials." You'll find more video (and text) tutorials at www.Apple.com/findouthow/mac that include many additional topics, from "Getting Started" to "Using iChat."

MobileMe tutorials

If you are a MobileMe member, take advantage of the **MobileMe page** where you'll find lots of tutorials and movies to help you learn more about how to take advantage (and have fun) using the features included with a MobileMe membership. You don't have to be a MobileMe member to see the video tutorials, just go to www.Apple.com/mobileme.

A MobileMe membership costs $99.95 a year and includes lots of features that make your Mac experience many times more empowering, creative, enjoyable, and just plain useful.

Enjoy Snow Leopard speed

In addition to great applications, powerful features, and ease of use, Snow Leopard also makes your Mac faster than ever. Compared to the previous operating system (Leopard), Snow Leopard is 75% faster shutting down, twice as fast waking from sleep with Screen Locking enabled, and up to 55% faster joining a wireless network.

2

GOALS

Become familiar with the various disk icons in your Finder windows

Understand the Library folders

Learn how to select multiple items in the different window views

Use Exposé to access windows easily

Take advantage of contextual menus

Use keyboard shortcuts to navigate Save As and Open dialog boxes

Access menus at the Finder without using the mouse

A Bit Beyond the Basics

If you're feeling comfortable with the techniques and features described in the previous lesson, then carry on into this lesson and learn a few more advanced (but still everyday and useful) features. If anything overwhelms you in this lesson, feel free to skip it and come back later.

Understand the Various Disk Icons

In the **"Devices" portion of the Sidebar,** you probably see something similar to the example shown below—you might see more icons and you might see fewer. These icons represent hard disks, networks, a CD or DVD, an iPod, or any other type of removable media.

Display the contents of each media item the same way you do any of the items in the lower portion of the Sidebar: single-click the icon.

You can choose what gets displayed in this upper portion of the Sidebar; see page 274.

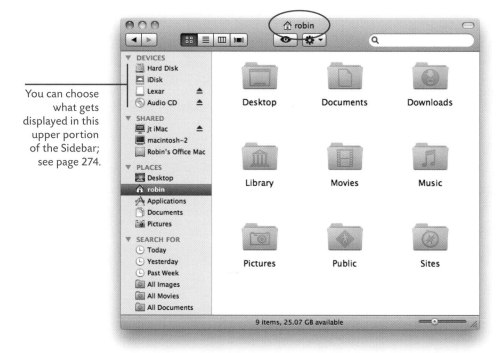

The **Hard Disk** is your computer, the disk that holds the operating system and all your files. You can rename your hard disk at any time, just as you rename a folder (as explained on page 11).

The **iDisk** is your personal storage space on Apple's computers, which is something you get when you sign up for a MobileMe account. A single click on the iDisk icon connects you to that storage space.

"Lexar" is a USB storage device (an extra hard disk) that I've got connected to my Mac. "Audio CD" is a music CD I inserted. Removable media such as these always have an Eject symbol to the right of the name.

⏏ When you see the **eject symbol** to the right of an icon (the triangle with a bar under it), that means it is a removable disk of some sort. It might be a CD, a DVD, an iPod, or even another computer that you are connected to over the network. Click on the symbol to eject or disconnect the item.

TIP ———— Choose which devices, if any, appear on your Desktop. See page 274.

Shared

The **Shared** section (if you have it in your Sidebar) displays any other computers or disks that you can connect to through your *local* network. A local network is one in which computers in a small area, such as a home or office, are all connected via wires or a wireless connection.

Places

The **Places** section displays folders and files on your own computer. To make a file or folder easily accessible, drag it to this section of the Sidebar. When you no longer need easy access to the item, drag it out of the Sidebar. It disappears in a poof of digital smoke. If you decide to put that item back in the Sidebar, just drag it into the Sidebar again.

Search For

The **Search For** folders are "smart folders" that automatically keep track of files and make it easier for you to find things. Please see page 348 for more details. Feel free to single-click on any icon in the "Search For" section to see the files it has organized for you.

View your Home folder from the "Hard Disk"

Below you see another way of looking at your Home folder, using the Column View (as explained on pages 16–17).

You can tell by the highlight that in the top portion of the Sidebar I clicked on the hard drive icon labeled "Hard Disk"; the hard disk is where all your files are stored (although you might have renamed your hard disk). This click displays the folders stored on that hard disk; you can see them in the column to the right.

Then I clicked on "Users," which displays my Home folder in the *next* column. If you make any other users, as explained in Lesson 18, you will see all of those users here.

Then I clicked on "robin," which displays my Home folders in the *next* column.

Do you see the Applications folder in the screen shot below? Notice that it's in the top level (first column) of the Hard Disk. Your Applications icon in the Sidebar makes it easy to access this folder.

Experiment with different ways of getting to your Home folders until you feel comfortable about where things are stored on your Mac.

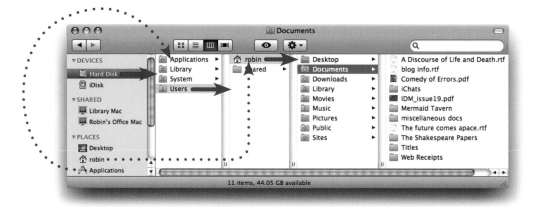

Understand the Various Library Folders

As you work with your Mac, you'll run across a number of folders with the same name: **Library.** Do you see the two Library folders in the illustration below? And if you open the "System" folder, you'd see another Library folder.

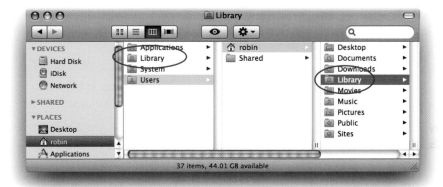

Library folders contain information that the operating system and certain applications need to function. Unless you have a really good reason and know exactly what you're doing, **leave the Library folders alone—don't put anything in them and don't take anything out.**

The Library folder you see above, the one directly to the right of the "Hard Disk," is at the "top level" of your hard disk. It contains files that are critical to running your entire computer, and those files pertain to all users who use this Mac. For instance, this Library folder has a folder inside called "Fonts," and all fonts that are installed into this top level folder are available to all users. (For details about multiple users and how to create them, please see Lesson 18.)

The Library folder in the far-right column, above, is in my Home collection, my user folder. This is where all my application preferences, web page bookmarks, Address Book contact information, email, and other personal information is stored. Each user you set up will have her own Library folder with all her own data. There is even a Fonts folder in here; any fonts a user puts in her own Fonts folder will be available only to that user.

That's all you really need to know about your Library folders—and leave them alone for now!

Select Multiple Items in the Finder

To select an individual item in a Finder window, you simply single-click it, as you probably know. But often you'll want to select more than one item at a time. **To select multiple items,** there are two ways to do it, as explained below. Once items are a group, you can move, trash, or open all the selected files at once, change their labels (see page 276 about labels), and more.

In the Icon View

To select multiple items in the Icon View, hold down the **Command key** *or* the **Shift key** and single-click as many items as you want to group together. You can only select items from one window while in the Icon View.

Or *press* a blank spot in the window and *drag* the mouse around the items you want to select. Any icon that is completely or partially enclosed by the rectangle you draw with the mouse will be selected.

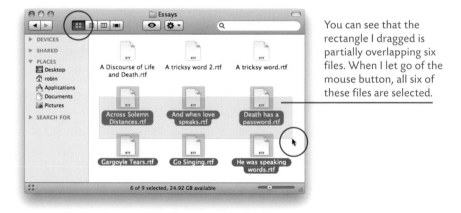

You can see that the rectangle I dragged is partially overlapping six files. When I let go of the mouse button, all six of these files are selected.

In the List View or Column View

In these views, using the Shift key is different from using the Command key.

Hold down the **Command key** and single-click multiple items.

In the *List View,* you can select items from several different folders in the same window, as long as their contents are showing in the list. See the example on the opposite page.

In the *Column View,* you can select multiple items from one column at a time.

Command-click to select non-contiguous items.

The **Shift key** lets you select a group of items that are *contiguous,* or next to each other in the list. Single-click on the *first* item you want to select in a list. Then hold down the Shift key and click the *last* item you want in the list. *Everything between the two clicks will be selected.* See the example below.

Shift-click to select contiguous items.

To deselect an item from any group in any view: Command-click it.

To deselect all items from any group in any view: Single-click any blank area in the window.

Exposé

If you like to keep lots of windows open (application windows, preference panes, Finder windows, etc.), Exposé is a feature you'll enjoy because it helps you find everything even if the Desktop is a mess.

Your Mac is already set up to use Exposé. Open several windows on your Mac, then press the F11 key at the top of your keyboard. Every window on your Mac disappears, leaving only the Desktop visible! Just hit the F11 key to bring them all back.

You might need to hold down the fn key while you tap F11. See page 288, Step 4 for more information about how and when to use the fn key (if your keyboard has one).

The keyboard shortcuts for Exposé are explained below, but if you need to change them, use the Exposé & Spaces system preferences, as shown below (go to the Apple menu, choose "System Preferences...," and click the "Exposé & Spaces" icon).

In the System Preferences pane, click this icon to open the preferences where you can change the shortcuts.

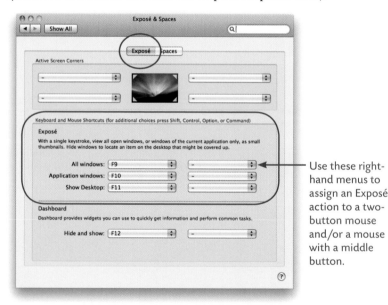

Use these right-hand menus to assign an Exposé action to a two-button mouse and/or a mouse with a middle button.

- **To show every window on the screen at once,** as shown on the bottom of the opposite page, press F9. On newer keyboards, F3 will also activate Exposé (you might need to hold down the fn key—see page 288, Step 4).

- **To show just application windows** (no Finder windows), press F10.

- **To hide every window so you can see your entire Desktop,** press F11.

- **To use your mouse** to activate Exposé, assign the actions in the preferences, as shown above.

Above is my messy Desktop. Rather than move windows around to find what I want, I can hit F9 and every open window lines up, as shown below. As my mouse hovers over each one, it is highlighted with blue (see below).

The blue outline is a visual clue that if I click on that particular item, it will come forward and everything else will be in the background, in the same stacking order as before.

The iCal window highlights in blue when I hover the pointer over it.

Dock Exposé

Dock Exposé adds even more flexibility to managing the pile of clutter on your Desktop. In the past, you may have *minimized* open windows (by clicking the yellow button in the window's top-left corner) and sent them to the Dock to keep them accessible, but out of the way. This technique works, but if you minimize a lot of windows, you'll be trading a cluttered Desktop for a cluttered Dock. Dock Exposé solves that delimma by sending minimized windows to hide behind their application icons in the Dock, completely out of sight.

To set up Dock Exposé:

1   Open System Preferences, then click the "Dock" icon in the top row of icons.

2   Checkmark "Minimize windows into application icon," shown below.

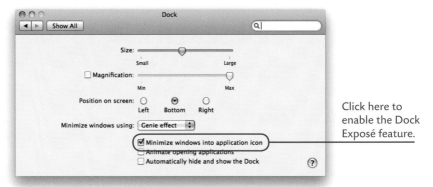

Click here to enable the Dock Exposé feature.

Now click the yellow minimize button in an open window's top-left corner and watch the window swoop down to the Dock to hide behind its application icon and out of sight. To show minimized windows from a specific application, press on the application icon in the Dock for a split second (shown on the following page).

When you *press* on an icon, in addition to showing an Exposé view of open files, a pop-up appears with options (Quit, Hide, Options) just above the icon. Press the Option key to show additional options (Force Quit, Hide Others).

When you press on an application icon in the Dock and hold for a split second, Exposé shows all open windows from that application, including both minimized windows and windows that are open and visible on the Desktop. If, however, that particular application is not currently open, Exposé will *not* be activated and you'll see only a pop-up menu with a limited number of commands and options.

A horizontal line separates open files and minimized files.

When you click a specific application icon, Dock Exposé shows files opened from that application. Press the Tab key to move to the next application.

The open windows shown in Dock Exposé (above) are separated by a thin, horizontal line. Windows above the horizontal line are open on the Desktop (not minimized). Windows below the horizontal line are currently minimized and hidden behind their application icon.

As you move your mouse over the windows in Dock Exposé, they're highlighted with a blue border. Click any highlighted window to make it the active window and return to a normal Desktop view.

To show all windows in Dock Exposé (as shown above), regardless of what application they're from, or whether they're open or minimized, click the F9 key.

To open all minimized windows in an application, Option-click one of the windows. **To minimize multiple open windows** from the same application, Option-click the yellow button of one. **To exit Dock Exposé,** click anywhere.

If the F9 key (the default Exposé key) doesn't work, you probably have a setting in Keyboard preferences that forces the F keys to act as "special feature" keys instead of "standard function" keys. Try holding down the fn key (if you have one on your keyboard) while you tap the F9 key. See page 288 and read Step 4 to learn about the fn key and how to change its setting in the Keyboard preferences.

Look for Contextual Menus

These are great. You can Control-click just about anywhere (hold down the Control key—not the *Command key*—and click) and a menu pops up right where you click. This is a **contextual menu** that is specific to the item you Control-click on, meaning what you see in the pop-up menu depends on what you click on (as opposed to menus in the menu bar or in dialog boxes that always contain the same items).

To display a contextual menu, hold down the Control key and click on an icon, a blank spot on the Desktop, inside a Finder window, on a title bar, toolbar, or just about anywhere. A little menu pops up, as you can see by the examples below.

If you have a **two-button mouse,** you don't need the Control key—just use the right-hand button to display a contextual menu.

There is *no visual clue* for a contextual menu—just keep checking. You'll find them in applications, on web pages, in toolbars, in the Sidebar, and elsewhere.

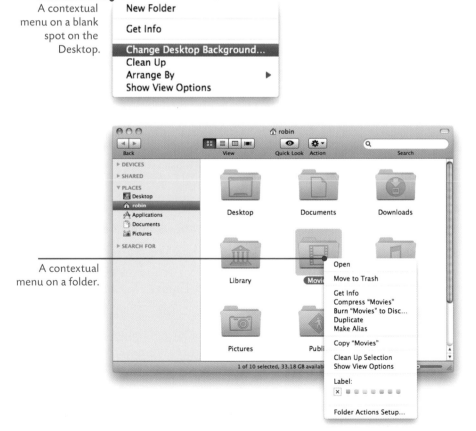

A contextual menu on a blank spot on the Desktop.

A contextual menu on a folder.

A contextual menu
on a Toolbar.

This is an example of a
contextual menu in an
application.

Control-click a misspelled
word in a new email message
to get a contextual menu with
possible spellings.

Select the correct word, let go
of the mouse button, and the
misspelled word is instantly
replaced with the correct one.

Try the "Speech" option—
your text will be read out
loud to you.

TIP ——— In Finder windows, the **Action button**
does many of the same things as the contextual menu,
and more.
Try it: Single-click to select a folder or file, then click the
Action button to see what the contextual options are.

Use Keyboard Shortcuts in Dialog Boxes

When creating and working with documents, you can use keyboard shortcuts in the **Save As** and **Open** dialog boxes. Use the Tab key to select different areas of the dialog box and the Arrow keys to select items in the columns. When you Save As, you can title your document, select the folder in which you want it stored, and save it—without using the mouse.

Visual Clues: Notice the **blue border** around this Save As edit box, and the blue highlight on the text; this means the edit box and text are **selected.** Simply type to replace the highlighted text.

If you don't see the full dialog box, as shown here, single-click this disclosure triangle.

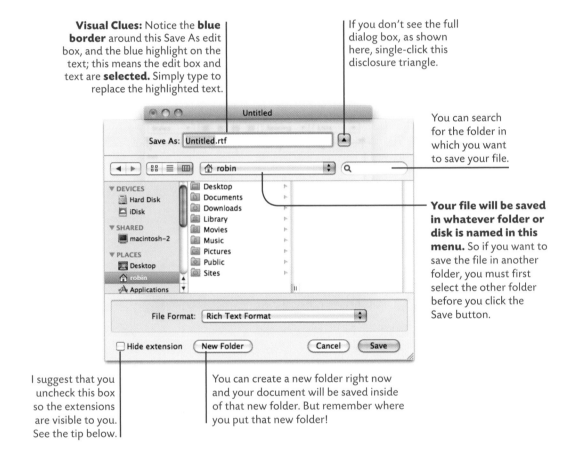

You can search for the folder in which you want to save your file.

Your file will be saved in whatever folder or disk is named in this menu. So if you want to save the file in another folder, you must first select the other folder before you click the Save button.

I suggest that you uncheck this box so the extensions are visible to you. See the tip below.

You can create a new folder right now and your document will be saved inside of that new folder. But remember where you put that new folder!

TIP —— **Extensions** are the three- or four-letter abbreviations at the ends of file names. Your Mac needs these extensions so it knows what to do with the files. You can "hide" the extensions so you don't have to see them, but it's a good idea to get used to them. They will help *you* keep track of what kind of files you're creating. See page 277.

If this checkbox is not visible, it's because a setting
in the Finder preferences is set to "Show all file
name extensions" (see page 277).

**Use the Tab key to select various parts of the Save As
or Open dialog boxes:**

❶ If the insertion point is in the field where you name the file,
then the first Tab selects the Search field.

❷ The next Tab selects the Sidebar. Use the up and down Arrow keys
to highlight the folder or disk you need.

❸ The next Tab selects the first column. Use the up and down Arrow keys
to select a file in the first column, then hit the right Arrow key to select
the next column.

❹ When you select the folder into which you want to save the file,
hit the Return key to activate the Save button.

Navigate the Desktop and Finder Windows

If you so choose, you can get around your entire Desktop and inside Finder windows using the keyboard. For instance, you can get to every menu across the top of the screen and choose commands, without ever touching the mouse.

Access the menus on the Desktop or in any application:

1   Press Control F2 to select the menu bar across the top of the screen (on a laptop, you might need to press **fn Control F2**).

2   Use the left and right Arrow keys to select menu items across the menu bar, or type the first letter of the menu you want to select. When a menu is selected, you'll see it highlight.

3   When the menu name you want is highlighted, press the Return key to drop down its menu.

4   Press the down and up arrows to choose a command in the list, or type the first letter or two or three. (If there is more than one command that starts with the same letter, type the first two or three letters quickly to select a specific one.)

5   Hit Return to activate the selected command.

6   To put the menu away without activating a command, press Command Period (Command .).

Try these shortcuts in a Finder window:

- Type the first letter or two or three to select files.
- When you're in the List View or Column View, use the Arrow keys to select the columns to the right or left, then use the letter keys to select files in that column.
- Select a document, hit Command O to open it, and get to work!

If you are interested in using more keyboard shortcuts, go to the "Keyboard" preferences, as explained on page 282. In that preference pane you see shown on the page, you'll find an extensive list of keyboard shortcuts. The shortcuts are not printed here in this book—they're in that preference pane on your Mac!

Mac OS X Applications in Snow Leopard

3

GOALS

Understand the
common features
of Apple applications

Realize what can NOT be
covered in this book

Introduction to Mac OS X Applications

One of the greatest things about Mac applications is that they are consistent, which makes them easy to learn and easy to use—what you learn in one application applies easily to just about any other application.

In this short introductory lesson, we're just going to present a brief overview of the major apps (applications) that you'll find in your Applications folder and the Dock. All of the Apple applications are integrated with other apps, and they all share certain features and tools. In the following chapters, I'll go into more detail about individual programs, and in Lesson 13 of this section, you'll learn how to use the tools that all Apple applications share.

Know your Applications Folder

In the Sidebar of any Finder window is an icon labeled **Applications.** Single-click this icon to display the contents of the Applications window. These are the programs you will use to create your work on your Mac.

At any time, you can put the application you use most often **in the Dock** so you'll have easy access to it: Just drag the application icon from this window and drop it on the Dock. If you accidentally lose something from the Dock, you can always come back to this Applications window to drag the item back in.

When you open an application that's not already in the Dock, its icon is automatically put in the Dock. When you quit the application, the icon disappears from the Dock. **To keep the application icon in the Dock,** *press* on it (in the Dock) to show a pop-up menu, choose "Options," then choose "Keep in Dock" (shown below-right).

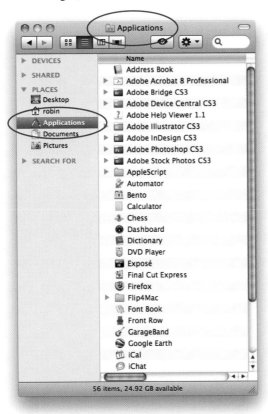

Some applications that you buy will display their *folders* here in the Applications window instead of the *applications' icons.*

If you see an application in a folder, open that folder and find the actual *application* icon to drag to the Dock.

Application Integration

All of the Apple applications share certain tools such as the Spell Checker and Grammar Checker, the Fonts palette, the Colors palette, the Special Character palette, and more. All of those common tool elements are explained in detail in Lesson 13.

Also keep in mind that all of these applications also work together in amazing ways. You can drag text and graphics from one app to another, save files into different formats, save to-do messages from Mail directly into iCal, create a PDF in TextEdit that you can read and annotate in Preview, and more. See the individual application chapters and Lesson 14 for details.

And be sure to read the last page of each of the application lessons to learn how many ways each app is integrated with others!

What We're Not Covering!

We introduce iTunes in Lesson 10, but we don't cover iPhoto, iWeb, iMovie, or iDVD because they are a special suite of apps called iLife, not part of the Mac operating system. Other authors cover those, however, in a variety of books published by Peachpit Press. There you'll find much more information than we can provide in this introductory book about such programs as Mail, iCal, and iChat. Some iLife books are more than 500 pages, so you can see why we don't cover all of that in this book!

Nor do we cover Pages, Numbers, or Keynote in this book because you have to buy those in the iWork collection of apps. If you have those programs, Peachpit publishes a book on iWork, plus the applications have good Help files built right in.

Know the Common Features of Mac Apps

Most Mac applications have these features in common.

Windows and window controls

When you open an application, you'll actually be working in a **window.** If you worked through Lesson 1, you already know all about windows, even ones you haven't seen before. You see the same red, yellow, and green buttons to close, minimize, and resize the window. The document name and a tiny icon appear in the title bar. You can drag the title bar or any edge to move the window.

Application menu

 The application menu (directly to the right of the Apple menu) always tells you the name of the currently **active application,** the one you're working in (even if there is no document window open on the screen). You'll always find the Quit command at the bottom of this menu.

File and Edit menus

You'll always find File and Edit as the first two menus to the right of the application menu.

Although each application includes specific features in its menus, in the **File menu** you'll always find the commands to *open* an existing document or create a **new** one, **save** the document or **save as** with another name, **close** the active window, and **print** the active document.

From the **Edit menu,** as shown below, you can always **undo or redo, cut, copy, paste, delete, select all,** check the **spelling and grammar,** and access the **Special Characters.**

Preferences Every application has its own preferences where you can **customize** the application to suit yourself. You'll always open the preferences from the application menu (see the previous page). Typically, you'll see a toolbar across the top of the preferences pane; single-click an icon in that toolbar to set the preferences for that particular feature.

Safari preferences. The Tabs pane is selected.

Toolbars Many applications have a Toolbar across the top of the window. Usually, you can **customize** this Toolbar: check the **View menu** for a command called "Customize Toolbar…," or use the contextual menu (Control-click or right-click the window's toolbar).

This is a typical sheet that drops down from a toolbar so you can customize it.

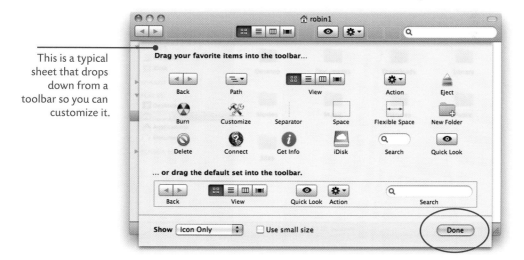

Sidebars or drawers

Many applications have a sidebar, a drawer, or some other sort of pane on the side of the window. Single-click the icons you see in a sidebar-like feature to display its particular contents in the window.

Here the iTunes Store is selected in the sidebar.

Special collections

Several applications use collection metaphors such as *Albums* in iPhoto, *Playlists* in iTunes, *Bookmark Collections* in Safari, *Mailboxes* in Mail, *Groups* in Address Book. Use these to store and organize your stuff.

Open and Save As dialog boxes

Whenever you open an existing document or save a new one, the dialog boxes you see to open a new document or save a document always look familiar. See pages 48–49 for tips on how to get around these dialog boxes and save into particular folders.

Help files   Every application has a Help menu with Help files specific to that application. You can either use the menu you see on your screen or press **Command ?** to bring up the files. You'll find a search box where you can type in key words, then hit Return to display the answers. See page 32 for more details.

Action button and menu

 In many applications, you'll see the Action button (shown to the left) that displays the Action menu. Every application has different options—always click on it to see what is available.

Preview before you print

At the bottom of the Print dialog box is a button called "Preview." Click this to open your document in the Preview application where you can see what it will look like when printed.

Search   Just about every application has a search feature. It's usually in the upper-right corner of the window, as you can see in the iTunes window on the opposite page and in the Address Book below. Just exactly what the search feature searches depends on the application. See the individual overviews in the lessons for each application.

Smart Folders

Many applications have some version of *Smart Folders* that automatically update themselves according to your specified criteria. See Lesson 19 on Spotlight to learn how to take advantage of this great feature.

Other applications have similar types of smart folders: The Address Book has *Smart Groups* that will add appropriate contacts to themselves; iTunes has *Smart Playlists* that will add music to themselves; Mail has *Smart Mailboxes.* See the individual lessons for each application.

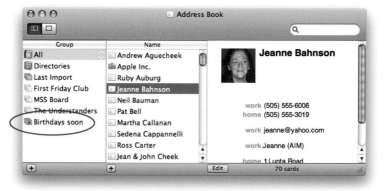

This Smart Group finds people in my Address Book who have birthdays coming up. iCal will add these birthdays to a calendar; see page 158.

4

GOALS

TextEdit for Word Processing

TextEdit is a small, yet surprisingly powerful word processor. Use it for writing memos, letters, diaries, novels, grocery lists, memoirs, or any other text documents. In TextEdit you can create simple tables and automatically numbered or bulleted lists. You can put shadows on type, insert images, search and replace text, and more. But it's not a full-blown word processor such as Apple's Pages or MarinerWrite (MarinerSoftware.com) or the sweet, new Pagehand (Pagehand.com). Although TextEdit can't do all the fancy things a big word processor can, it's excellent for many projects.

You'll find TextEdit in your Applications folder. If you use it regularly, drag its icon to the Dock.

If you've never used a word processor before and you don't know how to enter text, select text for formatting, cut/copy and paste, etc., please read *The Little Mac Book* first! This chapter assumes you know the basics of working in a word processor.

Read Microsoft Word Files

Do you work with people who send you **Microsoft Word files,** but you prefer to keep a Microsoft-free environment on your own computer? TextEdit can open Word files and save as Word files. Some of the advanced features will be missing, but this works great for basic text documents, including those with simple tables or numbered/bulleted lists.

If you don't have Microsoft Word installed on your Mac, file names ending with .doc (which are usually Word files) **automatically open** in TextEdit when you double-click them.

To force a Word document to open in TextEdit (if it's not your default), drag the file and drop it on the TextEdit icon.

(If the TextEdit icon is not in your Dock, it's in the Applications folder. If you want TextEdit in the Dock, drag it from the Applications folder and drop it in the Dock.)

Change the default application to open Word files

If you own Microsoft Word and want your **.doc files to open in Word,** not TextEdit, you can **change the default application**:

1   Control-click (or right-click) the Word document icon to get its pop-up menu.

2   While the menu is visible, also hold down the Option key. This changes the "Open With" command to "Always Open With."

3   Choose "Always Open With." If Microsoft Word is on your Mac, you'll see it listed in the pop-out menu. Or, select "Other…," then select the application you want to always open the selected file.

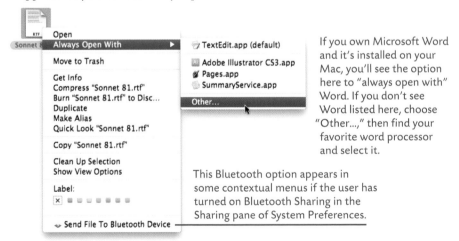

If you own Microsoft Word and it's installed on your Mac, you'll see the option here to "always open with" Word. If you don't see Word listed here, choose "Other…," then find your favorite word processor and select it.

This Bluetooth option appears in some contextual menus if the user has turned on Bluetooth Sharing in the Sharing pane of System Preferences.

Save TextEdit files as Word docs

You can save any TextEdit file as a Microsoft Word document to send to people who insist on that format.

To save a TextEdit file as a Word document:

1 Go to the File menu and choose "Save As...."

2 In the "File Format" menu at the bottom of the Save As dialog box, choose "Word 2007 Format (docx)." This automatically adds the Word extension, .docx, to the end of your file name.

As you can see in that Format menu, you can also save your files in several other formats. Keep these other formats in mind!

If you don't see the extension at the end of the file name—and you want to—see page 277. If you see a checked checkbox labeled "Hide Extension," click the checkbox to *unselect* that option to the extension is visible.

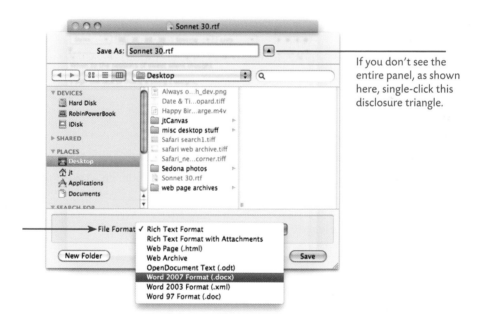

If you don't see the entire panel, as shown here, single-click this disclosure triangle.

Save TextEdit files as PDFs

From the File menu, choose "Print...," then click the "PDF" button (in the bottom-left corner of the Print dialog) and choose "Save as PDF...."

Find and Replace Words or Phrases

Did you write your entire novel using your sweetheart's name, Peter, as the hero? And now Peter's abandoned you and you want to **change** the hero's name to Heathcliff? No problem:

1   Go to the Edit menu, slide down to "Find," then from the pop-out menu, choose "Find...," *or* skip all that and press Command F.

2   Find "Peter" and replace with "Heathcliff."

If you create a lot of text in TextEdit, it will be worth your time to experiment with the options you see in the Find dialog box, as described below.

To replace:

Only the **currently selected occurrence** of the text, click "Replace."

All occurrences of the text in the document, click "Replace All."

All occurrences of the text **in a block of selected text,** hold down the Option key and click "In Selection" (it appears when the Option key is down).

To simultaneously select (but not replace):

All occurrences of the text, hold down the Control key; "Replace All" changes to "Select All."

All occurrences **in a block of selected text,** hold down both the Control key *and* the Option key; "Replace All" changes to "In Selection."

Paste Text to Match the Existing Text

This is one of my favorite features. Let's say you're writing a term paper and you copy a quote from a web page to add to your paper (properly cited, of course). Typically the copied text pastes in with the typeface, style, size, and color that were originally applied to it. But to add this quotation to your term paper, you want it to look like the rest of your page. Use this great feature instead of the regular paste:

> From the Edit menu, choose **Paste and Match Style,**
> *or* use the keyboard shortcut, Shift Option Command V.

The pasted text will pick up all the formatting *from the character to the left of the flashing insertion point.* This technique works in Mail as well.

Use your Favorite Text Styles Easily

TextEdit doesn't have the powerful style sheets of a full-blown word processor, but it does make your writing life much easier by letting you create **favorite styles** of basic type features so you can apply them quickly. A "style" contains all of the formatting information, such as typeface, size, color, indents, etc., so you can apply everything to selected text with one click of a button.

These styles are saved with TextEdit, not with an individual document, so you can use the same styles in different documents.

To create your own favorite style:

1 Type some text, any text, and set up the typeface, size, color, linespace, and the ruler the way you want it.

2 Click anywhere in that formatted text.

3 From the "Styles" menu in the toolbar, choose "Other..."

4 Click the button, "Add To Favorites."

5 Name your new favorite style and choose your options. Click "Add."

To apply a style, select the characters, then choose the style name from the Styles menu. All of the formatting that you saved with that style will be automatically applied with the click of that button.

Complete your Word Automatically

The **Complete** command in the Edit menu pops up a menu of possible completions for an unfinished word, as shown below. The list learns new words—type a word once, then next time you start to type it, that word appears in the list. Frequently used words appear at the top.

1   Start to type a word that you're not sure how to spell or one that is long enough that you don't want to type the whole thing.

2   From the Edit menu, choose "Complete," *or* press Option Escape (the **esc** key in the upper-left of the keyboard). A menu like the one shown below will appear.

3   If the word you want is already highlighted at the top of the list, just hit Return. If not, use the Down arrow key (or scroll) to select a word and then hit Return, *or* click on the word you want.

Use Typographer's Quotes!

TextEdit automatically provides typographer's quotes, or **smart quotes.** Smart quotes (and apostrophes) are the curly ones, not the lame, straight, typewriter quotes. Nothing will make your work look as amateurish as typewriter quotes.

typewriter quotes

It's "Baby Doll."

smart quotes

It's "Baby Doll."

There are three places where you can turn "Smart Quotes" on or off. In the TextEdit preferences (explained below), you can turn them on or off *for the application.* But you can also *override* this application setting in individual documents with a command from the Edit menu, or with a contextual menu command.

To turn on Smart Quotes for every new TextEdit document:

1   From the TextEdit menu, choose "Preferences…."

2   Click the "New Document" tab, if it isn't already blue.

3   Check the box for "Smart quotes."

To turn Smart Quotes off or on, as needed,
for an individual document:

1   From the Edit menu, slide down to "Substitutions."

2   In the sub-menu, click "Smart Quotes." A checkmark means they're on, and no checkmark means they are off.
    You can also Control-click (or right-click) anywhere in the document, slide down to "Substitutions," then choose "Smart Quotes."

Why would you want to turn them off? So you can type the feet and inch marks without looking dumb. For instance, I am 5'8" tall, *not* 5'8" tall.

Tabs and Indents

The tab and indent markers in TextEdit function as in any word processor. Drag tab markers from the Tab box to the ruler; drag them off the ruler to remove them. Drag the indent markers shown below to indent either just the first line of text or both the left and right edges.

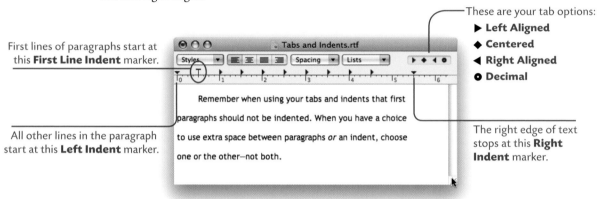

These are your tab options:

▶ **Left Aligned**

◆ **Centered**

◀ **Right Aligned**

● **Decimal**

First lines of paragraphs start at this **First Line Indent** marker.

All other lines in the paragraph start at this **Left Indent** marker.

The right edge of text stops at this **Right Indent** marker.

Remember when using your tabs and indents that first paragraphs should not be indented. When you have a choice to use extra space between paragraphs *or* an indent, choose one or the other—not both.

Examples of tab and indent settings

Below are some examples of how to set up your tabs and indents to create certain effects. Remember, for a tab, first set the marker, then hit the Tab key *before* you type the text. Once you've got tabs set up, you can move the tab and the text will follow; *just make sure you select the text before you move the tab!*

Follow the directions as explained in each window below to achieve the look you see in the window. *The tab applies only to the selected paragraphs.* Because of the way paragraphs work on the Mac, you need only click inside a paragraph to select the whole thing. To select more than one paragraph, press and drag to highlight several characters in each paragraph.

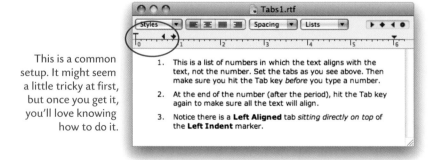

This is a common setup. It might seem a little tricky at first, but once you get it, you'll love knowing how to do it.

1. This is a list of numbers in which the text aligns with the text, not the number. Set the tabs as you see above. Then make sure you hit the Tab key *before* you type a number.

2. At the end of the number (after the period), hit the Tab key again to make sure all the text will align.

3. Notice there is a **Left Aligned** tab *sitting directly on top of* the **Left Indent** marker.

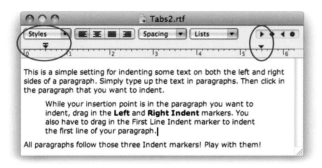

This is an example of an individual paragraph indented on both sides.

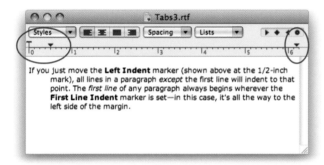

You can call this an outdent, where the first line is outdented further than the other lines.

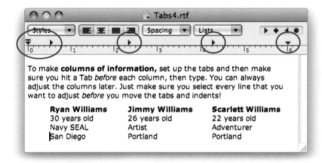

Columns are easy to create. Just remember to hit ONE tab to get to the next column.

Create Lists that Number Themselves

If you have a list of items, TextEdit can number them for you with numbers, capital or lowercase letters, or other options. When you add or delete items from the list, TextEdit automatically updates the numbering.

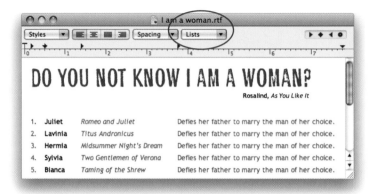

When you click on the Lists menu (circled above) and choose a numbering option, the numbers apply to **either** of the following:

> If you **selected text** on the page before you went to the Lists menu, your choice of list numbering will apply to the selected text. Each time you hit a Return, TextEdit considers that line to be the next item in the list.

> If there is no selected text, the flashing **insertion point** is "filled" with the list specifications, and everything you type from that point on will be in the list format. This is a good way to start a new list: Just make sure your insertion point is flashing where you want the list to begin, *then* go to the List menu and choose your numbering system, *then* start typing.

Choose "Other…" in the Lists menu to set up the specifications of your choice.

To end the sequencing of numbers in a list, hit the Return key twice at the end of the last item.

To delete the list numbers, single-click anywhere in the list. Open the Lists menu and choose "None."

To easily access the List options after you've started a list, click anywhere within a list, then Control-click (or right-click) in the list to show a contextual menu and choose "List…."

Create Tables

You can create simple tables in TextEdit. This table feature also helps ensure that tables created in a Word document will open in some form in TextEdit.

To create a table in TextEdit:

1   Position your insertion point where you want the table to begin.

2   Go to the Format menu and slide down to "Table...."

3   The Table palette appears, as shown below. Choose how many rows and columns you want in the table. You can determine how the text is aligned vertically as well as horizontally in each cell (use the "Alignment" icons), and more. Spend a few minutes to familiarize yourself with the tools.

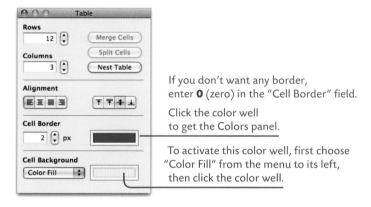

If you don't want any border, enter **0** (zero) in the "Cell Border" field.

Click the color well to get the Colors panel.

To activate this color well, first choose "Color Fill" from the menu to its left, then click the color well.

As you **type in a cell,** the cell expands downward to fit the text.

Change the formatting of the text as you do on a regular TextEdit page: select the text first, then choose formatting from the menus or palettes.

4   **To resize rows and columns,** position your pointer over the edge of a cell. The pointer turns into a two-headed arrow. With that two-headed arrow, press-and-drag on a cell edge to resize it.

Create Live Web Links and Email Links

It's easy to create web links and email links on a TextEdit page. If you send someone the TextEdit file, that person can click on a web link; her browser will open and go to the page you specify. An email link in the document opens her email program, pre-addressed to whomever you specified.

If you make a PDF of your document (see page 63), the links will still work in the PDF.

Create links as you type web addresses:

1 Simply go to the Edit menu and slide down to "Substitutions."

2 In the pop-out menu, choose "Smart Links." If there is a checkmark next to "Smart Links," it's already on!

   Or Control-click in the document, slide down to "Substitutions," then choose "Smart Links."

3 On your TextEdit page, just type the web address. It needs the *www* part of the web address. If your address doesn't have *www,* then be sure to include the *http://* in the address on the page. You'll know if it's working or not because the text will turn into an underlined link.

Sometimes the text on the page is not the actual address, but you do want the *link* to go to the address. For instance, perhaps you wrote, "Please visit our Mary Sidney web site," and you want the link attached to "Mary Sidney" to go to MarySidney.com. Or you want to say, Email me! as a link to your actual email address. In either case, use the manual process.

To manually create a web link on a TextEdit page:

1 Type the text that you want to turn into a web link. *This text can be anything— it doesn't have to be the email or web address itself!*

2 Select the text that you just typed in.

3 From the Edit menu, choose "Add Link…."

4 Enter the web page address. Make sure you include this code at the beginning of the web address: **http://**

5 Click OK.

To manually create an email link on a TextEdit page:

1   Type the text to which you want to apply an email link. This text can be anything—it doesn't have to be the email address itself.

2   Select the text that you just typed in.

3   From the Edit menu, choose "Add Link...."

4   Type into the field: **mailto:**

5   Immediately after the colon you typed (shown above), enter the entire email address just as you would address it.   mailto:**name@domain.com**

6   Click ok.

Select Non-Contiguous Text

This is really quite wonderful. "Contiguous" means "sharing a common border." Very few applications allow you to select individual sections of text that are not physically next to each other (text that is *non-contiguous*). This technique lets you apply formatting or copy, cut, or delete separate sections of text all at once.

To select non-contiguous text:

1   Press-and-drag to select a section of text.

2   Hold down the Command key. Press-and-drag to select some other text that is not contiguous!

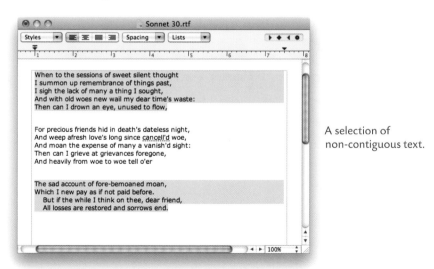

A selection of non-contiguous text.

Print Automatic Page Numbers

You can add page numbers to a *printed* document (the numbers won't appear on the screen). This feature also automatically adds the name of the document in the upper-left corner (including the extension, probably .rtf), the date and time in the upper-right corner, and the words "Page ___ of ___" in the bottom-right corner. That is, in TextEdit you can't choose one or the other of these—they all appear on the page, or none.

To print the page numbers (and everything else), press Command P (or go to the File menu and choose "Print..."). In the Print dialog box, shown below, make sure "TextEdit" is chosen from the menu. Check the box to "Print header and footer."

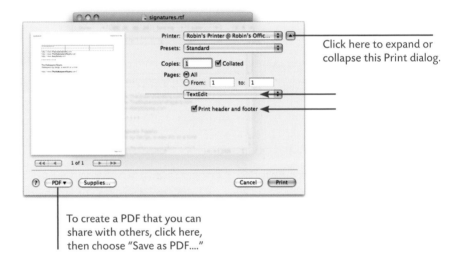

Click here to expand or collapse this Print dialog.

To create a PDF that you can share with others, click here, then choose "Save as PDF...."

Automatic spelling correction

TextEdit can automatically correct many spelling errors as you type. To enable this feature, open the TextEdit Preferences, then click the "New Document" tab. Near the bottom of the window, checkmark the "Correct spelling automatically" item.

Use Data Detectors

Data Detectors is one of several **Substitutions** available in TextEdit that enhance your text. I've already mentioned a couple of others: Smart Copy/Paste, Smart Quotes, and Smart Links. The Data Detectors feature, like Smart Links, makes your text interactive. When you hover the cursor over a street address or phone number in a TextEdit document, the cursor turns into a Data Detector and draws a marquee around the address (or phone number). Click the triangle button that appears at the end of the address to show a contextual menu of options (Create New Contact, Add to Existing Contact, Show Map, Large Type).

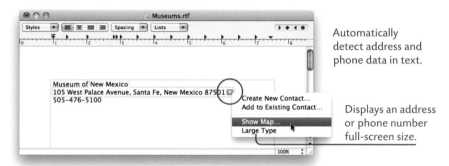

Automatically detect address and phone data in text.

Displays an address or phone number full-screen size.

To turn on Data Detection, check the Substitutions option in the Edit menu: A check next to a Substitution item means it is turned on; select it again to turn it off.

You can right-click on any empty spot in the document to open a contextual menu (below). Slide down to "Substitutions," then choose "Data Detectors." *Or* from the Edit menu, slide down to "Substitutions," then choose "Data Detectors."

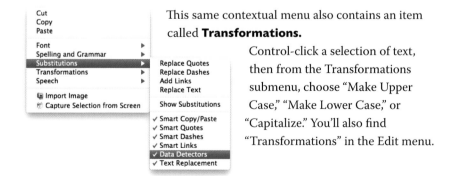

This same contextual menu also contains an item called **Transformations.**

Control-click a selection of text, then from the Transformations submenu, choose "Make Upper Case," "Make Lower Case," or "Capitalize." You'll also find "Transformations" in the Edit menu.

Show Substitutions

To access the entire range of Substitutions in a convenient floating panel, from the Edit menu slide down to "Substitutions," then choose "Show Substitutions." *Or* Control-click in the document window to get a similar menu.

The Substitutions panel provides extra controls for Smart Quotes so you can activate automatic quote styles for other languages.

This panel also provides a checkbox for **Text Replacement.** When Text Replacement is turned on, you can easily create professional typographer's symbols and fractions without memorizing special keyboard commands. For example, to type a copyright symbol (©), you can type (c) instead. When you tap the Spacebar or hit Return, the text turns into the proper typographical version. When you type a fraction, such as 7/8, it turns into a real fraction.

Click the "Text Preferences" button (shown above) to open the "Language & Text" window, then scroll through the "Symbol and Text Substitution" list and checkmark the items you want to turn on. **To add other replacements of your own,** click the Plus button below the list, then type an abbreviation of a long word or phrase. To the right, type the entire word or phrase. Now you can type the abbreviation, then tap the spacebar to replace it with the long word or phrase.

Extra Tips and Notes

Ruler: If the ruler isn't showing, press Command R. Without the ruler showing, you can't set tabs, indents, or margins.

Formatting: If text won't let you apply formatting, go to the Format menu and choose "Make Rich Text."

Wrap to Page: If text stretches the entire width of the window, you might want to switch to "Wrap to Page." Go to the Format menu and choose "Wrap to Page."

If your text prints really tiny, go to the Format menu and change "Wrap to Window" to "Wrap to Page."

Standard Mac OS X Application Features

Don't forget that TextEdit includes all of the standard Mac features as explained in Lesson 13, such as spell checking and grammar checking, creating shadows for text, applying color, using special characters, previewing before you print, making PDFs, and more.

TextEdit is Integrated With:

Safari: Web address links open in Safari.
            Control-click a word in TextEdit to search for it in Google.

Dictionary: Control-click a word and choose "Look Up in Dictionary" from the pop-up menu to get that word's definition and thesaurus entry. Snow Leopard includes the Oxford American Writer's Thesaurus, second edition.

Mail: Email address links in TextEdit open a pre-addressed email message in Mail.

Preview: Create a PDF in TextEdit (see below) that opens in Preview. You can also annotate the PDF in Preview (see Lesson 11).

Speech: Have your text read aloud to you. Select some text to read, then go to the Edit menu, slide down to "Speech," and choose "Start Speaking." A voice (named Alex) starts to read the text aloud. To turn the voice off, you have to go back to the Edit menu and choose "Stop Speaking," or use the contextual menu (Control-click or right-click in the document) and from the contextual menu, choose "Stop Speaking."

Other Relevant Lessons for TextEdit

Search: Besides the search-and-replace feature explained on page 64, you can also do a Spotlight search, as explained on page 362.

PDFs: All TextEdit documents can be turned into PDFs with the click of a button: just go to File and choose "Print…." In the Print dialog box, click the "PDF" button and choose "Save as PDF…."

Fax: You can fax any TextEdit page with the click of a button. See Lesson 17.

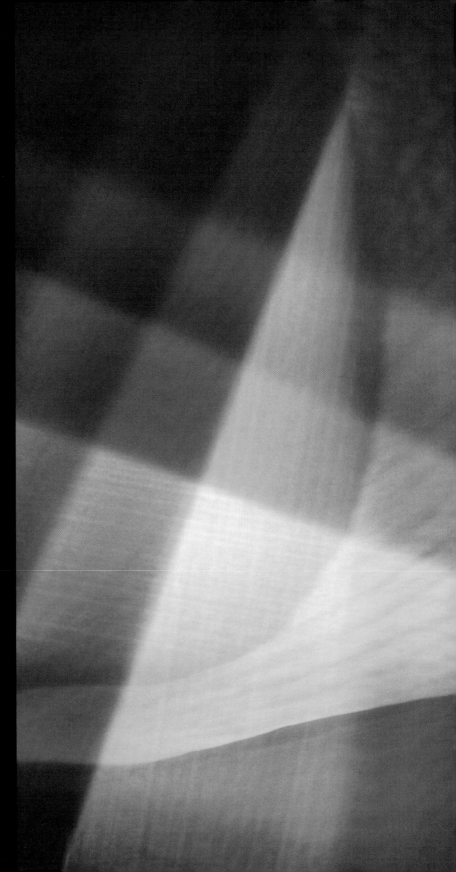

5

GOALS

Mail for Email, Notes, and To Do Lists

Mail is Apple's application for sending and receiving email. If you have more than one email account on more than one server, Mail can check them all at the same time. You can send mail from any of your accounts right through Mail.

A really wonderful feature is "stationery," where you can create fancy HTML email messages with special fonts, images, and design—all with the click of a button.

And take advantage of the Notes and To Do lists in Mail. They even coordinate instantly with your iCal information to expand their usefulness.

For those who use Windows systems at work, Snow Leopard has built-in, seamless support for Microsoft Exchange Server 2007. Now you can use your Mac apps (Mail, iCal, Address Book) to access Exchange services, such as email, calendar invitations, and Global Address Lists.

New Account Setup Assistant

It's easy to add your email account to Mail if you didn't do it when you first installed Leopard or turned on your new Mac. **If your account is already set up, skip to page 84.**

1   In Mail, go to the File menu and choose "Add Account…."

2   A sheet, shown below, appears. If you enter your MobileMe account name and password, you're done—your Mac will fill in everything else and your email will appear in the viewer window. Skip the rest of these setup instructions (except take a look at the SMTP info on page 82).

   If you have an email account that is not a MobileMe account, enter the information required, then click "Continue."

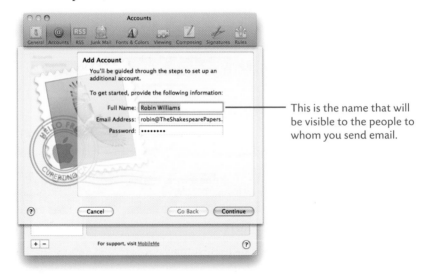

This is the name that will be visible to the people to whom you send email.

3   The next sheet asks technical details about your account. If you don't know what kind of account it is, call your Internet Service Provider and ask. *Generally speaking,* this is how to **choose the type of account:**

   Choose POP if you have an email account with your ISP, or if you have a domain name that you paid for and you opted for an email account with it (regardless of whether there are actually web pages for that domain name). **This is the most common.**

   Choose IMAP if your account is the kind that you can use on different computers and always see your mail. This is usually with a paid service or a large company intranet (although most POPs can be set up as IMAP if you ask your provider).

Choose Exchange if your company uses the Microsoft Exchange server and the administrator has configured it for IMAP access. See your system administrator for details.

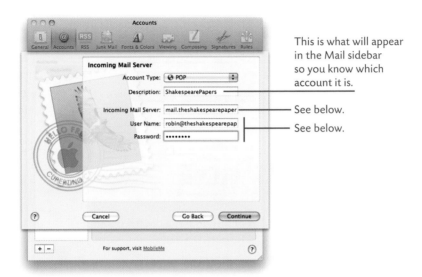

This is what will appear in the Mail sidebar so you know which account it is.

See below.

See below.

Each account type has slightly different information to enter.

For instance, if you choose a POP account, Mail wants to know the **Incoming Mail Server.** It's usually something like *pop.domain.com* or *mail.domain.com.* The "domain," of course, is to be replaced with the domain name of your email. For instance, I use *mail.TheShakespearePapers.com* for my mail that comes from that web site. If you're not sure, check your email host's web site or call and ask for the "incoming mail server."

If you use a **webmail** account, such as Hotmail, GMail, AOL, Yahoo, etc., it's a wee bit trickier to set up Mail. It's not difficult at all, but you have to know certain information. Because this information changes all the time, check this great web site: www.EmailAddressManager.com. Look for the "Mail server settings" link and from there find the information about incoming and outgoing mail servers and ports for your particular kind of account.

The **User Name** for a POP account might be different from your email name, or it might be your entire email address (most often) or it might be something different altogether. If your email address doesn't work, ask your provider.

Enter your password as provided by your provider or set up by you when you opted for the email account.

Click "Continue." *—continued*

4 The **Outgoing Mail Server,** or **SMTP,** has a couple of options. For instance, your MobileMe account will be automatically set up with a MobileMe smtp. However, I've found that the most reliable smtp is the one provided by your Internet service provider. For instance, if you use Comcast, your best smtp is "smtp.comcast.net." That is, *your most reliable outgoing mail server is the company that you pay to connect you to the Internet.*

Some providers may have a low-end broadband option that does not allow you to have an outgoing mail server, requiring you to use web mail to check and send your mail. If that's your situation and you don't like it, call them and upgrade your service so you can get an smtp address (or change providers).

The **Description** field lets you name this smtp so you can choose it from certain menus. Enter something that will make it clear to you.

Unless your provider insists, you usually don't have to enter a user name and password for authentication, so for now you can leave those blank.

5 In the Account Summary pane that opens, checkmark the "Take account online" checkbox, then click "Create." The new account should now be listed in the Inbox of Mail's sidebar.

To add another account or edit an existing account:

At any time you can add another account or edit an existing one by using the Mail preferences.

1 Go to the Mail menu and choose "Preferences...."

2 Click the "Accounts" icon in the toolbar.

3 **To add a new account,** single-click the ✚ sign at the bottom of the Accounts pane. Fill in the information on the right.

   To edit an existing account, single-click the account name in the pane, then use the pane on the right to edit.

4 When finished, just close the preferences or click on another icon. A message will appear asking if you want to save these changes.

Check your Dock Icon

When email is received, your Mail icon in the **Dock** displays a little red badge telling how many messages are unread.

Single-click this Mail icon to bring the Mail window to the front. You don't have to quit Mail when you're finished working in it.

Right-click (or Control-click) the Mail icon to open a pop-up menu of commands and options (below-left), such as "Compose New Message." These commands are also available in the File menu and the Application menu.

Press (hold down the mouse button) the Mail icon to pop up a menu with other options (below-right), such as "Quit," "Hide," and "Keep in Dock."

The appearance and content of these contextual menus change, depending on if the application is already open, or not. If the application is already open, Dock Exposé is activated (shown below-right). See pages 44–45 for information about Dock Exposé.

Read and Send Email

The default in Mail is to automatically check your mail every five minutes. This, of course, assumes you use a full-time broadband connection. If you use a dial-up connection, go to the Mail preferences (from the Mail menu), click the "General" tab, and change it to "Manually."

As mentioned on the previous page, when you have messages in Mail that are yet unread, the Dock icon puts the number in red so you always know.

To read mail that has arrived:

1   If you have more than one account, your "Inbox" will have a disclosure triangle next to it. Click the triangle to see the individual accounts (shown below).

2   On the left, single-click the account you want to see. The messages are displayed in the message pane to the right. Unread messages have a **blue orb** next to them.

3   **To read a message,** single-click it and the message will be displayed in the lower pane. **Or** double-click a message and it will open into a new window.

Click "New Message" to compose and send a message.
Enter the recipient's email address, plus a subject.

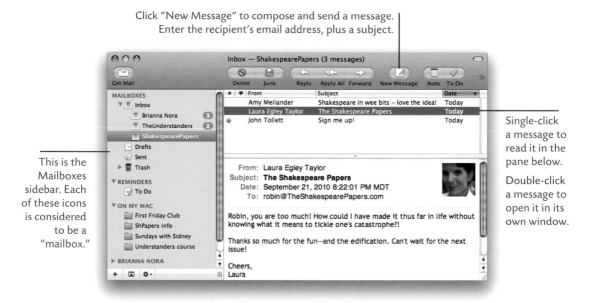

This is the Mailboxes sidebar. Each of these icons is considered to be a "mailbox."

Single-click a message to read it in the pane below.

Double-click a message to open it in its own window.

To send an email message:

1   Click the "New Message" button in the toolbar, or press Command N.

2   In the "To" field, enter an email address.

   Or if you have an address in your Address Book or if you've sent a message to this person before, as soon as you start typing, the rest of the email address appears. If there is more than one person with those beginning letters, you'll get a list of possibilities. You can use the arrow keys to go up or down the list and select the addressee you want; hit Return to put that address in the field.

   Or click the "Address" icon in the toolbar to bring up the Address Book pane, a limited version of your Address Book. Double-click on anyone's name to add it to the "To" field. To add someone's email address to the Cc or Bcc fields, select a name in the list, then click the "Cc:" or "Bcc:" button.

3   In the "Subject" field, enter a subject. Do not type something that might be construed as junk mail! For instance, don't type "Hi" or "Thought you might like to know" or "About last night" or "I've got a great opportunity for you—all I need is your bank account number." Be specific so the recipient will actually open your message instead of immediately deleting it because it sounds like spam.

4   In the message pane, type your message. Mail will automatically check your spelling and display suspect words with a red dotted underline. You can change the font, the color, the size, the alignment, and more—using the Format menu. You can also use the Font panel, Colors panel, Spelling Checker, and all the other Mac OS features—see Lesson 13 for details.

5   If you want to send a file of some sort, just drag it into the message window and drop it (see pages 106–108 for more details).

6   When you're ready, hit the "Send" button. **Or** click the "Save As Draft" button in the toolbar to save it for later. To open that letter later, go to the Drafts folder in the sidebar.

TIP ———— If you can't format the text in a message, such as color it or even make words bold, go to the Format menu and choose "Make Rich Text." If it says "Make Plain Text" in that menu instead of rich text, that means you're already working in rich text. If you still can't make bold or italic text, then the font you chose does not have bold or italic versions. Check the Fonts panel (press Command T) to see if the font you're using includes bold and italic versions. See pages 246–247 for details.

Customize the Message Window

It's easy to customize the message headers, the toolbar, and to add or delete various columns of information.

To add or delete columns of information in the message pane:

1 Make sure the Mail viewer window (the main window) is open in front of you.

2 Go to the View menu, slide to the first item, called "Columns," and slide out to the right. Choose the information that you want to see from that list.

To customize the toolbar:

1 From the View menu, choose "Customize Toolbar...."

2 Drag anything into the toolbar from that pane. While the pane is open, drag anything *out* of the toolbar that you don't want—drag it off the toolbar and drop it on the Desktop. Drag icons left or right to rearrange them.

To reorganize the existing items in the toolbar *without* opening the Customize Toolbar pane, hold down the Command key and drag icons to different positions in the toolbar, or drag them completely out of it.

To customize the message headers:

1 Open any new message (click the "New Message" button in the Mail toolbar).

2 Click the Action button (shown circled, below), and choose "Customize..." to get the pane shown below.

3 Check the boxes of the items you want to see in your messages. Click OK when you're done.

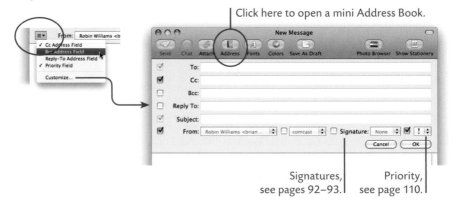

Click here to open a mini Address Book.

Signatures, see pages 92–93.

Priority, see page 110.

Do Not Display Junk Mail!

Some junk mail sends an invisible message back to its sender as soon as you open it, telling the despicable junk-mailing scumbag that this is a working email address. To prevent opening and displaying that mail at all, get rid of the message pane, as shown below. Then, when you click on a message to delete it, it doesn't automatically appear in that pane. **When you want to read a message,** double-click it and it will open in a separate window.

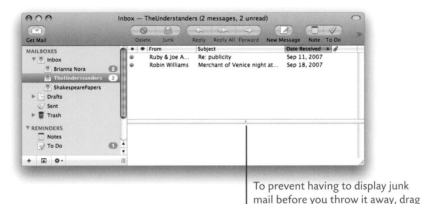

To prevent having to display junk mail before you throw it away, drag this bar all the way to the bottom.

Delete Junk Mail Without Ever Seeing It!

Mail has a **junk mail filter** that can toss your spam automatically. Actually, while in "training," it will put spam in a special brown "Junk" folder where you can check to make sure messages really are garbage before you toss them. Once you are confident the junk mail filter is doing a good job, use the instructions below to send junk mail to the Trash immediately.

To turn on Junk Mail filtering, go to the Preferences pane (in the Mail menu), click the "Junk Mail" icon, and check the box to "Enable junk mail filtering." Carefully read the other choices in the pane and choose your options.

To move junk mail directly to the Trash, select "Perform custom actions," then click the "Advanced…" button. The dialog sheet that opens contains some default settings for handling junk mail, which you can modify if you want to. In the lower section of this sheet labeled "Perform the following actions:," choose to "Move Message" to mailbox "Trash."

Use Stationery to Send Fancy Email

It's actually called "HTML" mail, not "fancy" mail. HTML just means it has HTML code written into the message for you that creates the layout, the space for photos, the fonts, etc. *You* don't have to write one single piece of code. All you do is choose the stationery template, type your message, and drag photos to replace the existing ones.

To create an email with stationery:

1 Open a new email message (Command N).

2 Single-click the button on the right side of the message toolbar called "Show Stationery." (If you don't see that button, open the message window wider, or click on the arrow you see where the button should be—that will pop out a menu with "Show Stationery" on it.)

3 A row of stationery templates appears, as shown below. Single-click a category on the left, then choose a template on the right.

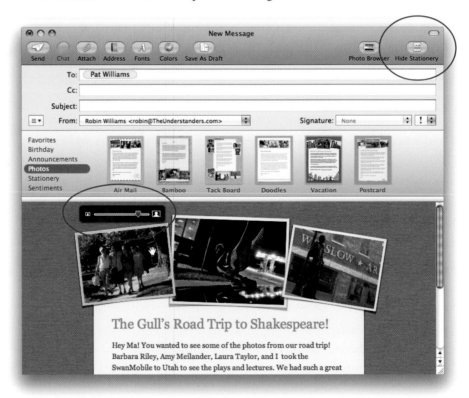

4 **To replace the text,** click it and Mail automatically selects all the text in that section. Whatever you type will replace that text, but will retain the font.

5 **To add photos,** you can do several things.

- Click the "Photo Browser" button in the toolbar. This opens the Photo Browser and displays all the photos you have in iPhoto, Aperture, or Photo Booth. Just drag an image from the Photo Browser and drop it directly on top of the image you want to replace.

- Drag an image from anywhere on your Mac and drop it on an existing image.

- Open iPhoto and drag an image directly from iPhoto onto an existing image.

6 **To resize photos,** click an image and a little slider bar appears, as shown on the previous page. Drag the slider right or left to enlarge or reduce the image.

7 **To reposition the image within the frame,** click the image. Then press-and-drag on the image to reposition it within its frame (you can't reposition the frame itself).

You can **change templates at any point**—if there are fewer photos in the new template, some of them will disappear. Your text will reappear in the new template.

Click the "Hide Stationery" button to put the row of templates away so you have more room in which to write.

Save as stationery

You can save your own designs as stationery. You can't use the templates that Apple provides, but you can set up an email message with the fonts you like to use, as well as colors, links, and images that you want to appear in the message. When you've got it the way you want it, go to the File menu and choose "Save as Stationery."

A new category appears in the list of stationery, called "Custom." Click on that new category and you'll see your own stationery.

To delete stationery you made, position your mouse over it and a little **X** appears in the upper-left corner. Click the **X** to delete the stationery.

Create Mailboxes to Organize your Mail

Organize your mail with mailboxes in the same way that you make folders in a Finder window to organize all the files on your Mac. (In fact, most of the mailboxes look just like folders.) Use the "Mailbox" menu to create new ones, or Control-click in the Mailboxes sidebar. If you Control-click directly on an icon in the sidebar, the new mailbox will be a subset of that icon.

The items in the sidebar are reorderable. They can be dragged up or down to new positions in the sidebar, just the way you want them.

Once you've got your mailboxes set up, drag messages to your mailbox folders to organize your email. Use filters (called Rules; see the next page) to automatically send incoming mail to the different folders/mailboxes. Also check out pages 95–97 about Smart Mailboxes.

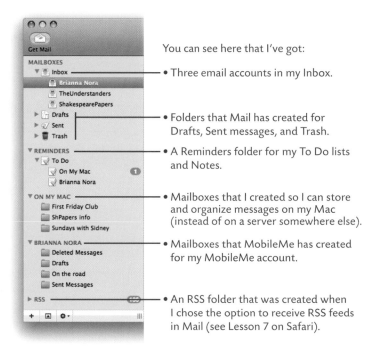

You can see here that I've got:

• Three email accounts in my Inbox.

• Folders that Mail has created for Drafts, Sent messages, and Trash.

• A Reminders folder for my To Do lists and Notes.

• Mailboxes that I created so I can store and organize messages on my Mac (instead of on a server somewhere else).

• Mailboxes that MobileMe has created for my MobileMe account.

• An RSS folder that was created when I chose the option to receive RSS feeds in Mail (see Lesson 7 on Safari).

Filter your Incoming Mail with Rules

Create rules, or filters, to **sort incoming mail** into the appropriate mailbox. First, create the mailboxes you want for organizing (see opposite page). Then:

1 From the Mail menu, choose "Preferences…."

2 Single-click the "Rules" icon. Single-click "Add Rule."

3 Choose your parameters for the type of mail coming in and what to do with it. (If you forgot to make a special mailbox for something, you can actually do it while the Rules pane is open on your screen; use the Mailbox menu. The new mailbox will immediately appear in the pop-up menu, shown below.)

> In the example below, I first made a new mailbox called "NancyD" (although you *can* make one while this dialog box is open).
>
> Then I created a new rule to find any incoming mail from my editor, Nancy Davis.
>
> When found, I want that message to move straight into the "NancyD" folder and play a little sound so I know it arrived.

Click the pop-up menu button (under here) to choose the mailbox this Rule will move messages into.

Add Signatures to your Messages

An **email signature** is the little blurb you can automatically add to the bottom of your messages. A signature might include your contact information, promotion for your upcoming art show or book publication, your favorite quote, or even a small graphic. You can make more than one signature, then choose which one you want for an individual email message, as a default signature that automatically appears, or you can let Mail randomly choose one for you.

This is a signature.

If you have created more than one signature, you can choose which one to use in the message—see the opposite page.

To create a signature:

1   From the Mail menu, choose "Preferences…."

2   Single-click the "Signatures" icon. You'll see the window shown on the opposite page.

3   At the top of the left-hand pane, single-click "All Signatures."

4   In the middle pane, single-click the plus sign (**+**). The new one is called "Signature #1." Double-click it to name it something more relevant.

5   In the right-hand pane, type your signature. From the Format menu at the top of your screen, choose "Show Fonts," then choose a font, size, style, alignment, and color. You can use Returns and Tab keys in your signature.

Don't choose a font that you have bought or acquired along the way because most of your recipients probably won't have that same font installed. Use one of the fonts that came with your Mac.

6 If you want an **image** to appear in this signature, drag the image from the Finder and drop it into the right-hand pane. Keep in mind that this should be a very small image, both in file size and in visual size!

If you like, drag an image from the Finder and drop it in this pane.

7 Drag a signature from the middle column and drop it on the account name in the left column to add it to that email account. You can have lots of signatures, yet have only certain ones available for different email accounts.

8 Each email account can have its own **default signature** that automatically appears in each email message you write: First select an account in the left-hand pane, then use the "Choose Signature" menu circled above.

To use a signature, put the "Signature" menu in your message window:

1 Open a new message as if you're going to write a letter.

2 Single-click the Action button, then choose "Customize…."

3 Put a checkmark in the box next to "Signature."

4 Click OK. Now you will see the Signature menu in every new mail message, as shown below. Choose the one you want to use for each individual message.

Action button.

You won't see an option to add signatures if you haven't made any yet!

Search your Mail

In Mail, Spotlight searches very thoroughly. It's very simple.

1   If you want to limit the search to a particular mailbox or to Notes, select that mailbox or the Notes mailbox. Or click the "Inbox" to search all mail.

2   Enter a word or phrase in the search field; results immediately appear.

3   A new bar also appears, as shown below. In this bar you can choose which account to search, and choose which part of the email to search.

Choose "All Mailboxes" or click on one in the sidebar, then choose it here in this header.

"Entire Message" includes not only the message, but the From, To, and Subject lines as well.

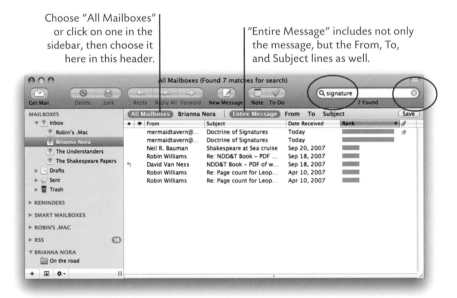

4   **To display all your messages again,** click the gray **X** in the search field. As long as there is even one character in the search field, you will see the search results instead of your mail.

Smart Mailboxes

You can create **Smart Mailboxes** that will hold all the email messages that meet certain search criteria. If you are familiar with Rules (filters), as explained on page 91, you'll notice there are a couple of differences between Rules and Smart Mailboxes.

- A Rule is an *action* that is applied to incoming messages, such as filtering certain email into a certain folder. The *original* email is *moved* into the folder.

- A Smart Mailbox contains messages that match search criteria. No action is taken on the messages.

- A Smart Mailbox does not contain the *original* message, thus the same message can be "stored" in a number of Smart Mailboxes.

- A Smart Mailbox automatically updates itself as messages come in or are deleted.

- A Smart Mailbox applies your search criteria to mail that is already in your box, not just to future incoming mail.

Below you see an example of several Smart Mailboxes in the sidebar. The ones named "Understanders" and "The Shakespeare Papers" are actually Smart **Folders** that each contain Smart **Mailboxes.** The folder is just for organizational purposes. Both are explained on the following page.

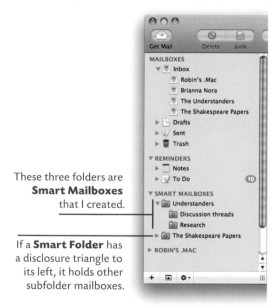

These three folders are **Smart Mailboxes** that I created.

If a **Smart Folder** has a disclosure triangle to its left, it holds other subfolder mailboxes.

Create Smart Mailboxes

There are several ways to **create a Smart Mailbox.** One is from the Mailbox menu (below) and another is to use the parameters you've designated in a saved search, explained on the opposite page.

To create a Smart Mailbox from the Mailbox menu:

1 If you go to the Mailbox menu, you'll see there are two similar options, "New Smart Mailbox Folder…" and "New Smart Mailbox…."

   The **Smart Mailbox Folder** creates a folder with no search parameters; it is simply for organizing other **Smart Mailboxes** inside (as shown on the previous page). If you choose to make a Smart Mailbox, you will only be asked to name the folder and click OK.

   If you want your Smart Mailbox to be *inside* of an existing Smart Folder, first select that folder in the Mailboxes sidebar; if not, make sure that folder is *not* selected.

2 When you choose "New Smart Mailbox…," the dialog sheet shown below appears. Name your Smart Mailbox, choose your parameters, and click OK.

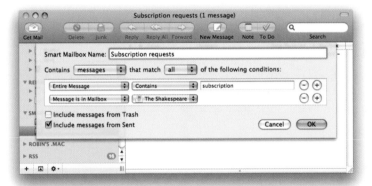

3 If you need to edit the parameters of your new Smart Mailbox, select it, then either Control-click, right-click, or go to the Mailbox menu and choose "Edit Smart Mailbox…."

To create a Smart Mailbox by saving a search:

1 Do a search as usual, as explained on the previous pages.

2 If the search gives you what you need and you think you'll want to use the same search again, click the "Save" button.

3 The saved search is automatically named with the search phrase you just used. You can refine your search in the edit box, if you like. When ready, click OK.

4 If you need to edit the parameters of your new Smart Mailbox, select it, then either Control-click, right-click, or go to the Mailbox menu and choose "Edit Smart Mailbox...."

TIP —— If the command to make a Smart Folder is gray, it's probably because something is selected in the sidebar and Mail can't put a Smart Folder inside of whatever is selected. Click on an empty space in the sidebar, and the option to create a Smart Folder will become available.

Amazing Data Detectors

Mail is able to detect certain kinds of data, such as addresses, days, dates and airline flight numbers. When you hover your pointer over certain kinds of data in an email message, Mail puts a dotted border around the data and adds a pop-up menu button on the right side of the data. Click the button to open a menu of options that changes with the type of data selected. In the example below, when I choose "Show Map...," Safari opens Google Map and shows a map of the address.

Click the Data Detector menu of a day or date and the pop-up menu lets you choose to create a new iCal event on the selected date.

If someone sends you an email with a flight intinerary attachment, you can click the data detector's highlighted flight number to open Dashboard's Flight Tracker widget and instantly see up-to-date information about the flight, including arrival and departure times, and the current location of a flight if it's in the air. See page 101 for more information about data detectors.

To Do Items

Mail is no longer just an email program—it's the message center for your digital lifestyle. When you use Mail to create To Do lists and Notes, you stay organized and can find all your information quickly and easily. Mail keeps track of everything and integrates with iCal to make sure you never miss a date.

To create a To Do item from text in an email message:

All you do is select the text in a message you've received, then click the "To Do" button in Mail's toolbar (or Command-click the selection and choose "New To Do"). You can create as many To Dos from one message as you like.

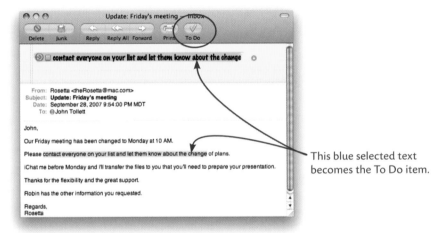

This blue selected text becomes the To Do item.

Your To Do items appear at the top of the message, and also in Mail's sidebar, and they have their own viewer pane with their own **columns of information.** Control-click any column header to see the other columns you can add.

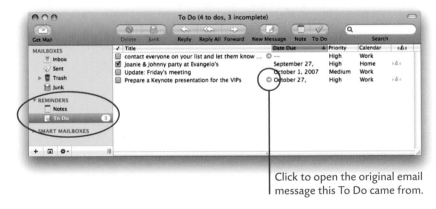

Click to open the original email message this To Do came from.

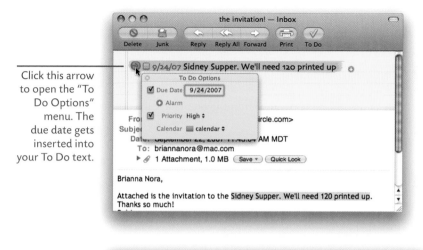

Click this arrow to open the "To Do Options" menu. The due date gets inserted into your To Do text.

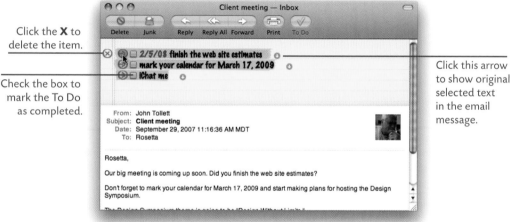

Click the **X** to delete the item.

Check the box to mark the To Do as completed.

Click this arrow to show original selected text in the email message.

To create a To Do item related to an email message:

Control-click a selection of text in a message. Or Control-click in a blank area of the message. From the pop-up menu that appears, choose "New To Do." A yellow note pad graphic slides down from the top of the window. Type a brief note.

To create a To Do item without using an email message:

Just click the "To Do" icon in the toolbar. Type your message in the field provided. Control-click the message to get options for setting priorities, due date, etc. This To Do item will be associated either with the last email account you made a To Do in, or the one you choose in Mail preferences, in the Composing pane.

To Do items in Mail's sidebar

To Do items are in their own section of the sidebar, as shown below. If you have more than one MobileMe account, the To Dos are sub-categorized into the different accounts. All non-MobileMe mail accounts go into a category called "On My Mac."

You won't see those categories in your sidebar until you make a To Do item, and then they appear automatically.

The title bar tells you how many
To Do items are not completed.

You can add or delete columns
of information: Control-click any
column header to see the options.

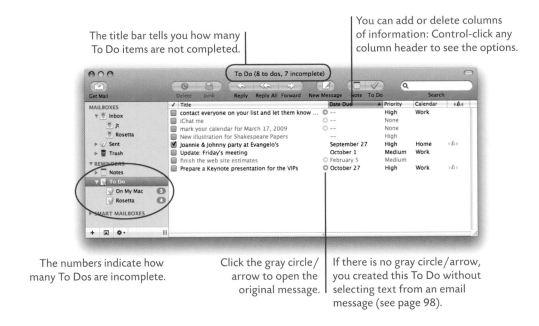

The numbers indicate how
many To Dos are incomplete.

Click the gray circle/
arrow to open the
original message.

If there is no gray circle/arrow,
you created this To Do without
selecting text from an email
message (see page 98).

TIP —— The Mail To Dos are intimately connected with iCal (another Apple application on your Mac). Dates will be inserted as events on the appropriate day, and you can send email invitations out from iCal. Please see Lesson 8 for details.

Automatic data detection for events

This is amazing. As in TextEdit, when you hover your mouse over a day or date in an email message, it highlights with a gray dotted outline and adds a menu button (a triangle symbol). If you click the menu button, you can choose to immediately open iCal and see what's going on for that date, or choose "Create New iCal Event…." Notice this is not creating a To Do item, but an *event* in iCal.

An info dialog box opens in which you set all the information, then click "Add to iCal." In this example, even though a numerical date was not available (just the word "Monday"), iCal automatically assumed the message meant the next Monday following the date of the email.

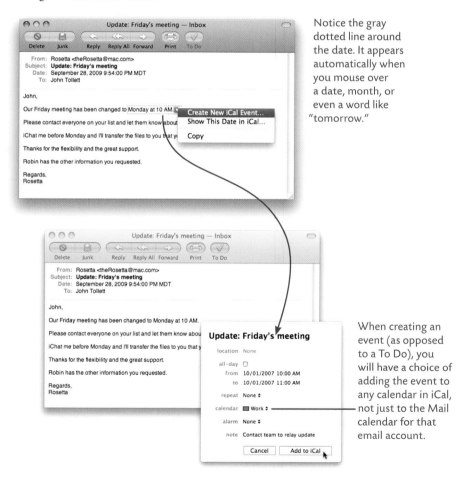

Notice the gray dotted line around the date. It appears automatically when you mouse over a date, month, or even a word like "tomorrow."

When creating an event (as opposed to a To Do), you will have a choice of adding the event to any calendar in iCal, not just to the Mail calendar for that email account.

About the calendars

To Do items and events are automatically sent to iCal. If you have already set up iCal with a number of calendars, you can send events and certain To Dos to any of those pre-existing calendars.

If your email account is a MobileMe account, Mail/iCal makes a special Mail group for you in iCal with a default calendar in it cleverly called "calendar." You can rename it, of course. Any To Do item you create from your MobileMe email account will be assigned to a calendar in this Mail group *only;* you cannot assign a To Do item to any of your other calendars. Any To Do items in this Mail calendar will be available to you automatically anywhere in the world through your MobileMe account online.

To Do items from any other email message or in any other email account besides a MobileMe account can be assigned to any calendar in the Calendars group.

These are the calendars I made in iCal. They're in the **Calendars group.**

Events (as opposed to To Do items) that you create in Mail can be assigned to any calendar, regardless of which email account it originated from.

The instant you make your first To Do item in Mail in a MobileMe email account, a **MobileMe group** like this is created for you.

From within Mail, you can create new calendars; these calendars instantly and automatically appear in iCal.

- If you make a new calendar from a **MobileMe account,** the calendar goes in the **MobileMe group,** shown above.

- If you make a new calendar from **any email account that is not MobileMe,** that new calendar goes into the **Calendars group,** as shown above.

To make a new calendar in Mail, Control-click a To Do account in the sidebar.

Use the columns to assign options

Take advantage of the information you can display and change in the columns of the To Do items. Control-click in the column header area and you'll get a list of possible columns you can add, or you can delete ones you don't need. You can also use the View menu (the "Columns" sub-menu) as long as you are showing the To Do pane when you go to the View menu. (That is, if you're looking at email messages, the Columns sub-menu shows you column headings for email, not To Dos.)

To set a due date for items that don't have one, move your pointer over the "Date Due" column; a small triangle appears. Click that triangle to get the pop-up menu shown below. To set a specific date, click "Other...."

You can also **assign a calendar** to a particular To Do item from the Calendar column, or switch the item to a different calendar. Just click in the Calendar column for that To Do item. A little menu pops up with the calendars available to that particular email account, as explained on the opposite page.

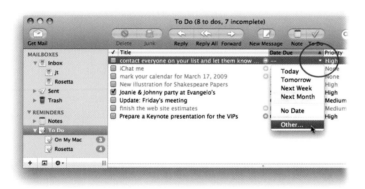

The little menu arrows appear when your mouse hovers over the column.

Notes

While the To Do items are great for tracking things that need to get done, Notes are a handy place to store ideas, thoughts, or any other information you want to keep track of. Mail becomes a central location for information—messages, Notes, and To Do lists.

Create a new Note

To create a new Note, click the "Note" button in Mail's toolbar. (This button is only available when you're in the main viewer window, *not when an email message is open and active.* To Do items can be created from email messages, but not Notes.)

A "New Note" window opens in which you can type a brief or lengthy note. Mail uses the first line of text as the subject of the note (keep that in mind as you write the note), and shows the first line in Mail's list of Notes.

To create an automatically bulleted or numbered list, go to the Format menu, slide down to "Lists," and choose the type of list you want. Type your list, hitting a Return after each item. **To stop the list** so you can type regular text, hit the Return key twice.

When finished, click "Done."

If multiple Mail accounts are active, the note is added to the Mail account that was selected in the Mailboxes category in the sidebar, unless you have specified otherwise in the Composing pane in the Mail preferences.

Format and add attachments to a Note

You can format the text in a Note just as you do in an email message, and you can add attachments and To Do items. Just click the appropriate buttons in the Note toolbar. When you choose to "Send" a Note, an email window opens with the note inside the message area.

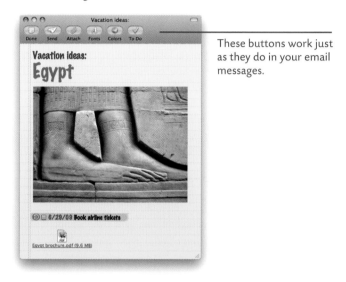

These buttons work just as they do in your email messages.

View Notes in Mail

The Mail window includes a Notes mailbox in the sidebar, which displays all your notes, as shown below. But you'll also see the Notes appear in your list of email messages when viewing an inbox. Notes are identified by an icon in the "Message Status" column on the far left, as you can see below.

To sort Notes by Mailbox, click the Mailbox column heading.

Attachments

One of the greatest things about email is the ability to send files and photos back and forth. Mail has some great features for attachments, making it easier than ever to share files.

To send an attachment:

1   Open a new message window and type your subject, message, etc.

2   To attach a file or photograph, single-click the "Attach" icon.

This opens the standard Open dialog box. Find your file, select it, and click "Choose File." You can hold down the Command key to click on and select more than one file to attach.

Or drag a file or photo from a window on your Desktop and drop it directly into the message window.

3   A file icon appears in your window. If it's a one-page PDF or a photo, the actual image will probably appear, as shown below, instead of a file icon.

4   If the file in the window appears as the actual image, you can change it into an icon if you like (you don't have to): Control-click (or right-click) on the image. From the pop-up menu (below), choose "View as Icon." This does *not* determine how the person who *receives* the file will view it.

Click here to attach a file.

If the photograph is too large, you can choose to send a smaller version right here.

5   Send your email.

To receive and download an attachment:

1   An attachment appears in someone's Mail message, or yours, as an actual image or as a file icon, shown below.

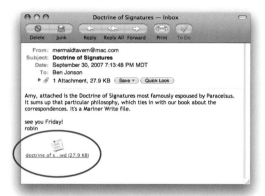

2   There are several ways to deal with this file:

If it's a photograph and you can see it in the window, then you see it and maybe that's all you want to do with it. So you're done. Or . . .

If it's **one file or photograph,** you can do any of several things:

Either drag the file to the Desktop or directly into any window or folder on your Mac.

Or single-click the "Save" button in the header information at the top of the message; the files are instantly added to the Downloads folder; see page 109.

Or save the image directly into **iPhoto** (if you have iPhoto installed): *Press* (don't click) the "Save" button and choose "Add to iPhoto" (shown on the following page).

Or Control-click (or right-click) the photo or file icon and choose any of several options, shown below.

—continued

If you have a **series of photographs** in your email message, you have even more options. You can do everything mentioned on the previous page, plus:

> **Save only one file** from the collection. *Press* (don't *click*) the "Save" button and a menu appears, as shown below. Choose the file you want to save.

> You can view a **full-screen slideshow** of the photos. Simply click the "Quick Look" button in the header information.

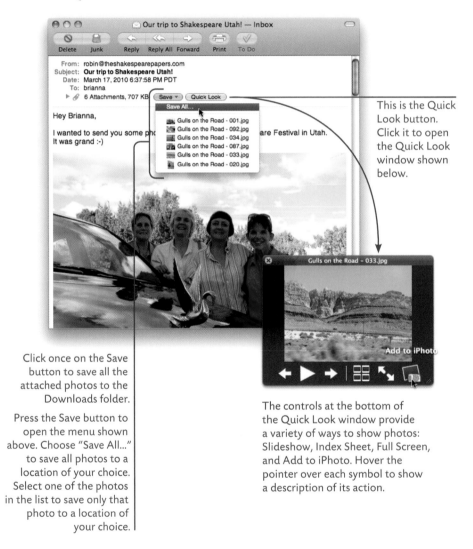

This is the Quick Look button. Click it to open the Quick Look window shown below.

Click once on the Save button to save all the attached photos to the Downloads folder.

Press the Save button to open the menu shown above. Choose "Save All…" to save all photos to a location of your choice. Select one of the photos in the list to save only that photo to a location of your choice.

The controls at the bottom of the Quick Look window provide a variety of ways to show photos: Slideshow, Index Sheet, Full Screen, and Add to iPhoto. Hover the pointer over each symbol to show a description of its action.

Downloads Folder

When you click the "Save" button in an email to save the files that someone sent you, the files are automatically stored in the **Downloads folder** in your Home folder; a copy of this Downloads folder is in the Dock. Open either folder to get to the files. These folders in the Dock can be viewed as a "Stack" (a stack of icons), or as a "Folder," as shown in the examples at the bottom of the page. Press the Downloads folder in the Dock to show a pop-up menu, then select the view you want— Fan (below-left), Grid (below-middle), or List (below-right).

You can see that the files in the Downloads folder above are exactly the same as the ones in the Downloads folder in the Dock, no matter which view you choose: Fan, Grid, or List.

Single-click the Downloads icon in the Dock to display its contents, as shown in the examples below. Single-click a file to open it in its application. Click "Open in Finder" to show the files in a Finder window, as shown above.

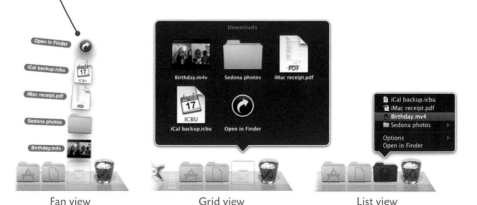

Fan view   Grid view   List view

Priority Options

You can set one of three **priority** options in Mail messages so your recipient understands how urgent (or not) a particular message is—provided the recipient's email program can display the priority marker. If someone sends you a message marked as high or low priority, Mail will mark it as such.

To set a priority:

With an email compose window open, go to the Message menu in the menu bar, slide down to "Mark," and choose the priority option you want for this message.

If you would like to have the priority options handy, put this tiny menu in the message window. See page 86.

To check the priority of an incoming message:

If the Flag column is visible in Mail, you will see two exclamation marks to denote a message that has been labeled **High Priority.** A dash indicates **Low Priority.** (One exclamation point means the message is **Normal Priority,** but you won't see any symbol for this kind of message.) If the Flag column is not visible, Control-click on a column heading, then from the pop-up menu, choose "Flags."

Use the Standard Application Features

Mail includes all of the **standard Mac features** as explained in Lesson 13, such as spell checking, text with shadows, text in color, special characters, creating PDFs, previewing before you print, reading text aloud, and more.

The "Complete" feature, as explained on page 66, can be used in email messages. Any styles you created in TextEdit, as described on page 65, are also available in Mail messages—from the Format menu, slide down to "Style," then out to "Styles...."

Mail is Integrated With:

Parental controls: See Lesson 18 to make another "user" for your child or children and have full control over their email access.

Address Book: Click the "Address" icon in the Mail Toolbar to open a mini Address Book panel.

iChat: A green dot in a column in your Viewer window indicates an iChat Buddy is online and available. If you don't see that column, go to the View menu, select "Columns," then choose "Buddy Availability."

iCal: Email announcements to all attendees of an event. All To Do items can go straight to iCal. Calendars created in Mail appear instantly in iCal.

MobileMe Sync: Synchronize your MobileMe mail with the MobileMe web mail site so you have access to your mail on any computer in the world.

TextEdit: Click an email link in TextEdit to open Mail and automatically address the email.

Safari: Safari will email complete web pages or just the links, as well as send email from email links.

Dashboard: When you send an email flight itinerary, or recieve one, Mail's flight data detector can identify flight numbers, then open Dashboard's Flight Tracker widget for up-to-date flight information. See page 97.

6

GOALS

Address Book for Contact Info

The **Address Book** is a great **contact list** integrated with so many other parts of your Mac. It's much more complete than its simple appearance might lead you to believe—take the time to explore its possibilities!

Enjoy the drag-and-drop ease of creating groups and sending everyone in the group a message. Create Smart Groups so that new contacts that meet certain criteria are automatically added to the group. Show a Google map of an address with a single click. Start a new email message, or an iChat conversation, with a click.

Mail and iCal are integrated with Address Book so you can easily and quickly send messages and invitations to your contacts. And it's easy to sync your entire Address Book, or a single Group, to your iPhone (or other mobile phone).

For people working in a Windows environment, Snow Leopard supports Microsoft Exchanger Server 2007.

How you'll Use your Address Book

Before I explain how to do specific tasks, such as create new address cards, add a photo to a person's card, send email, etc., first let me briefly describe how you can use this great application.

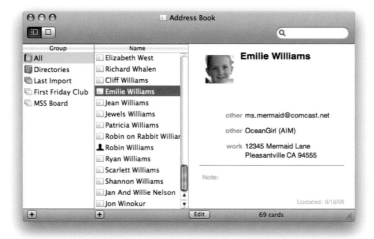

You can customize individual cards and/or add new *fields* (those places where you type in information) to all of them. For instance, you can add a "birthday" field or a nickname field. You can change the labels, add a photo or image, and customize the address for another country.

You can create Groups of addresses to make a mailing list so you can mail everyone in the Group with one click.

In Mail, all the contacts you put in your Address Book will be available via the Address Pane (see page 86). In the Address Pane in Mail, you can't add or edit or delete or group addresses—you can just access them for emailing.

While in Mail (not Address Book) **you can automatically add an address from an email you receive:** open the email in Mail, right-click (or Control-click) the email address in the "From" field, then from the pop-up menu, choose "Add to Address Book." If that contact information is already in your Address Book, the pop-up menu item says "Open in Address Book."

Your iPhone will synchronize with all the addresses or with certain Groups that you specify. As you add contacts to your iPhone, they will automatically be added to your Address Book on your Mac next time you connect and sync your phone.

Make and Edit New Cards

To make a new card, (sometimes called a vCard), click the **+** sign at the bottom of the "Name" pane, which displays the new card in the right pane, ready for you to add information.

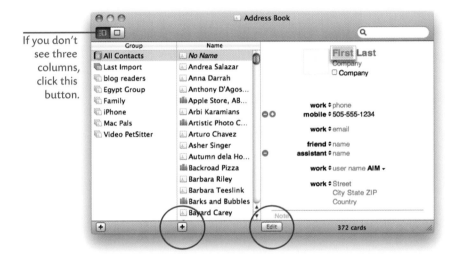

If you don't see three columns, click this button.

⊕ Click the green button to **add another field** for that particular type of information, like another phone or email address. You won't see this green button until you have filled in the blank area and are ready for another one.

⊖ Click the red button to **delete** that field.

▼ Click labels that have tiny triangles to **change the existing field label names.**

To edit an existing card, select the card in the "Name" column, then click the "Edit" button (circled above). Edit the card to your heart's delight. When you're finished, click "Edit" again.

> **TIP** ——— Only the fields that contain information will be visible on the card.
>
> Also, be sure to check out the preferences for Address Book (under the Address Book application menu). Use the "Phone" preferences to automatically format phone numbers, and use the "General" preferences to customize your contacts and several other features. Use the "Accounts" preferences pane to synchronize your contacts with your MobileMe, Yahoo!, or Google accounts.

Add a photo to a card

You can add a photo to any contact card. That photo will appear in email that you receive from that person; it will be transferred to your iPhone so you can see his handsome face when he calls; and you can print it with his contact info.

To add a photo to a contact card:

1   Go to that card in your Address Book and click the "Edit" button (if it isn't already).

2   Double-click the empty photo space to the left of the name. A sheet appears:

The empty photo space on the card looks like this, a ghost.

Effects button.

3   Drag any type of image into the pane, **or** click "Choose..." to find a photo on your hard disk, **or** click the camera icon to take a picture of someone, even someone you are iChatting with. (If there is no camera attached to your computer, your camera icon is gray.)

4   Drag the blue slider bubble to the right or left to enlarge or reduce the image. Press on the image to drag it around inside the space.

Click the effects button to choose from different weird effects.

5   Click "Set" when you like it.

Add photos via your iPhone

If you have an iPhone, next time you are with someone whose contact information is in your Address Book (or whose contact info you are adding into your iPhone), edit her contact info in your phone and take her photo. The next time you sync your iPhone to your Mac, this photo will automatically apppear in your Address Book and when you get email from this person, it will include her photo in the upper-right corner of the message.

Designate your Own Card

In your Address Book, you can designate the card with your contact information on it as "My Card." Other applications, Safari and iChat in particular, will use that information in various ways, such as filling in forms online, accessing your email address, and displaying your photo.

Your card name has a little human silhouette next to the name.

Enter a **card** for yourself in the Address Book (Apple might have done that for you already). Then go to the Card menu and choose, "Make This My Card." (Apple might have already done that for you too).

To keep some of the information private so it won't show up if you send your vCard (virtual card) to someone else (as explained on page 123):

1   Go to the Address Book preferences (under the "Address Book" menu).

2   Click the "vCard" icon in the toolbar.

3   Check the box to "Enable private me card." Close the preferences.

4   Go to your own card and click the "Edit" button. You'll see a blue checkbox for each item on your card; the checkmark means it is public information. **Uncheck** the boxes that you want to be private.

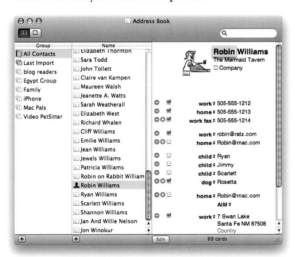

Customize One Card or All Cards

The fields for data only appear on the card if there is data in them; otherwise the fields disappear, which is kind of nice. Select a card and click the "Edit" button to see what fields you might have on a card that are not filled in.

You can add a number of other fields to an individual card or to all cards.

To add a field to ONE card:

1 Select that card.

2 From the Card menu in the menu bar across the top of your screen, slide down to "Add Field," and make a choice from the pop-out menu.

To add a field to EVERY card:

1 From the Card menu, slide down to "Add Field" and then choose "Edit Template...."

   Or go to the Address Book menu and choose "Preferences...." From that toolbar, click on the "Template" button.

2 Click the "Add Field" button to display its menu. All the field names in gray are already on the card template. Choose any field name that is in black and it will be added to *all* of your cards. Until you enter information into that field, you'll only see it when you click the "Edit" button on individual cards.

Check Out the Options

There are lots of hidden options in the Address Book. Single-click the labels to the left of the fields on a card. You'll get little menus, depending on what you click on. Check them out! Below you see where I chose the option "Show in Large Type" to display a fax number. (This option only shows up on phone or fax numbers, but you could put a love note instead of a phone number to surprise your sweetheart.) You can send text messages to cell phones, dial numbers with your Bluetooth-enabled cell phone, send email, chat, and more. If you have Skype installed, even more options will appear.

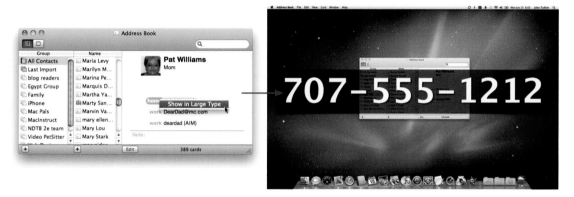

Map It

You can instantly get a Google map of any address in your Address Book. (You must be connected to the Internet, of course.)

Click the label to the left of an address in Address Book. A little menu pops up where you can choose "Map this Address." Safari opens to Google Maps and displays the location of that address. Freaky, but cool.

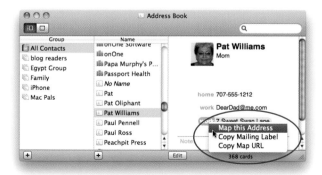

Create Group Mailing Lists

After you've made a Group mailing list, you can **send email to the name of that Group** and your message will go to everyone in the Group.

To make a new group:

1 Click the **+** sign at the bottom of the "Group" column.

2 Change the existing name of the Group to something you'll recognize.

3 Click the "All" group.

4 Drag names from the "Name" column of the "All" group and drop them on the Group name. You can put the same name in many different Groups.

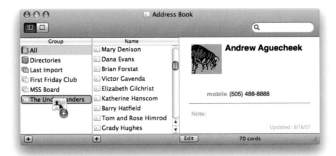

To email a message to a Group:

■ **In the Address Book,** Control-click (or right-click if you have a two-button mouse) the Group name and choose "Send Email to (group name)."

■ **OR in the Mail application,** type the name of the Group in the "To" field of an email message.

To prevent all the addresses from appearing in everyone else's email:

1 Open Mail (not Address Book).

2 From the Mail menu, choose "Preferences...."

3 Click the "Composing" icon.

4 Uncheck the box, "When sending to a group, show all member addresses."

TIP ——— Select a person's name, then press the Option key to highlight all the Groups in which he is included.

Create Smart Groups in Address Book

A Smart Group is a list of contacts that automatically updates itself as contacts meet its criteria. For instance, you might want a Smart Group that automatically adds people who work for a certain company or who are part of your literary salon. You can create a Smart Group that tells you when someone's birthday or anniversary is approaching. Or you might want to gather a list of everyone in a particular city without having to find them all in your Address Book—a Smart Group will find existing contacts and automatically collect them.

Most of these searches require, of course, that you have a particular field on your card and that it has data in it. For instance, you can't have a Smart Group that tells you when a birthday is coming up if you don't have the Birthday field on your cards. For directions on how to **add new fields** to individual cards or to all cards, please see page 118.

To create a Smart Group:

1   From the File menu at the top of the screen, choose "New Smart Group…."
    Or Option-click the **+** sign under the "Group" column.

2   In the sheet that drops down, shown above, choose your parameters.

3   If you need more parameters to narrow down or open up the possible items in the Group, click the **+** sign (circled above).

4   If you want to see a visual clue when a new item has been added to the Smart Group, be sure to check the box to "Highlight group when updated." Then when a new item is automatically added, the Smart Group will change color to let you know someone's been added to it.

Search your Address Book

You can do a standard, simple search for anyone or any information in your collection of contacts. And you can do a Spotlight search of anyone in your Address Book that searches your entire hard disk for everything related to that person.

To search your Address Book for a contact:

1   **To search for a contact within a Group,** single-click the Group name you want to search.

   To search your entire database of contacts, click the "All" group, as shown below.

2   Single-click in the search field.

3   Type the first couple of letters of the name of the person you want to find, either first or last name or the business name. As you type, results will appear in the center "Name" pane.

4   Type more letters to narrow your search, or single-click one of the contacts in the "Name" pane.

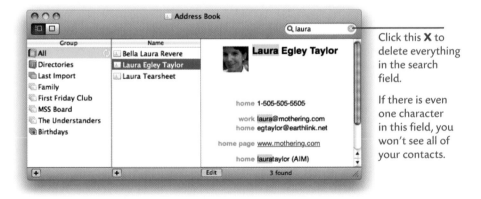

Click this **X** to delete everything in the search field.

If there is even one character in this field, you won't see all of your contacts.

5   **To display all of your contacts again,** click the **X** in the search field, and single-click the "All" group.

To search for a person or business in Spotlight:

1 Find the person you want to Spotlight, as explained on the previous page.

2 Control-click (or right-click) the person's name; from the pop-up menu that appears, choose "Spotlight *'This Person'*" (where *'This Person'* is the name of the contact you just searched for; that name automatically appears in the menu). See the illustration below.

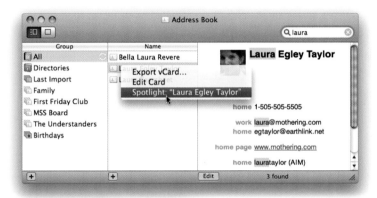

3 You will get the Spotlight window (a Finder window), as explained in Lesson 19. It will show you every file on your computer that is connected with this person, such as email she's sent, files she's mentioned within, documents she has created and sent to you, images of her, and more.

Send your Address Book card to others

To send your personal contact info to someone else, Control-click your name in the "Name" column.

1 From the pop-up menu, choose "Export vCard…" (*or* from the File menu, choose "Export…," then choose "Export vCard…").

2 Select a location in which to save the file, such as the Desktop. Click "Save." This creates a vCard icon in the location in which you saved it.

Now you can drag that exported vCard icon into a new message window. The file is now attached to that email message and you can send it to others. If the receiver has a Mac, she can simply double-click on your vCard and the contact info will be added to her Address Book.

Share your Address Book Contact List

If you are a MobileMe member (see www.Apple.com/mobileme), you can **share your entire contact list** with other MobileMe members. This can be useful for families, teens and their friends, organizations, businesses, and others. And you can **subscribe** to someone else's shared Address Book, provided that person has already put you on their shared list.

Remember, you must have a MobileMe account to share, and the only people who can share your Address Book are other MobileMe members running Tiger (Mac OS 10.4), Leopard (10.5), or Snow Leopard (10.6). The people you want to share with must already be in your Address Book as contacts, so if they're not there yet, add them before you follow these steps!

1   From the Address Book menu, choose "Preferences...."

2   Single-click the "Accounts" icon.

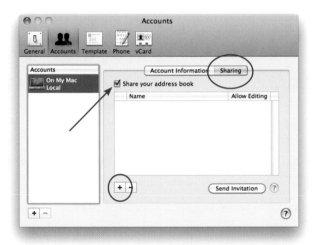

3   In the window that appears, click the "Sharing" button, then check the box to "Share your address book."

4   You must choose who is allowed to access and share your Address Book: Single-click the **+** sign at the bottom of the window.

5   This drops down a sheet displaying the people who are in your Address Book, as shown at the top of the next page. Select the names you want to share with; hold down the Command key to select more than one name.

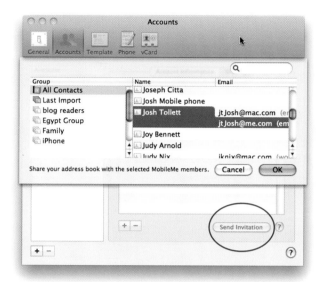

6 Click OK. After you add names, you can send an email inviting someone to share your Address Book: Single-click a name (or Command-click several names), then click "Send Invitation."

Subscribe to someone's Address Book

You can only subscribe to an Address Book that someone else has already set up as shared, as explained above. And that person must have already chosen you as someone who is allowed to access her Address Book. Once that's done:

1 In your own Address Book, go to the File menu and choose "Subscribe to Address Book...."

2 Enter the MobileMe account name of the person whose Address Book you want access to. After you enter the account, click OK.

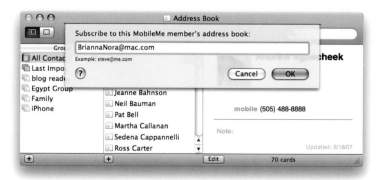

Print in a Variety of Ways

From Address Book you can **print** mailing labels, envelopes, customized lists, and even pages that fit into a standard pocket address book.

1 First, in Address Book, select the names or the Group that you want to print.

2 Press Command P to get the Print dialog box. If you don't see the full window as shown below, click the small blue triangle to the right of the "Printer" pop-up menu (circled below).

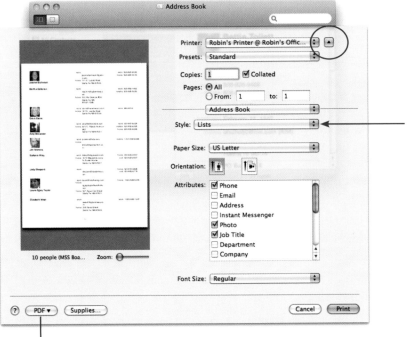

You can save the job as a PDF and then send that PDF to someone else to print.

3 From the "Style" pop-up menu, choose what you wish to print—lists, envelopes, mailing labels, or pocket address book pages. Each "style" has different parameters to experiment with. Whatever you choose will be displayed in the preview window.

Spend some time poking around this dialog box so you know what all your options are. As you can see below, you can add an image to your return address, choose different fonts and colors for the text, choose different envelope sizes, and so much more that it's just amazing.

To print a return address, check the "Print my address:" box. Address Book automatically uses your "Me" card for the return address. If you want it to use another card, go back to the Address Book, select that other card, go to the Card menu, and choose "Make This My Card." You can switch it back when you're done printing. Of course, you can uncheck the box so it doesn't print any return address at all.

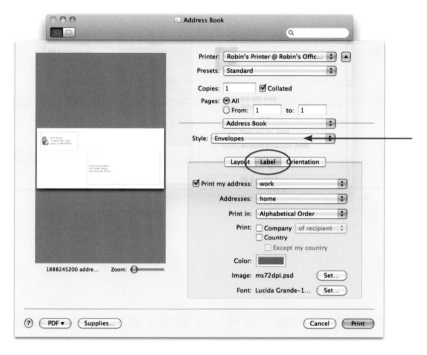

To add an image to your return address, click the "Label" tab above.
You'll have options to change fonts, colors, add an image, and more.

Backup your Entire Digital Database

There are few things more annoying than losing your entire Address Book that you have carefully created over the past year or two. You have a couple of options for backing up your entire Address Book.

■ One way is to select everyone in the Name column (or just select the important names), then drag that block of names to the Desktop. This creates a vCard file, shown below, that you can then store on another disk for safekeeping.

Andrew Aguecheek
and 69 others.vcf

You can send this vCard to someone else on a Mac; she double-clicks it and the addresses get automatically entered in her Address Book.

■ **Or** go to the File menu and choose "Export," then "Address Book Archive...." Your Mac will make a file for you and ask you where to store it. When you want to restore your Address Book, double-click this file or use the Import option in the File menu.

Address Book
2008–...8.abbu

Remember, a backup is only useful if it's not in the same place as the original. That is, don't keep it on your hard disk—if your hard disk goes bad, it will take both the original and the backup! Copy the file onto a disk, upload it to your iDisk if you have a MobileMe account, or email it to a colleague for safekeeping.

Address Book is Integrated With:

Dashboard: Pop up a mini-version of your Address Book for quick and easy access. See Lesson 16.

Safari: Put your Address Book in the Bookmarks Bar and you have instant access to any web sites listed in the Address Book. To do this, open Safari, and in the Safari preferences, in the Bookmarks pane, check the box to "Include Address Book."

The AutoFill feature in Safari uses the data you enter in your "Me" card.

iCal: iCal can create a Birthday calendar from your Address Book so everyone's birthday is automatically placed on its appropriate day; see page 158.

Mail: Send email to a selected contact email address with a contextual menu. The photos you put in the Address Book will appear in other Mac users email messages when they send you mail.

To automatically add someone's email address to your Address Book, select a message in Mail, then press Command Shift Y.

iChat: iChat will pick up the data and pictures you add in Address Book. And when a Buddy is online and available, his address card displays a green dot.

With a camera connected, you can add a photograph of someone you are chatting with through iChat.

MobileMe: Synchronize your other Macs and your MobileMe account so you have your entire Address Book accessible on the web, anywhere in the world.

Spotlight: Send your Address Book search out to your entire computer through Spotlight. See page 122.

iPod: Transfer your entire contact list to your iPod using iSync.

iPhone: Transfer your entire contact list or selected Groups to your iPhone using iTunes.

7

GOALS

Safari for Web Browsing and News

Safari is Apple's beautiful web browser for viewing web pages on the Internet. You've probably already used it, but you might be surprised at the tips and tricks it offers that you haven't taken advantage of yet.

Safari also includes its own "news reader" that brings in RSS feeds. RSS stands for Really Simple Syndication. It's an Internet technology that "feeds" you news and information of your choice from a huge variety of sources. Safari can gather the RSS feeds you are interested in and display the headlines from many sources in one place—a web page. You'll have access to them with one click of a button, and you can organize the information, filter the feeds, automatically update them, and more.

Safari Web Browser

Below is a brief overview of the main features of the Safari window. Although it looks simple, it holds a lot of power in subtle ways.

Customize the toolbar; choose "Customize Toolbar" from the View menu **or** Control-click the toolbar.

Type a web address, then hit the Return or Enter key.

Click to reload a web page.

Enter a Google search right here!

Bookmarks Bar.

Bookmarks Cover Flow.

Top Sites.

Status Bar. If you don't see this bar in your browser, go to the View menu and choose "Show Status Bar."

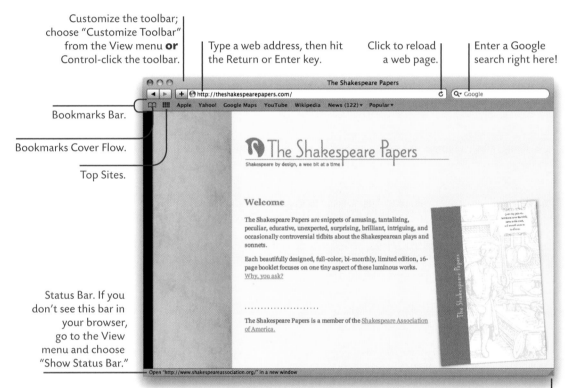

Drag this corner to resize the window.

Watch for visual clues

When a web page is loading in Safari, you'll see an indicator in the address field, as shown to the right.

Enter a new web address quickly

This is one of my favorite features in Safari: If you double-click between www and .com, it selects *just* the domain so you can change it. This means you don't have to drag the mouse across tiny little letters when you want to change the address. Try it.

And don't forget you never need to type "http://." If it's a .com address, all you need to type is the main word. For instance, to go to www.apple.com, just select everything in the location bar, type *apple*, then hit Return.

Quickly Access your Top Sites

 Safari keeps track of your top sites, based on how often and how recently you visited them. **To display your top sites as a wall of previews,** click the Top Site icon (shown below, left) in the Bookmarks Bar. The top sites displayed on this page change, depending on your browsing activity.

To open a top site in the browser window, click its preview. **To open one or more sites as a tab,** Command-click the preview (see page 138 for more about tabbed browsing). **To search your browsing history,** enter a keyword in the "Search History" field. **To edit your Top Sites display,** click the Edit button.

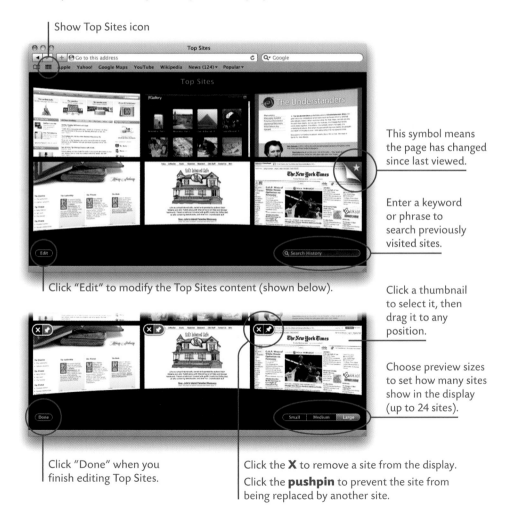

Show Top Sites icon

This symbol means the page has changed since last viewed.

Enter a keyword or phrase to search previously visited sites.

Click "Edit" to modify the Top Sites content (shown below).

Click a thumbnail to select it, then drag it to any position.

Choose preview sizes to set how many sites show in the display (up to 24 sites).

Click "Done" when you finish editing Top Sites.

Click the **X** to remove a site from the display.
Click the **pushpin** to prevent the site from being replaced by another site.

Bookmarks in Cover Flow View

To show a Cover Flow view of all your bookmarks (the Bookmarks Library), click the "Show all bookmarks" icon on the left side of the Bookmarks Bar (the book icon, shown on the left and circled below). If the Bookmarks bar isn't visible, go to the View menu and choose "Show Bookmarks Bar."

To search a Bookmarks Collection listed in the Sidebar, or a specific folder of bookmarks you've created and organized, select the item in the Sidebar, then enter a keyword or phrase in the search field located in the top-right corner of the Cover Flow pane.

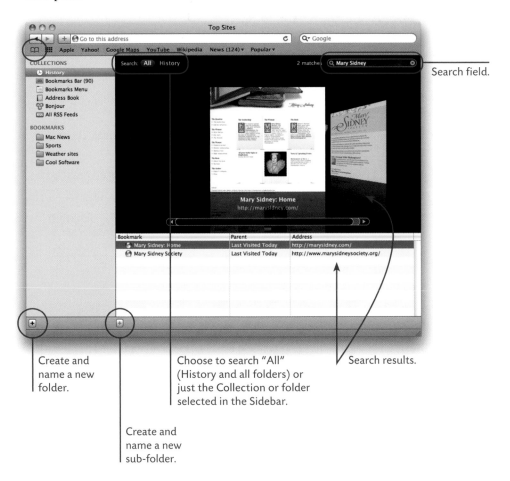

Search field.

Create and name a new folder.

Choose to search "All" (History and all folders) or just the Collection or folder selected in the Sidebar.

Search results.

Create and name a new sub-folder.

Bookmarks

The bookmarks in Safari are powerful and easy to use.

Choose this to display the Bookmarks Library.

The **Bookmarks Menu,** shown above, is what drops down from the menu bar at the top of your screen.

The **Bookmarks Bar** is that strip in the browser window, just below the address field, as shown on the opposite page. To show it (if it isn't already showing), go to the View menu and choose "Show Bookmarks Bar."

The **Bookmarks Library** and the various **Collections** you create let you organize hundreds of bookmarks, but you don't have to put them all in the Bookmarks Menu, which would make your list a yard long. Click the "Show all bookmarks" button ( ) at the far-left of the Bookmarks Bar when you want to open the Bookmarks Library and make new folders for **organizing your bookmarks.**

When you hit Command D to **create a bookmark,** a little sheet drops down and asks you where you want to store it. You can rename the bookmark at that point and choose to store it in any folder *you have already made* in the Bookmarks Library.

Organize your bookmarks with folders

You can organize all your bookmarks in the Bookmarks Library.

1 From the Bookmarks menu, choose "Show All Bookmarks," or click the bookmarks icon on the far left of the Bookmarks Bar.

2 In the bottom-left of the window, click the **+** sign. This puts a new bookmark folder, called a Collection, in the left-hand pane.
   When you make bookmarks, as mentioned above, you can choose this folder in which to store the bookmark.

3 To put this folder in the Bookmarks Menu so you can access it in that menu, first click the "Bookmarks Menu" item in the Library. Now drag the folder from the left pane and drop it into the large right pane, which is the list that will appear in the Bookmarks Menu. You can drag the items into the order you want them listed. You can also drag folders or bookmarks directly into the Bookmarks Bar.

Fill in Forms and Passwords Automatically

This is wonderful. Safari will **fill in online forms** with the information you have entered into your Address Book; it takes the data from the card you have designated as "My Card" (use the Card menu in Address Book to do that; see page 117). You can also tell Safari to remember your **user ID and password** for specific sites, which is great if no one else uses your Mac or if you have set up different users.

To enable Safari to fill in forms and passwords, go to the Safari Preferences and click the "AutoFill" icon. Check the appropriate boxes.

Notice the "edit" buttons. You can delete the information from any web page that was hanging on to your info or passwords.

Next time you start to fill in a form, Safari will fill it in for you. Next time you go to a page that needs an **ID and password,** go ahead and fill them in, then Safari will ask if you want to save that information. Try it on your MobileMe log in page.

To delete saved user names, passwords, or forms, go back to the AutoFill preferences. Click the "Edit..." button next to the items you want to remove. In the sheet that opens, select one or more specific sites, then click "Remove." Or, click "Remove All."

AutoFill is turned off when you turn on private browsing, explained on page 144.

Block Pop-Up Windows!

Go to the Safari menu and choose "Block Pop-Up Windows." Woo hoo! Only pop-up windows that you click on will appear—none of those obnoxious ads.

Occasionally, however, this can cause a problem. You might run across a web site where you click on a link for extra information and nothing happens. This might be because the extra information appears in a pop-up window. If so, go back to the Safari menu and choose "Block Pop-Up Windows" again to take the checkmark off.

SnapBack to a Results Page or Other Page

Do you see those little **orange arrows** in the location field and the Google search field below? Those indicate "SnapBack" pages.

When you do a search in Google, either at Google.com or through the Google search field in the upper-right corner of Safari, you get a page of results. As soon as you click on a link on that page, the SnapBack arrow appears. Wherever you surf, you can always click the SnapBack arrow **to return to the original results page.**

You can **mark any page** you want as a SnapBack page: Go to the History menu and choose "Mark Page for SnapBack." As soon as you leave that page, the arrow appears in the location field, ready for you to click to return. You'll also see the SnapBack arrow anytime you type in a web address yourself (as opposed to getting there from a link or bookmark).

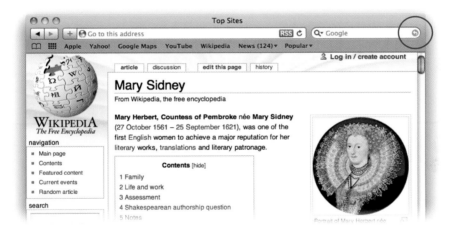

Quickly Enlarge or Reduce a Web Page

Safari can scale entire web pages, both text and graphics, to show the page elements large or smaller. This technology is called "resolution independent scaling." Make the **a web page larger or smaller** with Command **+** (larger) or Command **–** (smaller). You don't have to select anything first.

You can also add a "scaling" shortcut button to your Toolbar. From the View menu, choose "Customize Toolbar…." From the sheet that opens, drag the "Zoom" buttons to Safari's Toolbar. Click the small "A" to reduce a web page, and click the larger "A" to enlarge a web page.

Tabbed Browsing

When you click a link, of course, Safari takes you to another page and thus you lose track of the one you were on. Besides taking advantage of the SnapBack feature described on the previous page, you can also choose to open web pages in **tabs**.

Instead of losing your original page, a tabbed page gets loaded and displays as a tab, as shown below. **To open any link into a tabbed page,** Command-click the link (hold down the Command key and click the link).

Command-click lots of links and they will all load themselves into individual tabs. Then when you're ready, click any tab to display that page, while leaving your original page still available (as a tab).

Hover your pointer over a tab to show this **X** symbol. Click the **X** to close the tab.

Tabs.

Click a tab to display that page.

Option-click the **X** to close all open tabs except the one you clicked.

Drag a tab left or right to change its position.

To use tabbed browsing, go to the Safari preferences and click the "Tabs" icon. Take a few minutes to check out the options. For instance, if you check the second box, shown below, the tabbed window will immediately come to the front instead of lining up behind the current page.

Also see page 150 about "Auto-Click:" displaying all bookmarks in a folder as individual tabs, all at once.

Find a Word or Phrase on the Current Page

To find a word or phrase on the *page* you are looking at (as opposed to searching the Internet for it), press **Command F**. Then just type—Safari knows to put the search term in the search field that appears in the top-right corner.

To make it easy for you to see the found word or phrase, Safari dims out the rest of the page and highlights every instance of what you're looking for, as you can see below. Just click on the page to un-dim it.

To make Safari put the strong yellow highlight on successive results, press **Command G**. Each time you hit that shortcut, Safari puts the yellow highlight on the next found result.

Safari holds onto that search. You can go to another page and hit **Command G** again—Safari will search for the last word or phrase you requested. In fact, you can close or even quit Safari and the next time you open it, Command G will find results of the last word or phrase you were looking for.

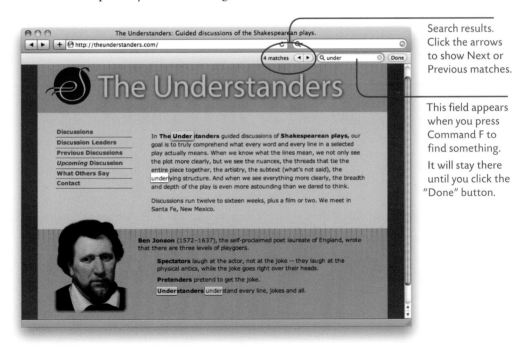

Search results. Click the arrows to show Next or Previous matches.

This field appears when you press Command F to find something.

It will stay there until you click the "Done" button.

Email a Web Page or a Link to a Web Page

Safari makes it especially easy to **email an entire web page** to anyone, complete with images and links.

1   Open the web page in Safari.

2   From the File menu, choose "Mail Contents of This Page."

3   The Mail application opens with the name of the web page as the subject. The entire web page is in the body of the email. All you have to do is add the recipient's address and click the "Send" button.

Or you can **email just the link.** Follow the steps above, but choose "Mail Link to This Page."

If you want to make emailing the link to a web page even easier, customize the Safari toolbar with a "Mail" button. Control-click (or Right-click) on the Safari toolbar, then choose "Customize Toolbar…." From the sheet that slides down, drag the "Mail" button to the Safari toolbar.

View PDF Documents

To view a PDF document right in Safari, just drag the PDF file and drop it into *the middle* of any Safari page.

To enlarge or reduce the size of the PDF on the screen, Control-click (or right-click) anywhere on the PDF page. From the menu that appears, choose one of the sizing options (Automatically Resize, Actual Size, Zoom In, or Zoom Out). Or, hover your pointer over the bottom edge of the document to show controls for Zoom, Open in Preview, and Save to Downloads Folder.

If the PDF has **more than one page,** but all you see in Safari is one page, Control-click (or right-click) and choose "Next Page" or "Previous Page." You can also, Or, choose either "Single Page Continuous" or " Two Pages Continuous," and use the scroll bar to scroll through the document pages.

Save a Page and Everything on It

Safari lets you save a web page and all the images and links and text on the page. It creates one file, an archive, that you can open at any time; all the links will work (as long as the destination pages haven't changed). This is particularly handy for pages that you know aren't going to last long, such as online newspaper articles or purchase receipts. Keep in mind that some web pages can prevent you from saving items on the page.

1   Open the web page you want to save.

2   From the File menu, choose "Save As…." Or, Control-click on a web page, then choose "Save Page As…."

3   From the Format menu in the dialog box, choose "Web Archive," as shown.

4   Choose the folder you want to save into, then click "Save."

To save a frame of a web page, Control-click (or right-click) the frame. From the menu that pops up, choose "Save Frame As…."

Make a Web Clip Widget

This is pretty cool. There's a button in the Safari toolbar that lets you make a Dashboard widget of any section of any web page. Any buttons, fields, or links that are captured in that widget will work in Dashboard. If you delete this widget, you'll have to remake it from scratch to get it back.

To make a web clip widget:

1   Go to any web page in Safari.

2   Click the Web Clip Widget button in the toolbar. (If the button is missing, Control-click the toolbar and choose "Customize Toolbar...," then from the sheet that slides down, drag the Web Clip button, above-left, to the toolbar.)

3   The page turns gray, except for a clear box that follows your mouse around. Click in the area that you want to capture as a widget. Immediately eight handles appear on the clear box. You can drag any of these handles to reshape the box. Press and drag inside the box to move it.

4   When you like where it's positioned, click the "Add" button in the upper-right.

5   Immediately Dashboard opens up, displaying the new widget.

Click the tiny *i* that appears in a bottom corner (cirlced, below-right) to flip it over and add a fancy border, if you like.

The selected area above (baseball scores) becomes the Dashboard widget shown to the right.

With this Wikipedia web clip, I can go to Dashboard, enter a search term, click Go, and I'm there.

Print Web Pages

You can see a preview of how your web page will print. You can tell the background not to print, and you can make sure the web address and date appear on the page.

To print a web page:

1 Just go to the web page you want to print, then press Command P to get the Print dialog box, as shown below (or go to the File menu and choose "Print...").

2 If you don't see the expanded box shown below, click the blue disclosure button shown circled below.

3 Make sure the "Safari" option is chosen in the menu in the middle of the pane, shown below. You'll see the preview on the left.

4 Check or uncheck the boxes to print the background or the headers and footers, shown below.

5 If the web page needs more than one piece of paper to print, the preview will show you every page; use the arrows under the preview pane to navigate the previews of each page.

6 Click "Print."

Click this disclosure button to contract or expand the sheet you see here.

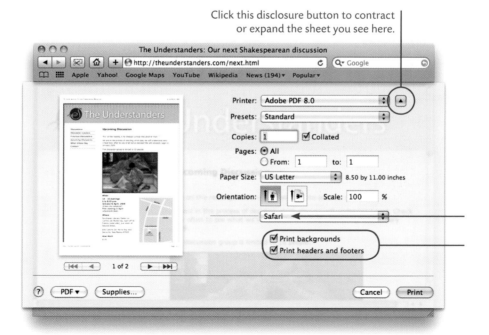

Private Browsing

You may have noticed that Safari keeps track of where you've been and what you've entered into search fields and what web pages you've asked to see. Safari's AutoFill feature even keeps track of user names and contact information you've entered on sites, as well as passwords and credit card numbers. If there are other people who use your computer, or if you are using Safari on someone else's Mac or at a school or an Internet cafe, you probably don't want Safari keeping track of all that information. That's where **private browsing** comes in handy.

When you turn on private browsing:

- None of the information you enter on any page is saved.
- Any searches you do will not be added to the pop-up menu in the Google search field.
- Web pages you visit are not added to the History menu. However, you can still go back and forward to pages you've viewed during the current session.
- If you downloaded anything, those items are automatically removed from the Download window when you quit Safari or turn off private browsing.
- Cookies are automatically deleted when you turn off private browsing or quit Safari.

To turn ON private browsing, go to the Safari menu, choose "Private Browsing." A checkmark appears next to the menu item to indicated it's turned on.

To turn OFF private browsing, go to the Safari menu and choose "Private Browsing" again to remove the checkmark.

When you **quit Safari,** private browsing is automatically **turned off,** even if you left it on before you quit. So each time you open Safari, you need to turn private browsing on again if you want to use it.

To further secure your privacy, when you are finished go to the Safari menu and choose "Reset Safari…." You can eliminate any trace of your whereabouts from the options you see listed here. This, however, will remove *everything* from that feature in Safari, not just the ones you used today!

Parental Controls

If you have a young child (or anyone acting like a young child), you can set up some serious parental controls to limit access to web sites. It involves multiple users, which are explained in detail in Lesson 18. You'll need an admin user (you) to set up another user for the child. The child will be able to view only web sites you have placed in the Bookmarks Bar. He won't be able to enter web addresses in the Address field, modify any bookmarks, or use the Google search field in the toolbar.

To limit web access to a young user:

1 Using the Account preferences, set up another user (details in Lesson 18). In the "Accounts" pane, choose "Enable Parental Controls."

2 Click the button to "Open Parental Controls...."

3 Choose the account to which you want to add parental controls.

4 Click the tab labeled "Content."

5 Click the button to "Allow access to only these websites."

6 To remove a site listed, select it and click the **–** button.
   To add a web site, click the **+** button and type a web address of your choice.

7 Log in to that user's account, open Safari, and make sure it's what you expect. Safari puts the web sites chosen in Step 6 into the Bookmarks Bar, as shown below, and the user will not be allowed to go anywhere else.

This icon (a padlock on top of the bookmarks icon) shows that Parental Controls are enabled.

The Bookmarks Bar contains the sites you chose in Steps 5 and 6.

Note: This does not prevent the user from surfing the web with any other browser. If you want to limit the *applications* this user can use, do so in the Parental Controls, as above.

So What is RSS?

All major news organizations, as well as thousands of personal web logs (blogs) and individual web sites, offer article summaries and headlines in the form of RSS feeds.

To see RSS feeds, go to a site that provides an RSS feed page and click the RSS icon in the web adddress field (see page 148). An Apple RSS feed page is shown below.

You can **customize the display** of an RSS feed page. To display more or less of an article, drag the "Article Length" slider (circled above-right). Take note of the other categories in the sidebar that can help you organize the presentation of information.

To open an RSS aticle's web page, click the headline, or click the "Read more..." link that appears at the end of each RSS blurb.

You can **bookmark RSS feeds** to keep them organized. In the example above, I dragged the RSS feed icon (circled) from the address field to the Bookmarks Bar to create a bookmark in that location. The number of unread articles from this RSS feed is now displayed in parenthesis next to the bookmark.

At any time you can add more RSS feeds to Safari, delete RSS bookmarks you don't want to keep, search RSS feeds for information, and even bookmark searches to which you want to return (enter a search term in the "Search Articles" field, then from the "Actions" sidebar group, choose "Bookmark This Search" (circled above).

View all existing RSS feeds in Safari

Apple has provided some RSS news feeds to get you started. Build your own collection of RSS bookmarks, as described on the following pages.

To see all of your RSS feeds:

1 Open Safari, your web browser.

2 If the Bookmarks Bar is not showing, press Command Shift B, *or* go to the View menu and choose "Show Bookmarks Bar."

3 Open the Bookmarks Library: Single-click the "Show all bookmarks" icon at the far-left end of the Bookmarks Bar (circled, below).

4 In the Collections pane, which appears in the sidebar that opens, single-click "All RSS Feeds." A list of all your RSS feeds will appear on the right, as Cover Flow previews and also as a list. You'll see the blue **RSS** icon next to each web site in the list.

5 Double-click a link in the list, or single-click a preview image in the Cover Flow pane to open its RSS feed page (shown on the previous page).

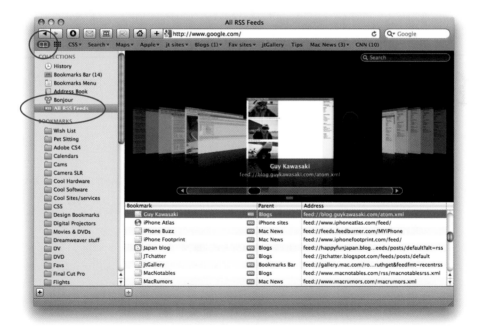

To view just the RSS feeds in a particular collection, choose a folder in the sidebar that contains RSS feed pages. Or, click on a bookmark in the Bookmarks Bar that contains RSS feed pages.

Find other feeds

When you come across a web site that has an RSS feed, Safari will display an RSS icon in the address field, as shown below.

To view the actual RSS feed, click the RSS icon in the address field.

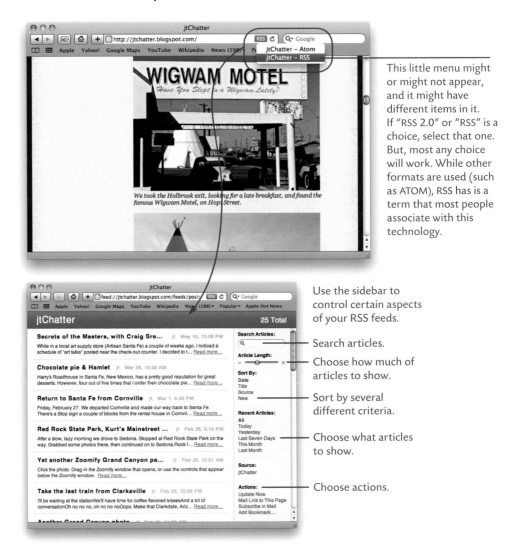

This little menu might or might not appear, and it might have different items in it. If "RSS 2.0" or "RSS" is a choice, select that one. But, most any choice will work. While other formats are used (such as ATOM), RSS has is a term that most people associate with this technology.

Use the sidebar to control certain aspects of your RSS feeds.

Search articles.

Choose how much of articles to show.

Sort by several different criteria.

Choose what articles to show.

Choose actions.

To find a directory of RSS feeds, go to your favorite search tool, such as Google.com. Search for **directory RSS feeds** or **directory XML feeds.**

View all RSS articles in a collection

When you click a bookmarks folder (such as "News," shown below) that contains RSS feeds, a pop-up menu opens. Choose an individual feed that indicates a number of unread articles are available. You can also choose to "View All RSS Articles," or "Open in Tabs." The latter option will open each feed in the list as a tab.

Bookmark your favorite feeds

There are at least three ways to bookmark a feed you want to follow.

To organize your bookmarks, first make folders in the Collections pane in the Bookmarks Library (click the plus sign at the bottom of the sidebar pane, then name the folder).

To bookmark a feed, do one of the following:

- Click the RSS icon in the address field, as shown on the opposite page. This takes you to the news feed page. *Bookmark that page:* in the little sheet that drops down, choose the folder (one you previously created in the Bookmarks Library) in which to save the bookmark *or* choose "Bookmarks Bar" to put that RSS feed bookmark directly into the Bookmarks Bar.

- Look on the web site page for a little **RSS** or **XML** logo, icon, or note (or also check for "Atom"). Single-click it, which takes you to the news feed page. Bookmark that page and choose the folder in which to save the bookmark.

- If you find a link to **RSS** or **XML** on a web page, Control-click it (or right-click). From the menu that appears, choose "Add Link to Bookmarks...." Be sure to give it a name that will describe what it is.

- A number in parentheses tells you how many unread articles are available in that feed.

Auto-Click to view all pages or feeds in tabs

Safari has a nifty little feature called "Auto-Click" that lets you load all the web pages in a Collection into different tabs with the click of a button. Instead of going to each individual page one at a time and then losing the previous page, you can open and peruse them all, each in its own tab.

To view all pages in tabs automatically:

1 In the Bookmarks Library, single-click "Bookmarks Bar" in the "Collections" group, as circled below.

2 Put a check in one of the "Auto-Click" checkboxes that you see next to each folder. (Of course, if there are no folders, you won't see any checkboxes!)

3 As soon as you check the "Auto-Click" box, you'll notice that the tiny triangle in the Bookmarks Bar has changed to a tiny square.

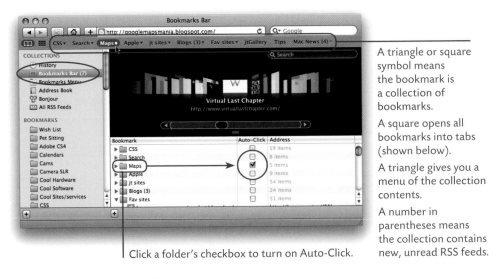

A triangle or square symbol means the bookmark is a collection of bookmarks.

A square opens all bookmarks into tabs (shown below).

A triangle gives you a menu of the collection contents.

A number in parentheses means the collection contains new, unread RSS feeds.

Click a folder's checkbox to turn on Auto-Click.

4 When you click a folder in the Bookmarks Bar that has the tiny square, every page in that folder opens, each with a different tab (which indicates a different page), as shown below. Single-click a tab to go to that page. Drag a tab left or right to change its position.

To close a tab, hover over it, then click the x that appears on the left side of the tab.

To close all tabs, Option-click the x.

View RSS feeds in Mail

To make it even easier to get your info fix, you can send the RSS feeds directly to Mail so whenever you check your email, you can see if you have news waiting.
To send the RSS feeds to Mail, make a bookmark (press Command D or click the **+** button in the toolbar) of an RSS feed and in the sheet that drops down, check the box to add the bookmark to "Mail."

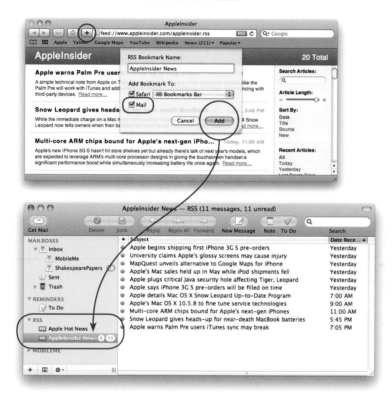

Change the RSS preferences

In the Safari preferences, you can tell Safari RSS how often to check for updates, what color to highlight new articles, when to get rid of old articles, and more.

To open the RSS preferences, go to the Safari menu and choose "Preferences...." Then click the "RSS" tab to get the RSS options.

If you choose to "Automatically update articles," Safari will put a number after the feed or folder of feeds to tell you how many new and unread articles there are. You can see that number in the Safari illustration above and on the previous pages.

Send an RSS feed to a friend

If you want to share a feed with someone, simply open that RSS feed page in Safari. On the right-hand side of the Safari window, at the bottom of the pane, is a link called "Mail Link to This Page." Click it, and your Mail program will open with the link to the page already in the message area and a subject line already written. Just add an email address and send.

Recent Articles:
All
Today
Yesterday
Last Seven Days
This Month
Last Month

Source:
MacRumors iPhon...

Actions:
Mark All As Read
Update Now
Mail Link to This Page
Subscribe in Mail

Subscribe in Mail

Put your favorite RSS feeds in Mail's sidebar, as shown on page 90. In Safari, go to an RSS feed page, then click "Subscribe in Mail" in the RSS feed page sidebar (circled above).

Use RSS feeds as a screen saver

Ha! This is very clever. You can use the current headlines from your favorite RSS feed as your screen saver. It's sexier than it sounds.

1   From the Apple menu, choose "System Preferences...."

2   Click "Desktop & Screen Saver," then click the "Screen Saver" tab.

3   In the left-hand pane, choose "RSS Visualizer."

4   Click the "Options..." button to choose your favorite feed. After you have made all the setting changes, close the pane.

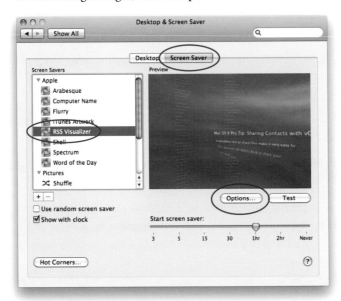

Cool Safari Tips:

The **New Tab** button (the Plus symbol in the top right corner of the Safari window) creates a new tab that, by default, opens the Top Sites display. You can change that behavior: open Safari Preferences, click "General" in the Preferences Toolbar, then set the "New tabs open with:" pop-up menu to Home Page, Empty Page, Same Page, or Bookmarks (opens the Cover Flow view of the most recently selected Bookmarks Collection).

Use the keyboard **Arrow keys** to scroll up, down, left, and right in a web page.

From the History menu, you can **Reopen All Windows From Last Session.**

Consolidate multiple open browser windows into one with multiple tabs: From the Window menu, choose "Merge All Windows."

To automatically **create a Bookmark folder from a group of tabbed windows,** from the Bookmarks menu, choose "Add Bookmark For These Tabs." In the dialog that opens, choose a Bookmark location for the folder. Safari automatically enables Auto-Click, so a single click on the folder re-opens all of the tabs in the group.

Safari is Integrated With:

Address Book: Put your Address Book in the Bookmarks Bar and go to the web site of any contact in your Address Book. In the Safari preferences, in the Bookmarks pane, check the box to "Include Address Book."

The AutoFill feature uses the Address Book contact you have designated as "My Card."

Mail: Email a web page or just the contents to someone; see page 140.

Email links open a pre-addressed message in Mail.

Subscribe to RSS feeds in Mail.

TextEdit: Web links on a TextEdit page will open in Safari.

iCal: Web addresses in events open in Safari.

Dock: Drag the tiny icon that you see to the left of a web address and drop it on the far right side of the Dock to create a web location. No matter which application you're in or which Space, you can click that icon in the Dock and Safari instantly opens to your favorite page.

8

GOALS

Create calendars

Add Events and
create To Do lists

Send email notifications
of Events

Publish your calendar
and subscribe to others

Print data in useful ways

iCal for Organizing your Life

iCal is a calendar program that keeps track of Events, creates a digital To Do list, and pops up reminders to you, among other things. You can publish your calendar over the Internet for other iCal users (publicly or privately), and they can subscribe to it and get automatic updates. Or publish it to a web page where anyone on any computer can view it. iCal supports Microsoft Exchange Server 2007, for people who need to sync their work calendars.

iCal is a great tool for keeping track of family activities or for coordinating corporate Events. And you can do it all in one application because you can create separate calendars for separate parts of your life.

If you have an iPhone, iCal syncs selected calendars to it so you never miss an important date.

The iCal Window

The iCal window is in a familiar calendar format, but because it's digital you can switch to different views with the click of a button. View a month at a time, a week, or a day; go back in time or forward into the future. Set recurring Events to happen every first Friday or every three months. Create To Do lists that are attached to certain calendars. Turn calendars on or off so you can view just individual ones, or view several at a time to see how they overlap.

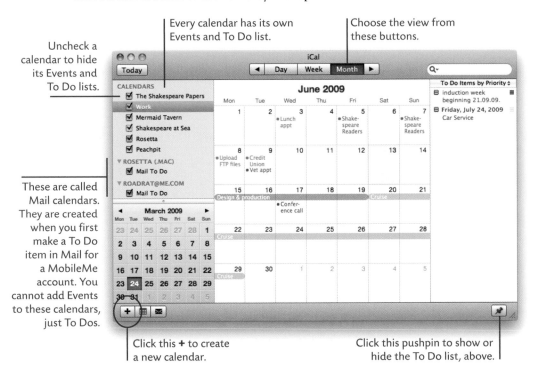

Uncheck a calendar to hide its Events and To Do lists.

Every calendar has its own Events and To Do list.

Choose the view from these buttons.

These are called Mail calendars. They are created when you first make a To Do item in Mail for a MobileMe account. You cannot add Events to these calendars, just To Dos.

Click this **+** to create a new calendar.

Click this pushpin to show or hide the To Do list, above.

Set Up Google or Yahoo! Calendars

If you have a Google or Yahoo! account, you can set up those calendars in iCal.

1   Open iCal's Preferences and click "Accounts."

2   Click the Add (**+**) button in the lower-left corner to create a new account.

3   Enter your Google or Yahoo! email address and password, then click "Create." iCal finds any calendar accounts associated with the email address you entered.

Create Calendars

To create a new calendar, go to the bottom-left corner of the iCal window, click the **+** sign, then name the calendar.

You can have lots of different calendars. The checkmark next to a calendar name indicates those Events are displayed. Thus you can have a calendar for each one of your kids' activities, plus your work calendar, and choose to see all the Events at once or just selected ones. You'll have a visual display of just how crazy your life is.

To change the color of the calendar or to give it a description, Control-click (or right-click) the calendar name, then choose "Get Info." You'll see the pane below where you can change the color or add information.

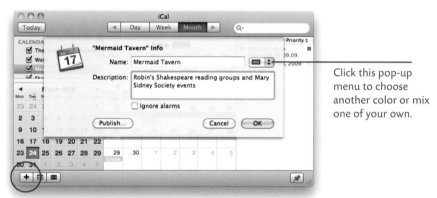

Click this pop-up menu to choose another color or mix one of your own.

Click here to create a new calendar. Shift-click to create a new group (explained below).

Create a Group of Calendars

Create calendar **groups** to organize related calendars. You might want to group together the calendars that all have to do with your children. Or perhaps a particular project has several different calendars associated with it.

To make a group, go to the File menu and choose "New Calendar Group." *Or* Shift-click the **+** sign in the bottom-left corner of the iCal window.

Name the new group, then drag other calendars into it. If a group is *selected* when you create a new calendar, the calendar is automatically added to that group.

Click the disclosure triangle to the left of a Group calendar to hide or reveal its contents.

Automatic Birthdays Calendar

iCal can work with your Address Book to create a Birthdays calendar that automatically updates itself.

1 First you must add the Birthday field to your Address Book, as explained on page 118.

2 Then, in iCal, go to the iCal menu and choose "Preferences...."

3 Click the "General" icon.

4 Check the box to "Show Birthdays calendar." The calendar will appear in the "Subscriptions" group. If you don't have a Subscriptions group in your calendar list, iCal will put it there now.

Double-click any birthdate showing in the calendar to open its Info pane. There you can click the link to go straight to that person's contact information in Address Book, from which you can send a birthday email.

You can't make any changes to the Birthdays calendar in iCal; in fact, you can't even add alarms to notify you of upcoming birthdays. You could, of course, manually create a birthday Event and add an alarm to it.

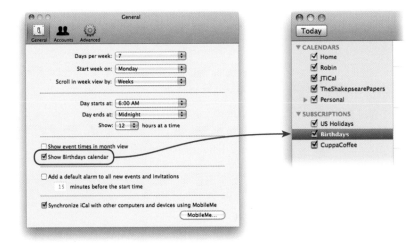

Create Events

An Event is what you'd expect it to be—something that happens on a particular day. You can **create Events** in a variety of ways.

First select the calendar in which you want the Event to appear. Then:

- In the "Month" view, double-click a day to create a new Event. A New Event Info pane opens so you can add more information; click "Done" to put it away, or click anywhere outside the Info pane. iCal arranges multiple Events of one day according to the times you enter.

- In the "Week" or "Day" views, double-click or press-and-drag on the time grid for your Event. Double-click the Event to open the Info pane and add information; click "Done" or click anywhere outside the Info pane to put it away.

- To stretch the Event out across multiple days, be sure to click the "all-day" checkbox in the Info pane, then enter the Event's dates in the "from" and "to" fields.

- To create a recurring Event, use the "repeat" feature in the Info pane. iCal automatically repeats the Event at a time interval you specify. For instance, the Shakespeare readings I host repeat the first Friday of each month.

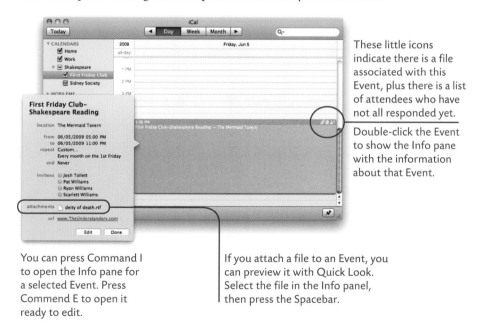

These little icons indicate there is a file associated with this Event, plus there is a list of attendees who have not all responded yet.

Double-click the Event to show the Info pane with the information about that Event.

You can press Command I to open the Info pane for a selected Event. Press Commend E to open it ready to edit.

If you attach a file to an Event, you can preview it with Quick Look. Select the file in the Info panel, then press the Spacebar.

Create To Do Lists

Each calendar can have its own **To Do list.** As you check and uncheck the calendar checkboxes, their attendant To Do lists show and hide accordingly.

To create a To Do item:

1 If the To Do pane isn't showing on the right side of iCal, click the pushpin button in the bottom-right corner.

2 Select a calendar from the calendar pane on the left.

3 In the To Do pane on the right, double-click in a blank space. *Or* Control-click (or right-click) and choose "New To Do" from the contextual menu.

4 Double-click directly a To Do item to open its Info pane (right). You can **prioritize** your item, add a note, give it a due date, change the calendar, and more.

5 When the item has been **completed,** click the "competed" checkbox.

Email a To Do item

You can email a To Do item, and if that person has a Mac, she can choose to click the link in the email to add the To Do item to her iCal.

To email the To Do from iCal:

1 Control-click the item in the To Do pane, and from the menu that pops up, choose "Mail To Do."

2 The Mail application opens with the To Do included as an attachment.

You can also create To Do items within Mail. They will automatically be added to iCal.

3 The recipient of the email clicks the email link (above-left), chooses a calendar (above-right), and the To Do is added to his iCal.

Email Notifications

You can send someone an email invitation to an Event, and she can send one to you. Mail automatically puts a notification in iCal and adds the new Event to the calendar.

To send an invitation/notification:

Command-click (or right-click) an Event in a calendar. From the pop-up menu that appears, choose "Mail Event." Address the message and send it.

To respond to an email notification:

1 When you get an email message from someone inviting you to an iCal Event, the Notifications box appears in the bottom-left corner of iCal. If the box isn't showing and you want to see it, single-click the Notifications button, shown circled below.

2 When an invitation comes in, the Notifications button displays a red arrow. In the Notifications box, shown below, click the button to indicate your response. An email message is immediately sent to the person who notified you.

3 If you accept the notification, that Event is added to your calendar on the appropriate day.

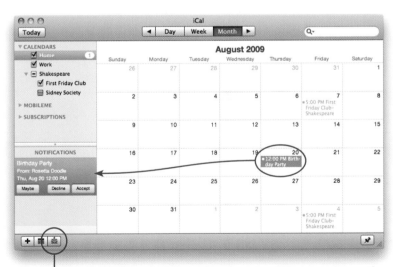

Click here to show or hide Notifications. A red arrow appears on the Notifications button when you've received an invitation to an Event.

Link Events and To Dos

To add an Event to a To Do list, drag the Event from the calendar grid to the To Do pane. The Event stays put, but now you also have a To Do item relating to it.

To turn a To Do item into an Event, drag a To Do item to a date in the calendar grid. The To Do item stays put, but now you also have an Event attached to it.

Sort (Organize) your Information

Automatically sort your To Do list by due date, title, calendar, or priority. Just click the tiny, double arrows in the heading of the To Do list and choose a sort option.

You can also manually drag a To Do item to a different position in the list.

Backup the Entire Calendar of Information

To make sure you don't lose the valuable information you have entered into your calendar, go to the File menu and choose "Back up iCal...." You will be asked where to save the file. If you have a lot of information you don't want to lose, you should save that file onto a CD and store it in a safe place.

Preview Files Attached to Events

Use Quick Look to preview Event attachments. Double-click an Event to open its Info pane, select the attachment (as shown to the right), then tap the Spacebar. Almost any kind of file will preview, without opening its native application.

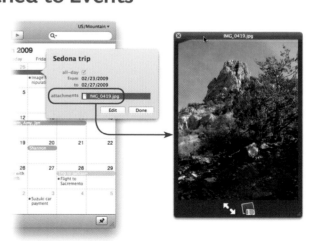

Publish your Calendar

If you have a MobileMe account (or a private server), you can **publish** your calendar of Events, including the alarms and To Do list if you choose, to a web page and anyone in the world on any computer can view it. It's really remarkable.

To publish, just select the calendar in the list, then go to the Calendar menu and choose "Publish…." A little dialog box (shown below) drops down. Make your choices, then click "Publish."

A message appears telling you the web address and asking if you want to email people with the address.

To notify others about your published calendar, select the calendar, go to the Calendar menu, and choose "Send Publish Email…."

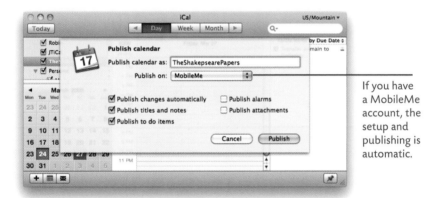

If you have a MobileMe account, the setup and publishing is automatic.

Subscribe to Calendars

There are many public calendars you can subscribe to, such as calendars for the PGA tours, NASCAR races, musician's tour dates, and many more.

To subscribe to a public calendar, go to the Calendar menu and choose "Find Shared Calendars…." This takes you to an Apple web site with dozens of public calendars. Browse through categories such as "Most popular" and "Most recent."

To subscribe to a private calendar, go to the Calendar menu in iCal and choose "Subscribe…." Enter the web address you have been given. If you received an email invitation to subscribe to a published calendar, click the link in the email invitation.

Print in a Variety of Ways

Check out the great features in the Print dialog box. Each "View" (Month, Day, Week, or List) you choose changes the options, so spend a few minutes here exploring the possibilities for each view. You can choose to print the data from as many or as few calendars as you like. They are all color-coded, so just as in iCal itself, you can see how different Events overlap.

From the File menu, choose "Print." In the "Print" dialog that opens (below) choose formatting, time range, calendars to print, and other options provided as checkboxes. After customizing your settings, click "Continue" to open the usual Print dialog where you select a printer and start the print process.

Change the view here; the preview
will immediately change.

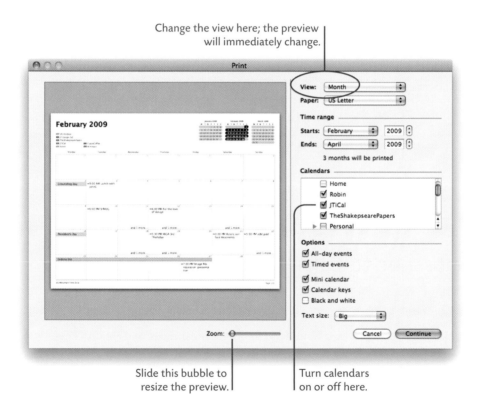

Slide this bubble to
resize the preview.

Turn calendars
on or off here.

iCal is Integrated With:

Address Book: Use the Address Book cards and groups to invite people to Events.

Any birthdays you enter in Address Book can automatically appear in iCal (go to the iCal preferences and checkmark "Show Birthdays calendar").

When you enter attendees names in the Info pane, iCal picks up their email addresses from the Address Book.

Open the Address panel from the Window menu. To quickly add people to the attendee list, drag them to the "attendee" button.

Mail: iCal will mail invitations and notifications of calendar updates, and Mail can automatically send notifications to iCal.

You can create iCal calendars in Mail and add Events to them from Mail.

You can create iCal Events in Mail: hover your pointer over a date or address in a Mail message to show a Data Detector outline and menu button, then click the menu button and choose "Create New iCal Event...."

To Do items you create in Mail are automatically added to the To Do list in iCal.

iPhone: Sync your iCal information to your iPhone through iTunes. You can also publish a calendar, then send a "Publish Email" to others so they can subscribe and access the calendar on their iPhone.

iSync: Synchronize the calendar on one computer with all the other computers in your office, as well as with your MobileMe account.

9

GOALS

iChat for Text, Audio, and Video Messaging

Using iChat you can communicate with others around the world with text messages, audio chatting, or video conferencing—free. You can text-chat with one other person or with a group of people, exchange files, and save printable copies of your chats. With a fast Mac and iChat, you can have audio chats with up to ten people at a time. You can have video conferences with up to three other people. You can even have one-way video chats with someone who doesn't have a video camera attached or built-in (or vice versa). Amazing.

Set up iChat

When you first open iChat, it asks you to fill in certain information to get started. You need a chat account of some sort.

> If you already have a MobileMe account, that will be your "screen name" or "buddy name." Include the **@me.com** part of your name when you tell others your buddy name.
>
> In the setup process, you can click the button labeled "Get an iChat Account…." This takes you to MobileMe.com where you can get a FREE iChat buddy name with a 60-day MobileMe trial account, and you can keep the buddy name after the free trial is over even if you don't convert the trial account to a paid one.
>
> Or go to www.AIM.com and sign up for a free AIM account; you can use that as your buddy name. This buddy name does **not** include @aim.com.
>
> If you already have a Jabber account, you can use that name as well.
>
> You can get a free Google Talk account at www.Google.com/talk. This is also a Jabber account. Include **@gmail.com** in your Buddy name in the iChat setup.

Save chat transcripts

To save a copy of chats, open iChat Preferences, click the "Messages" button in the toolbar, then checkmark "Save chat transcripts to:" In the pop-up menu, choose a folder, or use the default choice of "iChats" folder (located in the Documents folder).

As you chat, you can mark the conversation with a date and time stamp. From the Edit menu, choose "Mark Transcript."

Show a buddy's previous messages

If you save your iChat transcripts (see above), you can have iChat automatically show recent chats (5, 25, 100, or 250 recent messages) in the chat window when you start a new chat with a buddy. Open iChat Preferences, click the "Messages" button in the toolbar, then checkmark "In new chat windows, show:" Use the pop-up menu to select how many previous messages with a buddy you want to see in the chat window when you start a new chat with that buddy. This can be really helpful if you have lots of important chats.

A sample Buddy List and chat

So you'll know what to expect after you've gone through the process, below you see a typical Buddy List and text chat.

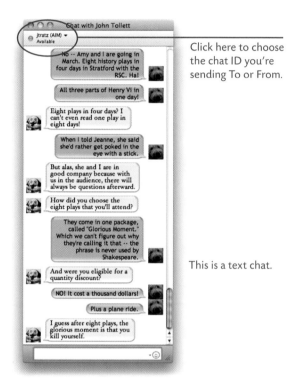

Click here to choose the chat ID you're sending To or From.

This is a Buddy List. Double-click a buddy name to open a text chat. The people whose names are gray are not available at the moment.

This is a text chat.

Customize your chat view through iChat preferences (from the iChat menu); use the "Messages" pane (get rid of Helvetica—it's hard to read on the screen)..

169

Create a Buddy List

To iChat with people, first set up a **Buddy List** of names. If you're using a Google Talk account or other Jabber account, your Buddy List is called **Jabber List.**

1   If you don't see the Buddy List when you open iChat, go to the Window menu and choose "Buddy List."

If the title bar of the Buddy List says you are "Offline," click on the word "Offline" and from the pop-up menu choose "Available."

2   To add a new buddy, single-click the **+** sign at the bottom of the list and choose "Add Buddy...."

3   In the dialog box that appears, enter the person's screen name or buddy name in the "Account Name" field. Choose whether it's an AIM or Mobileme account. If you choose MobileMe, it will enter the @me.com part for you.

Or click the disclosure button to display your Address Book, then choose a buddy from your list of contacts.

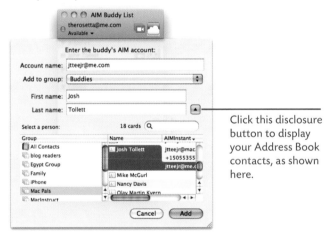

Click this disclosure button to display your Address Book contacts, as shown here.

4   Choose a Group in which to organize this buddy. Apple has provided several groups for you, and you can create your own.

5   Click the "Add" button.

This account is automatically entered in the Address Book for you, if your buddy isn't already there.

Chat with One Other Person

To have a **text chat** with someone around the office or around the world, simply open your Buddy List and double-click the name of the person you want to chat with. Double-click the person's name or icon, *not any camera or phone icon that might be visible.* A chat window opens. Type a message, then hit Return. *Or* select a buddy name, then single-click the "A" icon at the bottom of the Buddy List.

Chat with a Group of People

You can text chat with at least twenty-three different people around the world in one Chat Room.

1   From the File menu, choose "Go to Chat Room."

2   In the window that appears, type a name that will become the name of this chat room. Make it something distinctive because if anyone else around the world types the same word, they'll end up in your chat room.

3   A Participants drawer pops out to the side of the chat room window. Click the **+** sign and invite someone.

4   Click the **+** sign again and again to invite as many people as you like.

Or tell people ahead of time to all meet in a chat room called, say, "dogfood," at a certain time. At the prescribed time, tell everyone to do this:

1   Open iChat and go to the File menu; choose "Go to Chat Room...."

2   Enter the chat room name (in this case, dogfood) and click "Go." Everyone around the world who does so will end up in the room together. Remarkable.

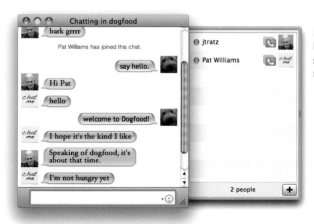

Here I've started a Chat Room and invited my sweetheart, John, and my mother, Pat.

171

Audio Chat with One or More

Talk, **literally talk,** with other people. Make sure you have a microphone built in or connected to your Mac, or an iSight or other video camera attached. Newer iMacs and laptops, of course, have built-in cameras. Your buddies will display little telephone icons next to their pictures if they are able to audio chat back to you.

To audio chat with someone, she has to be in your Buddy List (see page 170). In the list, as shown below, you can have a one-on-one audio chat with anyone who displays a telephone icon next to her name.

If a buddy shows *multiple* telephone icons, like "jtratz" and "roadrat," below, that means you can invite him to an audio chat that involves more than one person.

To audio chat, click directly on that person's phone icon. Or single-click his name and then click the phone icon at the bottom of the Buddy List.

If your Buddy doesn't have a microphone to chat back with you, select his name, then go to the Buddies menu and choose "Invite to One-Way Audio Chat." Your friend will hear you, but will have to send typed instant messages back.

This Mac has no camera attached, nor does it have a microphone. We can only text chat with each other.

TIP —— iChat picks up your photo from the Address Book; you can change the photo there.

TIP —— To add a photo to a buddy, select any buddy name and press Command I to get the Info window (or Control-click a buddy name and choose "Show Info" from the menu that pops up). Drag any image into the image well.

Open an audio chat and invite others to join you

To *initiate* an audio conference with more than one other person, you need a more powerful machine than you do to *join* an audio chat. Any machine purchased within the last couple of years is powerful enough to initiate an audio chat.

1   Single-click a buddy name that displays multiple phones, then single-click the phone icon at the bottom of the Buddy List (**or** just click directly on the phone icon next to the buddy's name).

2   That person hears a little phone ringing and sees a message on his computer; he clicks the message to see who it is, then clicks "Accept." This begins the chat. Your window looks like this:

3   Now click the **+** button to get a little menu that lists the other people in your Buddy List who are online and capable of joining an audio conference. Select a person, then add others in the same way.

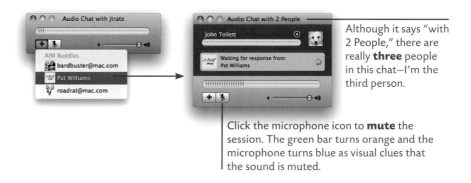

Although it says "with 2 People," there are really **three** people in this chat—I'm the third person.

Click the microphone icon to **mute** the session. The green bar turns orange and the microphone turns blue as visual clues that the sound is muted.

4   **To delete someone** from the audio conference, move your pointer up towards his icon. An **x** appears (shown above-right); click it and that person is gone.

5   **To terminate an audio session,** click the red close button in the upper-left corner of the Audio Chat window.

Video Chat with up to Three Other People

See other people on your screen while you talk (not type) with them. To video chat, of course you must have a video camera attached to your Mac. All of the newer iMacs and laptops have built-in video cameras. You can use Apple's cute little iSight camera if you already have one (they're not sold anymore), or you can attach any FireWire video camera to your Mac, or a USB video camera.

With whom can you video conference?

A video conference with more than one person takes a powerful Mac and a good broadband connection. If you are able to *participate* in a video conference with more than one person, the camera icon in your Buddy name shows a stack of camera icons. If someone in your Buddy List is able to participate, she shows multiple cameras, as well. It takes a powerful Mac and a fast broadband connection to *initiate* a video conference with up to four people.

To see a listing of what chat capabilities a buddy has, go to the Buddies menu, choose "Show Profile," and look in the "capabilities" category.

I can do a multiple video chat with two of my buddies, the two with multiple camera icons.

iChat AV preferences

You can make some minor adjustments in the Audio/Video pane of the iChat preferences. You might try changing the "Bandwidth Limit" to see if it affects your video chat one way or another. Depending on your Internet connection and how many other people use it, a different setting can work better (or worse).

Open a video chat and invite others to join you

To *initiate* a video conference with more than one other person, you need a more powerful machine than you do to *join* a video conference.

1   Single-click a buddy name that shows multiple video camera icons. That person hears a little phone ringing and gets a message on her screen inviting her to a video chat. When she clicks "Accept," she appears in your video window instead of you.

2   To add two more people to your video conference, click the **+** sign; a menu drops down with the names of the people in your Buddy List *who are online and capable of joining you.*

This machine doesn't have a camera attached, but that person joined the audio portion of the video chat.

If your Buddy doesn't have a camera with which to video chat with you, select her name, then go to the Buddies menu and choose, "Invite to One-Way Video Chat." Your friend will see you, but will have to send instant messages back.

iChat Effects

iChat Effects are useless but fun. You can distort your image, add artistic touches, and even add new backgrounds so it looks like you're somewhere else.

To preview the various effects:

1   Go to the Video menu and choose "Video Preview."

2   Now from the same menu choose "Show Video Effects."

3   Select an effect from the palette (shown below) to see what it will do.

To apply an effect during a video chat:

1   During a video chat, click the "Effects" button in the bottom-left corner of the chat window. This opens the "Video Effects" palette shown above.

2   The original, non-effect version appears in the middle of the palette. Click an effect to apply it as you chat.

3   To return to the original, non-effect image, click the "Original" image in the center of the palette.

Add backgrounds

In addition to distorting your video image with various effects, you can add a photo or a movie to replace the existing background that's really behind you. This background replacement feature works best if you have a simple, uncluttered, single-color background. We got the best results (but not perfect) by using a background wall that was smooth and almost white. Although you can do this in the middle of chatting, you might want to get it all set up before you call someone on a video chat and surprise them.

1   In the Video Effects palette, click the right arrow button until you get to the palette of background images. Look for photos, not your picture.

 To add your own background photos or movies, click through the effects until you find an empty well. Drag your image or movie into that well.

2   Click a background image to select it. A text prompt appears and asks you to move yourself out of the video frame. The prompt notifies you a few seconds later with a "Background Detected" message.

3   Move back into the picture. iChat replaces the original background with the photo or movie you selected and places you in front of it.

 If you want to change to another background, iChat will *not* ask you to step out again—it will just replace the existing one.

John's holding his nose because, as you can see, he's under water.

iChat Theater

Once you've initiated a video chat, you can use iChat Theater to show files, photos, slideshows, or movies while you continue your chat. This is amazing.

To share a file with iChat Theater:

1   Start a video chat with a buddy.

2   From the File menu, choose "Share a File With iChat Theater...."

3   In the Finder window that opens, select a file, photo, or movie you want to share, then click "Share." **Or** simply drag any file, photo, or movie from your hard disk and drop it onto the video chat window.

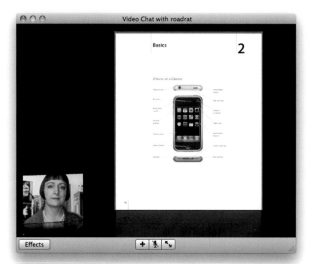

When you drag a file to the video chat window, the buddy's image minimizes to the bottom-left corner to make room for an image of the file. Your buddy sees you as a thumbnail video and sees the same file image that you see.

iChat Theater also opens a *file window* on your screen (shown to the right). It allows you to scroll through a shared multi-page document as your buddy watches, play or pause a movie, or show previous or next files in the chat window.

Click here to end an iChat Theater session.

This is the file window for a PDF in iChat Theater.

If the shared file is a movie, the file window displays a Play/Pause button and a scrub bar to drag the clip backward or forward.

To share *multiple* files of the same or different types, Command-click to select files on your hard drive, then drag the files to the video chat window. The files play as a slideshow.

iChat Theater's movie controls.   iChat Theater's window and controls for multiple files.

Share iPhoto with iChat Theater

You can also share entire iPhoto albums as a slideshow.

1 Start a video chat with a buddy.

2 From the File menu, choose "Share iPhoto With iChat Theater...."

3 In the iPhoto window that opens (below-left), select an album, then click "Share."

Select an album or multiple photos to show as a slideshow in the video chat window.   iChat Theater opens this file window and control bar so you can control the slideshow.

Bonjour on your Local Network

Bonjour is an integrated component of **iChat**. If you have two or more Macs connected through a local area network (an Ethernet network, wireless network, or a combination of both), Bonjour automatically detects and connects all of the computers on the network. You can send Instant Messages or files to Bonjour buddies on your local network. You can have audio or video chats with others on the local network (if a microphone or digital video camera is connected to your computer, of course). And you can use Screen Sharing to share your computer with others or to see another buddy's computer (see the following pages).

You don't have to have a MobileMe account or AIM account or any other kind of special account—just computers that are connected in some way.

To set up Bonjour:

1   Open iChat, then from the iChat application menu, choose "Preferences."

2   Click the "Accounts" button, then click "Bonjour" in the Accounts pane on the left side of the window.

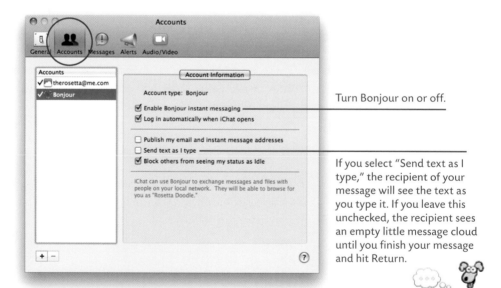

Turn Bonjour on or off.

If you select "Send text as I type," the recipient of your message will see the text as you type it. If you leave this unchecked, the recipient sees an empty little message cloud until you finish your message and hit Return.

Or you can just open iChat, go to the Window menu and choose "Bonjour List." It will give you a button to login to Bonjour.

The Bonjour List looks just like a Buddy List—except it's labeled Bonjour List. Your chat windows look similar too.

Bonjour automatically detects a local network and connects you to it. If you're in a public space, such as an Internet cafe, you should quit iChat and turn off Bonjour when you're not using it to ensure privacy and security.

To send a file to anyone on the Bonjour List, just drop the file on a buddy's name.

Or drag a file into the message field where you type to chat. Hit Return and off it goes. If the file is an image, the image itself will appear in the chat window, and your buddy can drag it to his Desktop, or double-click it to open it. Or, your buddy can Control-click (or right-click) the file and view it in **QuickLook.** To close QuickLook, tap the spacebar, or click the Close button (a circle-x) in the top-left corner of the QuickLook window.

> **TIP** —— If you're interested in sharing files on your network or sharing computer screens (where you can actually manipulate the other person's monitor wherever she is in the world), please see Lesson 21 on connecting and sharing files.

Record Chats

When an audio or video Chat is in progress, you can record the chat. Recorded video iChat files require a lot of storage space, approximately one megabyte for every five seconds of video.

1 Start an audio or video chat with a buddy.

2 From the Video menu at the top of the screen, choose "Record Chat."

3 The buddy's audio or video chat window reveals a "Recording Request" sheet (below-left). When the buddy clicks "Allow," the chat begins.

4 A red Record light alerts both participants that recording is in progress.

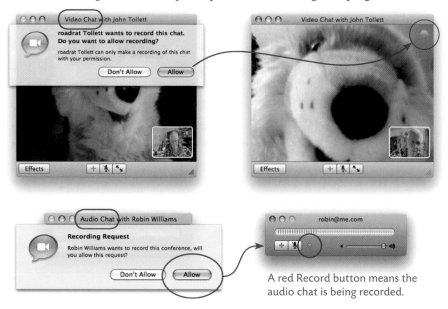

A red Record button means the audio chat is being recorded.

To stop a video recording, from the Video menu choose "Stop Recording."

To stop an audio recording, click the red Record button in the Audio Chat window (circled, above-right).

Find recorded chats

To locate a video or audio chat file, go to the Home folder, open the Documents folder, then look in the iChats folder.

The files are also found in iTunes. Look in your iTunes sidebar for a playlist named "iChat Chats." Click that playlist to show any recorded iChats.

iChat is Integrated With:

Address Book: The photo you put in Address Book appears in your Buddy and Bonjour List, and the photo you put in the Buddy or Bonjour List appears in the Address Book.

When an iChat buddy is online, a green dot appears on her card.

Mail: You can send email to a buddy through your Buddy List—Control-click (or right-click) a buddy name, then choose "Send Email...." And when a buddy in your list is online, a green dot appears in the "Buddy Availability" column in Mail.

iTunes: Let others know what music you are listening to; in the Buddy List, click on the word right beneath your name (it's a menu). Choose the option "Current iTunes Song."

iSight camera, built-in camera, attached video camera:

You video conference with this camera, of course, but you can also take a picture of the person on the other end to use for his buddy image—from the Video menu, choose "Take Snapshot," then from the Buddies menu, choose "Show Info." Drag and drop the snapshot from your Desktop to the image well in the Address pane of the Info window shown below.

Drop a photo or graphic image in this well. If you want this image to override the one your buddy uses, check the box to "Always use this picture."

Spotlight: To find any files or information you have on a buddy, perform a Spotlight search. Select a buddy in the Buddy List, then from the Buddies menu, choose "Search in Spotlight." Spotlight searches for files on your computer than have any reference (in the file name or contents) to the buddy's chat handle (buddy name) *and* real name.

10

GOALS

Buy music, movies, music videos, or television shows

Create Playlists and Smart Playlists of selected music

Watch movies or shows right in iTunes

Burn your own CDs of music

Listen to radio from around the world

Create playlists with iTunes DJ and Genius playlist

Use the Genius sidebar to find new songs

Print covers for your own CDs

iTunes for your Listening Pleasure

Import music into iTunes, create Playlists of your favorite songs, copy the Playlists to CDs so you have your own discs of customized music, or stream your music from your office down the hallway to hear it in the kitchen. You can buy music directly through the iTunes Store with the click of a button and download it right to your computer.

If you have an iPhone, your phone automatically opens iTunes to sync music and data to it. And, of course, your iPod gets its content from iTunes.

The iTunes Window

Below is an overview of the iTunes window. This short chapter is only an overview; if you want an entire guide to using iTunes, please check one of the iLife books from Peachpit Press (which publishes detailed guides for the iLife suite of applications from Apple). There is so much to iTunes! We encourage you to explore the menus, all the buttons, and the Help files.

Click these view buttons to display your collection in various ways.

Search for an artist or song title.

Click the Play button and all the *checked* songs in the window will play.

All of your songs, books, shows, etc., are imported into the **Library.**

The **Playlists** help you organize all the music in the Library.

Apple has made a number of **Smart Playlists** for you (see page 189 about Smart Playlists).

Click this arrow to send this album to someone as a gift or to publish it to iTunes as an "iMix" collection.

Click one of these arrows to find more of this artist's songs in the iTunes Store.

You only see these arrows on items that you have selected (single-click to select).

Buy Music, Movies, or Television Shows

To buy music, movies, or television shows, click on "iTunes Store" in the sidebar. You can search for music: Use the search field in the top-right corner.

The first time you click a "Buy" button, you will be asked to set up an account. If you have a MobileMe account or email address, use that. You'll be asked for a credit card number and contact info. After you've got an account, you can buy and download music, movies, and television shows with the click of a button. To watch a show or movie, see page 190.

Download Album Art

When you buy music through iTunes, you automatically get the **album art** with it. If the art is not showing at the bottom of the sidebar when you select a purchased song, click the "show artwork and video-viewer" button (shown to the right, and circled below).

You can add your own art here—select a song, then drag any graphic into this spot.
Click on this image to open a large version in its own window.

Create a Playlist

A Playlist is a **collection of songs** from your iTunes music Library. You might create one Playlist of your favorite jazz, another of Scottish folk songs, and another of a particular artist. The same song can be in any number of Playlists. You can take two songs from this CD, one from that CD, etc., to create your own personal collection, then burn that collection to a CD of your own.

1 Playlists are made from songs in your iTunes Library, so first import songs from CDs (see the following page) or buy songs at the iTunes Store (see the previous page).

2 Then click the **+** sign at the bottom of the sidebar. A new, untitled Playlist label appears in the sidebar.

3 Name this new Playlist.

4 Single-click the Music collection in the Library section of the sidebar.

5 Drag songs from the Library window to the Playlist name.

Another really easy way to make a new Playlist is to select multiple songs in the main iTunes window, then from the File menu choose "New Playlist from Selection." A new "untitled playlist" appears in the sidebar that you can rename whatever you want.

Click the iTunes DJ playlist to create an automatic, random Playlist.

Click the Genius playlist to create a playlist based on similarity to your current iTunes selection.

The purple Playlists (with a gear icon) that you see already in your sidebar are ones that Apple has created for you. They display the songs their labels describe—the recently played songs, the 25 you play most often, etc. These are purple and have a different icon because they are Smart Playlists, which are Playlists that automatically add items to themselves based on chosen parameters; see the next page.

Create a Smart Playlist

A regular Playlist holds the songs or music videos that you add to it by dragging items into it. A Smart Playlist **automatically adds certain music all by itself.** It's really great. Remember, buy the songs or import the songs to iTunes first.

1 Hold down the Option key; the **+** sign at the bottom of the sidebar turns into a gear wheel; click the gear wheel. **Or** go to the File menu and choose "New Smart Playlist… ."

2 In the dialog box that appears, click the menus from left to right and make your choices. Click the **+** sign to add more parameters. Click OK.

3 The Smart Playlist appears in the sidebar, waiting for you to rename it.

Import Songs from a CD

Put an **audio CD** in your drive and iTunes automatically opens. If you're online, iTunes goes to an online database and (if it can find the CD in the database) gets the artist, album title, song names, times, and more, and displays that information in the iTunes window.

Single-click the checkboxes to check or uncheck songs—checked songs are the ones that will be imported. (Command-click to check or uncheck all boxes.)

A button in the bottom-right appears called "Import CD." Click that button, and the *checked* songs will import into the Music library.

Share the Wealth

Share your Library of music with other computers in your office. Open the iTunes preferences. Click the "Sharing" tab, and then check "Share my library on my local network."

To find music that other computers are willing to share with you, check the box to "Look for shared libraries." Shared music libraries appear in the iTunes sidebar, under the "Shared" label (as shown on the previous page).

Adjust the Sound

Use the powerful **equalizer** for sound quality and enhancement. From the Window menu, choose "Equalizer." Experiment with the controls.

Watch Movies in iTunes

You can buy movies or television shows and watch them directly in iTunes. If you buy an Apple TV device and have a wireless system and widescreen TV in your home, you can stream the movies and shows from your computer to your television. (To do so, you'll have to read the directions that come with the Apple TV!)

To watch a movie in iTunes:

1   Go to the iTunes Store and buy a movie or television show. After it's downloaded, it will appear in the "Movies" or "TV Shows" list.

2   Select "Movies" in the Library section of the sidebar, then double-click the name of the movie or show. The film immediately opens in the iTunes window, as shown below.

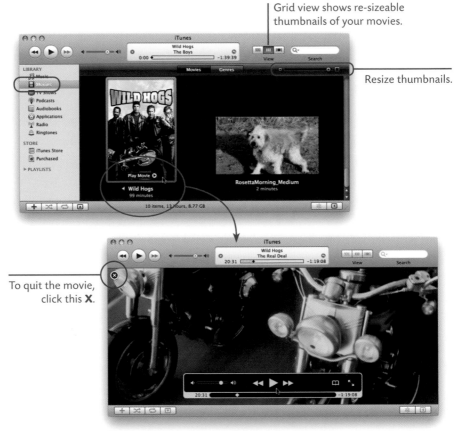

Grid view shows re-sizeable thumbnails of your movies.

Resize thumbnails.

To quit the movie, click this **X**.

These movie controls automatically appear when you hover your pointer over the playing movie.

Tune in to Visual Effects

To see **visual effects** that react to the music you're playing, go to the View menu and choose "Show Visualizer," *or* press Command T to turn on the visualizer.

Also, try these keyboard commands:

Command F—to view the effects full screen.

I—display track info.

C—toggle auto-cycle.

F—toggle freeze mode.

L—toggle camera lock.

N—toggle nebula mode.

P—change the color palette.

R—change mode (very fun).

The iTunes Visualizer. To choose other visualizers, from the View menu, choose "Visualizer."

Add a Ringtone to your iPhone

If you have an iPhone, you can buy ringtones and add them to your phone. You must first buy the song, and the ringtone costs another 99¢.

Add the "Ringtone" column to your window: Control-click (or right-click) any column header; from the pop-up menu that appears, choose "Ringtone."

Any song that is authorized for ringtones has a little bell in that column. Single-click the bell and you get an option to select whatever section of that song you want as a ringtone, up to 30 seconds. Drag either end of the blue clip, then click the "Preview" button to hear it. You can choose how long of a gap you want to hear before the sound repeats (loops). Experiment until you get exactly the clip you want, then click the "Buy" button. Plug in your iPhone and the ringtone is automatically synced to your phone.

Burn a CD of your own Collection

To burn a CD of your own collection, first import the songs and make a Playlist, as described on pages 188–189. You can't just select songs in the music library to burn to a CD—you must make a Playlist. Then:

1   Insert a blank CD-R (newer Macs can also burn to CD+R discs).

2   In iTunes, select a Playlist. You can only burn one Playlist onto a CD, so make sure it's got everything you want in it. You can burn about 600 MB onto one regular CD, so add as many songs from as many different artists and albums as you like. Check the status bar at the bottom of iTunes to know how many megabytes are in the selected Playlist.

3   Click the "Burn Disc" button in the lower-right of iTunes (this button only appears when a Playlist is selected). iTunes immediately begins the process of burning the songs to disc.

4   When it's finished, you'll see the name of the CD in the sidebar, along with an eject symbol. Eject the CD and enjoy!

TIP —— You can make a huge Playlist that holds many more songs than will fit on one CD. When you put in the first disc and click the "Burn Disc" button, iTunes will warn you that it will take more than one disc. Click OK and iTunes tells you when the first disc is full, ejects the completed disc, and asks you to insert another blank disc.

Listen to Radio from around the World

This never ceases to amaze me. You can listen to radio from around the world—all you do is click a button.

In the sidebar, click the "Radio" icon, circled below. Then double-click a category to see the variety of stations available in that genre, and double-click the radio stream you want to listen to. Amazing.

Once you've got the radio on, click the green zoom button in the upper-left of the iTunes window. That will reduce iTunes to just a tiny little window so it's out of your way, but the radio will continue playing. Click the green button again to enlarge iTunes to its full size.

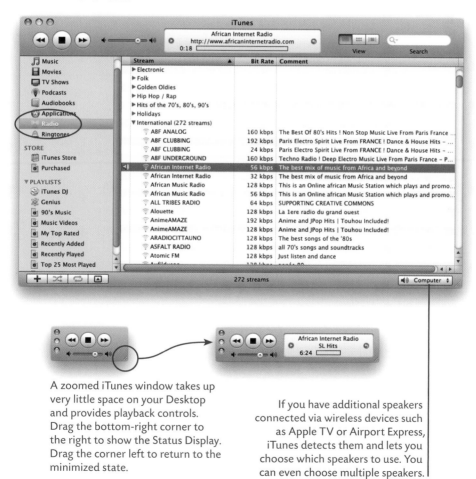

A zoomed iTunes window takes up very little space on your Desktop and provides playback controls. Drag the bottom-right corner to the right to show the Status Display. Drag the corner left to return to the minimized state.

If you have additional speakers connected via wireless devices such as Apple TV or Airport Express, iTunes detects them and lets you choose which speakers to use. You can even choose multiple speakers.

iTunes DJ, Genius Playlist, and Genius Sidebar

Why go to the trouble of making playlists when iTunes will do it for you? If you have an iTunes Store account, when you go to the "Playlists" section (in the left sidebar) and click **iTunes DJ,** iTunes automatically picks songs from your music collection and creates a random mix that updates after each song. You can change the list, or reorder it, at any time. You can even allow guests to request songs using Apple's Remote application on their iPhones or iPod touch.

Click the "Settings…" button (bottom-left corner) to set how many songs appear in the list at a time, or to give permission to guests to wirelessly request songs (using the Remote application), and to vote for songs (to control when a song plays).

Click the "Refresh" button (bottom-right corner) to change all songs in the playlist.

Instead of a *random* playlist, you can create a **Genius playlist** of songs *similar* to the current selection. Go to the "Playlists" section in the sidebar and click "Genius." iTunes automatically creates a collection of songs that go great together. Or, click the Genius icon (the atom symbol) in the Status Display.

Create a Genius playlist.

iTunes DJ playlist.

The **Genius sidebar** shows suggested songs from the iTunes Store you might like, based on your current selection. To show the Genius sidebar, click the "Show Genius sidebar" button (bottom-right). To hear previews of suggested songs, click the blue button next to the song. To buy a suggested song, click the "Buy" button.

Genius playlist.

Genius sidebar.

Show Genius sidebar.

Print a CD Cover Insert

You can print in a variety of ways from iTunes.

1 Select a Playlist, then hit Command P to **print.**

2 Experiment with the options in the window that opens (below). Choose a "Print" option, then choose a "Theme" for that print option.

iTunes is Integrated With:

iPhoto   Choose songs from iTunes to play during a slideshow.

iChat   iChat Buddy List and Bonjour List windows can display the songs you're listening to: In either window, click the tiny triangle under your name in the title bar; choose "Current iTunes Track."

Screen Saver   Your screen saver can display iTunes album art. Go to the System Preferences, click "Desktop & Screen Saver," click the "Screen Saver" tab, then select "iTunes Artwork."

iPod   Transfer songs to your iPod.

iPhone   Use iTunes to synchronize songs or videos to your iPhone.

Wireless connections

The AirPort Express wireless device includes built-in AirTunes software. Plug the AirPort Express device into any electrical outlet in your house, connect speakers, and stream iTunes from your Mac to that other room. If you have an Apple TV device, stream iTunes content to an HD television.

Dashboard   Display a small iTunes widget; see page 298.

11

GOALS

Learn to crop, color adjust, and resize images

Learn how to annotate and mark up a PDF

Search PDFs and create bookmarks for easy retrieval

Copy text from a PDF to paste into another document as editable text

Fill in PDF forms

Make screenshots

Print images or documents in a variety of ways

Save files into other formats

Preview for Viewing Images and PDFs

The small picture-viewing application called Preview does a great deal more than merely display photographs for you. It's actually quite a powerful program in which you can open and annotate PDFs, change file formats, crop images, adjust the color or size, make screen shots of what you see on your screen, import images from a camera, digital card reader, or scanner, and more. Take a few moments to explore the possibilities.

Open an Image or Folder of Images

If you haven't changed the settings, you can just double-click images or PDFs and
they open in Preview. Preview is in your Dock (if it isn't, see page 20 to put it there).

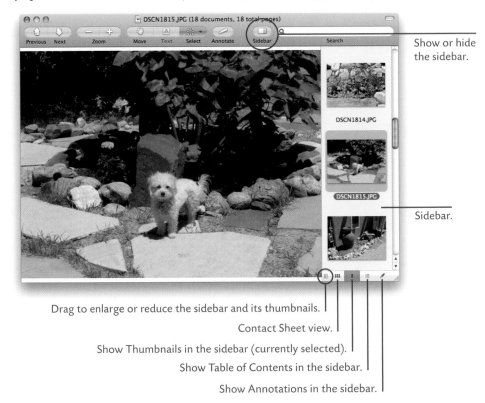

Show or hide
the sidebar.

Sidebar.

Drag to enlarge or reduce the sidebar and its thumbnails.

Contact Sheet view.

Show Thumbnails in the sidebar (currently selected).

Show Table of Contents in the sidebar.

Show Annotations in the sidebar.

To open an image or multiple images in Preview, do any of the following:

- Double-click the file.

- Drag one or more images (or PDF files) into the Preview sidebar.

- Drag-and-drop an image or PDF onto the Preview icon in the Dock.
  You can drag an **entire folder** of images to the Preview icon and they will
  all open and display themselves in the sidebar, as shown above.

- Control-click an image, select "Open With," and choose "Preview."

Check the Preview preferences for options about how to display your images.

To view multiple images as a contact sheet, click the Contact Sheet button
(shown above). Use the resize slider in the Contact Sheet view to resize thumbnails.

Sort the Images or Email Them

To sort the images into a particular order, or to **email an image,** Control-click a thumbnail in the sidebar, as shown above. From the pop-up menu, choose an action, such as "Sort By," or "Send to Mail." You can also use this menu to send an image to iPhoto, move an image to the Trash, and more. If you want to see more thumbnails at once in the sidebar, choose "Columns" from this pop-up menu, then choose how many columns of thumbnails to show in the sidebar.

Rotate, Reduce, or Enlarge the Image

If an image appears sideways, press Command L to **rotate** it to the left, or Command R to **rotate** it to the right. Or use the commands in the Tools menu. From the Tools menu you can also **flip an image horizontally or vertically.** To keep the changes, **save** the image (go to the File menu and choose "Save").

To enlarge or reduce and image, click the Zoom buttons (the **+** and the **−** buttons).

View a Slideshow

Drag a selection of images and drop them on the Preview icon in the Dock, the from the View menu, choose "Slideshow." Click the Play button in the Control bar that appears. To stop, click the **x** in the control bar, the Pause button, or the Escape key.

Display Facing Pages or Continuous Pages

You can display facing pages of PDF documents, as in a book (the first page will always display alone, like the first page of a chapter). This works whether or not the person who created the PDF saved the file in the "Spreads" format (which combines facing pages in the PDF). In fact, if someone *did* create the PDF pages in spreads, you can view them in Preview as individual pages. This comes in very handy when you need to print the document but don't want to print two-page spreads on one page.

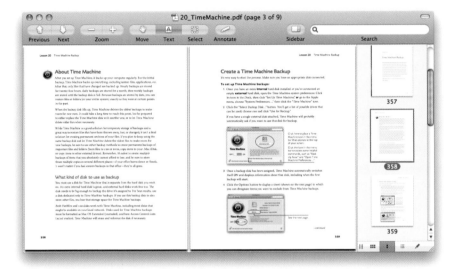

To switch back and forth from single pages to facing pages (above), go to the View menu, choose "PDF Display," then choose one of the options—"Single Page" or "Double Page" shows a page (or a two-page spread) at a time. "Single Page Continuous" or Double Page Continuous" shows the PDF as one long, scrolling page.

Open Multiple PDFs in a Single Window

To see multiple PDFs at once, drag them to Preview's Sidebar, then click the Contact Sheet button below the Sidebar. Drag the resize slider in the bottom-left corner to enlarge the PDFs. The PDFs are shown in the main window. When you hover your pointer over a PDF documents that contains multiple pages, a circled arrow icon appears on the right edge of the document. Click the arrow icon to show all of the document pages (including a slick animation effect of the front page peeling back and the other pages sliding into position in the window).

Crop a Photograph or Other Image

You can crop any photograph or image very easily in Preview. Keep in mind that when you crop an image, the part you get rid of *is gone from the original image forever.* You might want to make a copy of the file before you crop. (Cropping a **PDF,** however, is "non-destructive"; see pages 202–203.)

To crop a photograph or other image:

1 Open the image in Preview.

2 Choose a cropping tool from the "Select" button in the toolbar (you have to *press* on that menu to see the options; a *click* selects the option you see in the button menu). You can crop into a circle, oval, rectangle, or use the Lasso tool to draw a shape.

3 **To resize** the cropped area, press on any of the tiny round "handles" that you see on each corner and side. Drag any handle to resize.

4 **To move the cropped area** to a different part of the image, press in the middle of the cropping box and drag. **To cancel,** press the Escape (esc) key, or click anywhere outside the selected crop area.

5 When you are ready to crop, go to the Tools menu and choose "Crop." *Or* press Command K.

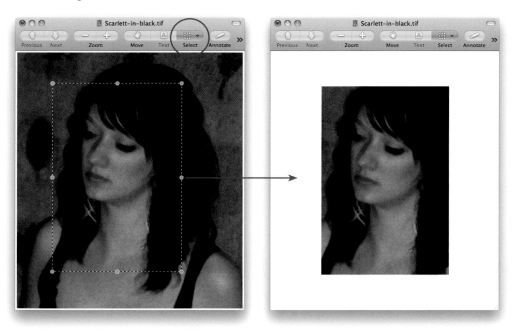

Crop a PDF

You can crop any part of a PDF. When you crop it, Preview actually keeps track of the part of the document you deleted and hangs on to it in case you want to uncrop the file, even after you've saved it.

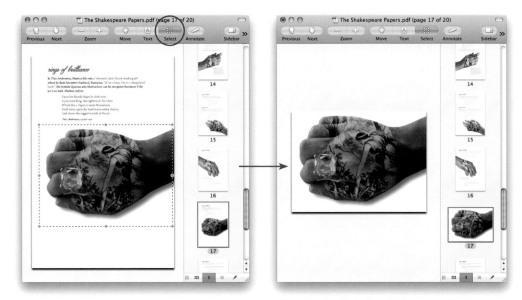

The thumbnails in the sidebar show that only the selected page was altered.

To crop a PDF:

1 Open the PDF in Preview.

2 Single-click the "Select" tool, circled above. If the little tools are not visible in the toolbar, drag the bottom-right corner of Preview to widen the window. *Or* go to the Tools menu and choose "Select Tool."

3 Starting in an upper corner, drag diagonally downward across the PDF to select the part of it you want to save. The light area is the part you're going to keep.

4 If you need to resize the cropped area, position the mouse directly over one of the eight "handles" you see on the corners and sides of the cropped area (see the previous page). Drag a handle to resize.

5 If you need to move the cropped area to another part of the page, position the pointer in the middle of the crop box. You'll notice the pointer turns into a gloved hand. Press the hand in the middle of the crop box and drag.

6   If you have a multi-page document, the cropping will apply only to the current page. When you have the cropped area finalized, go to the Tools menu and choose "Crop," *or* press Command K.

7   The cropped version of the page shows in the main viewing pane and also in the sidebar. All other pages of the document remain unaltered.

To switch between displays of the full page or the cropped page:

■ **Display the entire contents of the PDF page:** Go to the View menu, choose "PDF Display," and choose to see the "Media Box" (as shown below).

■ **Display the only the cropped image:** Go to the View menu, choose "PDF Display," and then choose to see the "Crop Box."

When you **re-open a cropped file,** it might open in the uncropped version. Just use the technique above to view the cropping again.

Search a PDF

The search feature in Preview is quite amazing. Use the standard keyboard shortcut for "Find," Command F. Once you have found an instance on the page, press Command G to find the next instance. These are the same shortcuts you've probably used in Safari to find text on a web page or in TextEdit to find text in your document.

To search a PDF:

1 With the PDF document open in front of you, press Command F.
   Or just type the word or phrase you want to find into the search field.

2 Click the "Sidebar" button to see a summary of search results. Use the buttons at the bottom of the sidebar to choose how to view the summary.

3 As you type, Preview starts finding and highlighting words that match. As you type, the search is focused more and fewer matches are found.

4 In the sidebar summary of results, click any item to go directly to that page. Click the Previous and Next buttons to cycle through the matches found.
   Or, press Command G to go to the next match in the document.

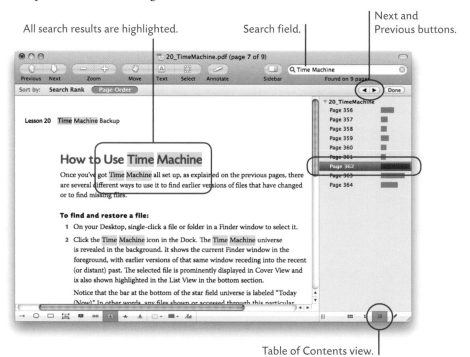

All search results are highlighted.   Search field.   Next and Previous buttons.

Table of Contents view.

Create Bookmarks

The bookmarks in Preview are not stored in the document itself. A bookmark puts the name of a file in the Bookmarks menu of Preview so you can open the document or photograph immediately without having to go look for it—open Preview, then choose a bookmark name listed in the Bookmarks menu (below-right), and the PDF file opens to display that particular page, even if that PDF document is not currently open. This is an easy way to access important pages from different documents.

To make a bookmark for an open document or image, press Command D (or from the Bookmarks menu, choose "Add Bookmark…" as shown above-left). You will be asked to name the bookmark. Give it a name that you'll recognize in a list.

> If the PDF is a **multi-page document,** you can make several bookmarks for the same document, each one to a different page. Just make sure you are viewing the page you want to bookmark before you press Command D.

To open a bookmarked file, open Preview, go to the Bookmarks menu, and choose the bookmark name from the list at the bottom of the menu (above-right).

To edit the name or to remove a bookmark, go to the Bookmarks menu and choose "Edit Bookmarks…." In the Preview preferences window opens (shown below). Click the "Bookmarks" icon in the toolbar, then:

> **To delete a file,** single-click the file name, then click the "Remove" button.

> **To edit the file name,** double-click its name, then edit.

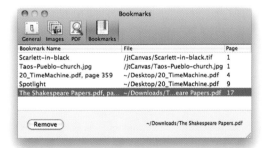

Annotate a PDF

You can add comments, highlights, shapes, and more to PDFs to call out items for other readers. Make sure the "Annotate" button is in Preview's toolbar. If not, go to the View menu, choose "Customize Toolbar…," and drag it into the toolbar. When you click "Annotate," a new toolbar opens across the bottom of the Preview window that contains all the annotation tools you need.

To create a text note on a PDF:

1   In an open PDF, click the "Annotate" button in the upper toolbar. Then click the "Note" button in bottom the Annotate toolbar at the bottom of the window.

2   Click anywhere on the page you need a note or comment. Preview places a small Note symbol on the page and immediately creates a text note to the side.

3   **To type the note,** just start typing and the text will appear in the note on the side. By default (see the Preview preferences) it adds your name and the date to the note. To **edit that note later,** triple-click it.

4   **To move a note symbol,** press-and-drag it on the page. The note text (on the side) will move up or down with the symbol.

5   **To delete a note,** click the symbol to select it, then hit Delete.

Annotation tools.

To draw an oval or rectangle annotation:

1 In an open PDF, click the "Annotate" button in the upper toolbar. Then click one of the shape buttons in the Annotate toolbar at the bottom of the window.

 To create an oval, click the "Oval" button.

 To create a rectangle, click the "Rectangle" button.

2 With the tool, press-and-drag anywhere on the page **to create a shape.**

3 **To resize a shape,** click it, then drag one of the handles to resize.

4 **To move a shape,** single-click the shape, then press-and-drag the shape around the page.

5 **To delete a shape,** single-click the shape to select it, then hit Delete.

To highlight, underline, or strike through text:

1 Click one of the Annotation buttons in the toolbar at the bottom of the Preview window (Highlight, Strikethrough, Underline).

2 Press-and-drag over the text you want to annotate.

 To delete all or part of a markup, select the markup tool that was used, then press-and-drag over the markups you want to delete.

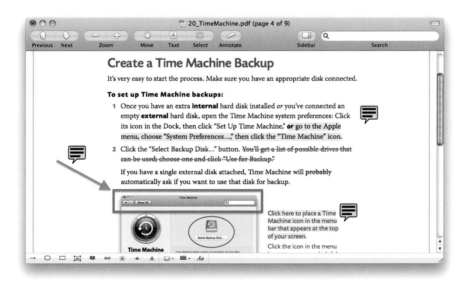

Create a link on an exisiting PDF

You can create a workable link on any PDF. Send the PDF on to someone else and the link still works. The link can go to any web page, in which case clicking on it opens Safari to that page. Or the link can go to another page in the same document. For instance, you might have a report with a table of contents. If there are no links from the table of contents to the actual pages in the existing PDF, you can add them.

To create a link:

1   In an open PDF, click the "Annotate" button in the toolbar, then click the "Link" button in the Annotation toolbar that appears across the bottom of the Preview window.

2   Press-and-drag over the existing PDF text (or an image) to which you want to apply a link. What the text says on the page has nothing to do with what you will enter as a link.

3   The Inspector palette (shown on the next page) automatically opens up to the "Annotations" pane. If it doesn't show up, go to the Tools menu and choose "Show Inspector."

Click here to create or show links.

If you don't see the same pane shown below, click the red oval in the Inspector toolbar to display the "Annotations Inspector" pane.

4 In the "Link type" pop-up menu inside this pane, you have a choice of linking to a "URL" on the web or to a "Link Within PDF."

If you choose to link to a URL (below-left), type in the *entire* web address including *http://*.

If you choose to link to another page in the PDF (below-right), go to the page you want to link to, then click the "Set Destination" button.

5 On the page, the link appears as a gray-striped box, as shown on the previous page. Click the link in Preview to make sure the link works. The links will be invisible unless you click the "Links" button in the bottom toolbar (shown circled on the previous page).

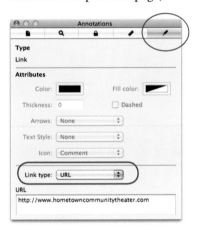 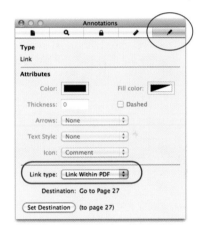

Copy Text from a PDF to Paste Elsewhere

You can copy text from a PDF file (as long as the person sending it to you hasn't locked it) and paste it into any other document as **editable text.** Or you can copy a section of text as a **graphic** and paste it into another document as a graphic image that can be resized as a unit.

To copy text:

1   Select the Text tool, shown circled below, *or* press Command 2.

2   Press-and-drag over the text you want to select.

To select just a vertical portion of text, as in one column, hold down the Option key before you start to drag, and keep it held down as you drag.

3   From the Edit menu, choose "Copy," *or* press Command C. Open your other document and paste it in (Command V).

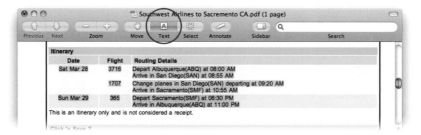

To copy any part of a PDF as a graphic, click the "Select" button in the Preview toolbar (below), then press-and-drag in the PDF document to select an area you want to copy. Go to the Edit menu and choose "Copy" (or press Command C).

Now you can go to any document in any application and paste that graphic in. To paste it, open the other document, press Command V, *or* go to the Edit menu and choose "Paste."

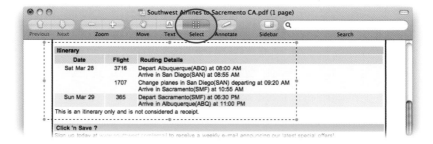

Adjust the Colors of Images or Photographs

You can do some editing in graphic images and photos. You can crop, as explained on page 201, resize, rotate, and resample (change the pixels per inch) images. And you have some pretty powerful color adjustments available. The only way to learn how to use them is to experiment! Always save a copy of the original photo before you start messing with it. Look for the image editing tools in the Tools menu.

To adjust the color of an image:

1   Open an image in Preview.

2   From the Tools menu, choose "Adjust Color." You'll see the panel shown to the right.

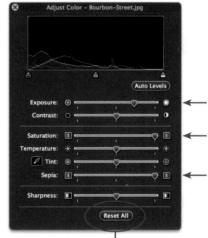

3   Move the sliders left and right to see what all the options do. The image will immediately change as you adjust the sliders. You can always click the button, circled to the right, to "Reset All" and restore the image to the way it looked in the first place.

4   When you're satisfied with the changes, press Command S to save. Then you can carry on with more changes that you can choose to save or not.

Reset all settings.

The original image.

The adjusted image.

Fill in PDF Forms

If you download forms from the web, you can actually fill them in by typing. *Then* you can print the fully completed forms, instead of printing them first and filling them in by hand. The PDF must have been created and saved in such a way that it has fields ready for you to enter data. That is, you just can't start entering data into any old PDF—it must be an actual form format.

After you save a form that you have filled in, you cannot edit any of the information you entered! You might want to save a clean copy of the file *before* you fill in the form.

To fill in a PDF form:

1 Open an appropriate PDF form in Preview. The example below is a tax form downloaded from the IRS site.

2 Click on the Text tool, shown circled below.

3 Click in the area where you are supposed to enter data. An insertion point appears and the text field becomes visible, as shown below.

4 Type! Be sure to save regularly (or *don't* save, in case you want to edit it later).

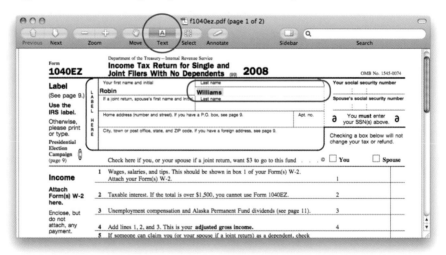

Import Images from a Camera or Scanner

If you have an image device connected, such as a camera, a digital photo card reader, or a scanner, you can use Preview to import images. From the File menu, choose "Import from Camera…" **or** "Import from Scanner…." If your scanner doesn't appear in the "Import from Scanner…" menu, go online and search for the latest "driver" software for that scanner. After you download and install the driver, the scanner name should appear in the "Import from Scanner…" menu.

Make Screenshots using Preview

A screenshot is a picture of what your screen looks like at that moment. It's useful to send to someone who's trying to help you or to show someone something cool that's only on your Mac. Preview uses the Grab utility to take pictures of items on your screen.

To make a screenshot:

1 Open Preview. You don't have to have any window open.

2 Go to the File menu, slide down to "Take Screen Shot," then choose either:

   From Selection: A crosshair icon appears. Press-and-drag around an area to take a screenshot of just that area. When you let go, it takes the shot.

   From Window: A camera icon appears, shown below. As you move the camera icon on top of different windows on your screen, it highlights each one in blue. When the window you want is highlighted, single-click. It takes a picture of the entire window, whether or not you can see the whole thing.

   From Entire Screen: Preview gives you ten seconds to get your screen set up the way you want it for a screenshot. For instance, you might want a picture of a particular menu and submenu. After ten seconds, Preview snaps a screenshot of the entire screen.

The screenshot immediately and automatically opens in Preview. From the File menu, choose "Save As...." Name the file, choose a format, and save in a location of your choice.

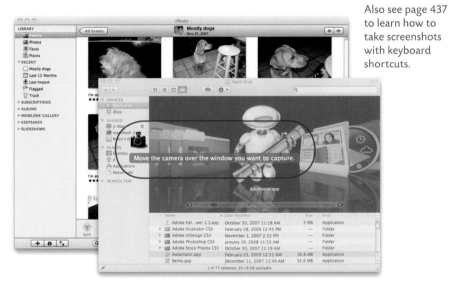

Also see page 437 to learn how to take screenshots with keyboard shortcuts.

Print or Fax from Preview

You can print any image or document from Preview, of course. But you can also print groups of photos or entire folders of images.

If you have multiple images open in Preview, select the ones you want to print: Choose them from the sidebar, or from the Contact Sheet view. From the File menu, choose "Print..." (if you want to print one image), or choose "Print Selected Images..." (if you want to print multiple selected images on the same sheet). You'll get the dialog box shown below. Be sure to spend a few minutes looking through all the options, then click "Print."

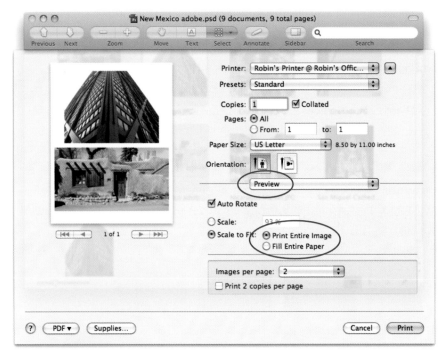

Above you see a preview of what the page will look like when printed with the specifications chosen in the dialog box.

To the left, you see a preview of what the printed page will look like with the option of "Fill Entire Paper" selected. If necessary, this option enlarges images and crops them.

To fax an image or selected images:

Not all computers today have an internal modem installed, and you can't fax without one. You must have a phone cable connected to a telephone outlet— you can't fax from your Mac over the Internet or through your broadband connection.

If your Mac has a modem that is connected to a phone line, it is automatically configured to send faxes. If you use your dial-up modem to connect to the Internet, your Mac will wait until you log off, then send the fax.

1 From the File menu, choose "Print...."

2 Click the button in the bottom-left corner named "PDF."

3 Choose "Fax PDF...."

4 Enter the fax number you want to send this to. Make your choices in this dialog box, similar to your choices when printing (as explained on the previous page).

5 Click the "Fax" button.

Also see Lesson 17 on printing and faxing.

Save as Another Format

If you know you need a particular image in another **file type,** go to the File menu and choose "Save As...." Click the "Format" menu, as shown below-left, and make a choice. Each choice will give you different specifications for that particular file format.

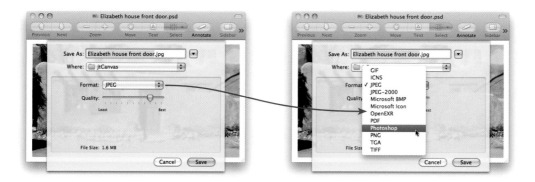

12

GOALS

Use the Burn Folder
to collect files for burning
to a CD or DVD

Create clips and bookmarks
in DVDs

Create a PDF from any file

Use Font Book to install
and preview fonts

Keep track of your life
with Stickies

Learn to use Photo Booth
to take still shots and
movies of yourself

Miscellaneous Tools on your Mac

Your Mac has a number of great tools in the form of small applications, some of which get overlooked. This lesson introduces you to some features and possibilities that you might not be taking advantage of yet.

Burn Folders make it easy to keep track of items you want to burn backups of at a later date. The DVD Player has some great features that may surprise you, especially if you teach a class and use DVDs as part of your presentation. You'll be surprised how easy it is to create a PDF from any file. Font management is simple when you use Font Book. And applications like Stickies and Photo Booth are both useful and fun.

Take a look at what you may have been missing!

Burn a CD or DVD with a Burn Folder

You'll want to burn backups of your important work. Be sure to burn backups of any applications or fonts or other files that you download straight from the Internet.

The steps below describe how to burn data files (as opposed to music or movies) onto a disc. A CD holds about 650 megabytes; a single-layer DVD holds about 4.3 gigabytes, even though the package might say it holds 4.7. (To burn a music CD, see page 192.)

The **Burn Folder** is the easiest way to burn a CD or DVD. Drag items into this special folder, and when you're ready, burn the contents to a disc. Your Mac automatically creates **aliases** of files in the Burn Folder (see page 435 for details on aliases). This means that after you burn the disc, you can throw away the entire Burn Folder without destroying any original files.

The wonderful thing is that you can collect items you want to burn without having to actually burn the disc at that moment—you can collect files over the period of a project and when finished, you have a folder ready to back up onto a disc.

To create a Burn Folder, put files inside, and burn it:

1   Open a Finder window and select the window in which you want the Burn Folder to appear. For instance, single-click your Home icon in the Sidebar, or single-click the Documents folder icon. Or click the Desktop, if you want the folder to appear there. (You can always move the Burn Folder to wherever you like, of course.)

2   From the File menu, choose "New Burn Folder."

3   A folder with the "Burn" icon on it (below-left) appears in the selected window.

Burn Folder.fpbf

I put this Burn Folder in my Home folder. Then I dragged it into my Sidebar so it's always available to me.

4 **To put a file (or a folder) in the Burn Folder** so you can burn it later, just drag the original file or folder and drop it into the Burn Folder. Your Mac will put an *alias* of the file into the Burn Folder and the original will stay right where it was, safe and sound.

5 **To burn the folder onto a CD,** first insert a blank CD or DVD.

6 **Then** single-click the Burn Folder in the sidebar; a bar across the top of the window appears with a "Burn" button, as shown on the opposite page.

You will be asked to name the disc, which of course you should do.

Click the "Burn" button that's in the window's Burn bar (circled on the opposite page).

TIP ——— If you drag the Burn Folder into the Sidebar, it displays a burn icon next to it. You can just single-click that burn icon to start the process.

TIP ——— You can make as many Burn Folders as you want. Rename them as you do any other folder. This makes it easy to have a separate Burn Folder for each project.

To check the amount of storage space used in the folder:

1 Single-click the Burn Folder icon.

2 Press Command I to display the Info window.

3 Click the disclosure triangle next to "Burning."

4 Click the "Calculate" button to see how much you have collected in the folder.

You can also check the status bar at the bottom of the Burn Folder window, shown on the previous page. The text in the status bar tells you how many items are there, and how much disc space will be required.

TIP ——— If you change your mind and want to take an unburned disc out of the Mac, Control-click (or right-click) on the disc icon and choose "Eject 'namehere CD.'"

DVD Player

DVD Player

Besides playing your DVDs and allowing you to control things as you do on your television, the DVD Player has several special tricks.

Display the thumbnail bar and controls

When a video plays in full screen mode (Command F), do the following:

To see the DVD playback controls, push your mouse down to the bottom of the screen and they appear.

To see the thumbnail bar that displays chapter markers, bookmarks, and video clips, push your mouse toward the top of the screen.

To show the DVD application menu bar, push your mouse all the way to the top of the screen.

These same controls can be found in the floating DVD player, in the Window menu, and in the Controls menu (important to know if you're not using full screen view).

Create bookmarks to find specific points in the video

A bookmark lets you skip immediately to certain points in the video that you choose. That is, you are not limited to the chapter markers that were created when the DVD was made.

To create a bookmark:

1 Play a DVD. Then . . .

2 Go to the Window menu and choose "Bookmarks." The Bookmarks palette opens. When you get to the point in the DVD where you want to insert a bookmark, click the + button at the bottom of the "Bookmarks" palette.

   Or go to the Controls menu and choose "New Bookmark...."

3 A dialog opens where you can rename the bookmark and easily identify it later.

Once you have created bookmarks, you can go to the Go menu and choose to skip straight to any bookmark you made. If you make more than one bookmark, use the Bookmarks palette to choose one of them to be the "default" bookmark: select a Bookmark thumbnail, click the Actions button (the gear icon), then choose "Make Default." These bookmarks are *not* stored with the DVD; if you loan the DVD to anyone, it will not include your bookmarks. They are stored only on your Mac.

Create your own clips with endpoints

Amazing. You can create individual video clips of selected segments of a DVD and then choose to play just those clips. This feature and the bookmarks feature are terrific for teachers or trainers who want to separate segments or start a scene in a DVD at a particular point. Or maybe there's a specific section of your dance or exercise video that you want to view over and over again—this makes it so easy!

To make a video clip:

1 Play a DVD. Pause the DVD, then move the playhead to the point where you want start a clip. Go to the Window menu and choose "Video Clips."

2 In the "Video Clips" palette that opens (below-left), click the + button.

Add video clip.

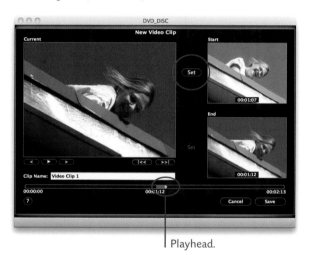

Playhead.

3 In the "New Video Clip" pane that opens (above-right), click the top "Set" button to set the beginning of the clip. Click the Play button (or drag the playhead) to get to the end point that you want to mark. Pause the playback, click the lower "Set" button to set the clip's ending, then click "Save."

To see your saved clips, from the Go menu, choose "Video Clips," then choose a saved clip from the submenu list. When in full screen mode, move your pointer to the top edge of the screen and click the film strip icon in the top-left corner to show clip thumbnails in a bar across the top of the screen.

Make adjustments

To adjust video color, sound, and zoom controls, go to the Window menu. Choose the adjustment you want to make and use the sliders.

Create your own personal disc jacket on the screen

This is great—you can add your own image to the DVD so whenever you stop the DVD, it displays the image of *your* choice.

To add your own image to the disc:

1 Open a DVD in the DVD Player.

2 Go to the File menu and choose "Get Disc Info."

3 Click the "Jacket Picture" icon in the toolbar, shown circled below.

4 Drag any image from your hard disk and drop it into the well. Click OK. Cool.

This is the image well.

Remember, changes like this don't really apply to the actual DVD—they are stored on your Mac. So the disc jacket will only appear if you show this DVD from the computer on which you added it.

Go back to the Finder

When a DVD is playing full screen, there are several ways to exit full screen mode without interrupting the DVD playback. Push your pointer to the top of the screen until the top menu appears, then go to the Go menu and choose "Switch to Finder." *Or* press Command Option F. *Or* tap the Escape key (esc). *Or* press Command F. *Or* go to the View menu and choose one of the size options there (including "Exit Full Screen").

Create PDF Files

A PDF (Portable Document Format) is a file created in such a way that most people can open and read it, no matter what kind of computer they use. The graphics, the images, the fonts, and all the formatting are held intact in the document. And it's usually compressed into a smaller file size (not physical size) so it can travel through the Internet quickly, or be stored efficiently.

To make a PDF in most applications, have the document open in front of you. From the File menu, choose "Print…," then click the "PDF" button.

Save as PDF   Saves a regular PDF that you can share with others. The graphics are at full resolution and the fonts are embedded. When you choose to save as a PDF, you'll get a window with a "Security Options" button where you can choose to require a password to open, copy, or print.

To view a password-protected PDF, enter the password, then tap the Return key.

—continued

Save as PostScript

This saves the document as a PostScript Level 2 file in ASCII format, meaning if you open it, you'll see a lot of code. But you can send it directly to a Postscript printer or run it through Acrobat Distiller. Don't choose this option unless you know you need it.

Fax PDF   If you have set up your fax specifications as explained in Lesson 17, then your Mac will make a PDF of the document and open the fax dialog box where you can enter the fax number and a message. Remember, you must have a phone line connected to the Mac.

Mail PDF   This creates a PDF of the file, opens Mail, creates a new message, and puts this PDF in the message ready to send. This is a great time-saver, but I've noticed that people using AOL or PCs often can't read these.

Save as PDF-X

The PDF-X standard from Adobe is designed for high-end printing. I don't suggest you choose this option unless you *know* you need a PDF-X file, and even then it would be best to create it in a high-end application.

Save PDF to iPhoto

Your Mac will turn this document into a PDF, open iPhoto (if you have it installed, of course), ask you which album to put it into (or ask you to create a new one), and then put the PDF in that album.

If you have an iPhone, this is a good way to get PDFs onto it. You might have tried putting a PDF directly into iPhoto and discovered that iPhoto won't accept it, says it's an unacceptable format. But iPhoto *will* take PDFs through the method described above. Next time you sync your iPhone in iTunes, go to the "Photos" tab in the sync pane and choose the album in which you're keeping the PDFs. They're kind of blurry, but if you need the info to take with you, it's an option.

Save PDF to Web Receipts Folder

Web Receipts

I love this. Have you ever bought something on the web and you got that page that says, "This is your receipt"? And you know you should print it but maybe the printer isn't turned on at the moment or it's three pages long and you know they're going to send you an email receipt anyway, but what if they don't send you the email receipt and you need this web page receipt? Well, this is a great solution: The Mac will save this web page as a PDF and it will make you a folder in your Documents folder called "Web Receipts" and it will store this PDF (and all others you make like it) in that folder.

Be careful, though—if you make a web receipt from the same site more than once, it will probably write over itself with the same name. Some sites automatically name their receipt file something generic like "Acme Receipt." So when you create another PDF from Acme, it gets named the same thing as all the other receipts from Acme and the newest version replaces the last one you created.

Since this method doesn't give you a chance to customize the file name, it's safer to just go ahead and choose "Save PDF" in the Print dialog (shown on page 223). You can still create a Web Receipts folder in the Documents folder, or wherever you prefer.

If you're adventurous, you can search on the Internet for an Applescript that will automatically append a date and time to the file name when you choose "Save PDF to Web Receipts Folder."

Font Book

Font Book allows you to install new **fonts** you acquire, disable fonts in your font menus that you never use, and view fonts before you install them.

Preview fonts you haven't installed

If you acquire new fonts or if you just have some fonts on a disk and you don't know what they are, simply double-click the font file. Font Book will open automatically and display the font. If you want to install it, click the "Install Font" button.

Install fonts

You can use the step above to install fonts. You can also:

1 Open Font Book (it's in your Applications folder).

2 In the Collection pane, single-click "User" (if you want the fonts available only to you as the user) or "Computer" (if you want the fonts available to every user of this particular computer).

3 Go to the File menu and choose "Add Fonts...."

4 Find the font you want to install and double-click it. Font Book *moves* the font from its enclosing folder and puts it in the Library Fonts folder. If the fonts don't appear in your application's Font menu, you might have to quit the application and restart it so they'll show up.

The default location for installing fonts is determined in the Font Book preferences.

Preview fonts you have installed

Single-click any typeface name in the Font pane of Font Book. A preview appears on the right. Use the slider to enlarge or reduce the typeface, or type in a point size.

Go to the Preview menu and choose:

- "Sample" to display the upper and lowercase letters, as well as the numbers.

- "Repertoire" to see every glyph (letter, number, punctuation, etc.) in the font.

- "Custom," and then type your own words to see them displayed in this typeface. Use the slider bar on the right to enlarge the font.

To disable an individual font, find it in the Font list. Single-click to select it, then click the little checkmark button at the bottom of the Font list. When the checkmark is removed, the font name is dimmed and the word "Off" appears to the right (shown above).

Create your own Collections

A **Collection** is simply an easy way to look at fonts you like instead of having to grope through a lengthy font list of typefaces you don't know or want.

To make a new Collection, single-click the **+** sign at the bottom of the Collection pane, then name it. Click the "All Fonts" collection (so you can access all fonts), then drag font names from the Font pane to the new Collection name.

To disable (turn off) an entire Collection, select it in the Collection pane. Then go to the Edit menu and choose, "Disable 'CollectionName.'"

Stickies

Stickies

The **Stickies** application lets you put little Stickie notes all over your screen, just like you'd stick them around the edge of your monitor (my kids tell me my monitor looks like a giant daisy).

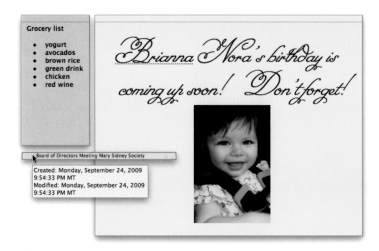

Notice in the examples above you can see these features:

- The grocery note above is a **bulleted list.** To make such a list, click Option-Tab on the note, then Control-click the note to open a contextual menu and choose "List..." from the menu. You can choose from a variety of bullets and numbers, plus you can add a prefix and suffix to the bullet. Thus you could create a numbered list that uses **(1)** or **Act 1:** or **•A•** or any other combination. The list options even include Greek characters and Asian characters.

- **Remember,** hit Option-Tab *before* you type the first item in the list. To continue the list, just hit a Return after each item. You can hit Option-Tab-Tab to indent an extra level.

  To end the list, hit Return twice.

  You can change the bullet formatting at any time—just use the List options from the contextual menu as explained above.

- You can **change fonts, size, color,** etc., just as in any other Mac application, using the Font dialog box (press Command T). See pages 246–247.

- Double-click in the title bar of any Stickie note to "roll it up" so **just the title bar shows,** as you can see on the opposite page. The first line of type appears in the title bar. Double-click the title bar again to unroll the note.

- Hover your mouse over any note to display a **tool tip** of information about when the note was created and modified, as shown on the opposite page.

- Drag a **graphic** image from anywhere on your Mac and drop it into the Stickie note.

- A note can hold many pages of text and graphics. You won't see **scroll** bars, but you can drag the mouse through the text and it will scroll, or use the arrow keys or the PageUp or PageDown keys. If your mouse has a scroll wheel, use it to scroll through long notes. **Resize a Stickie note** just as you would any other window—drag the bottom-right corner.

- Notice the red dots under the name Brianna. This is a visual clue that the **spell checker** is on and working. Control-click the note, choose "Spelling and Grammar," then choose one of the spell-checking options.

- If you prefer working with a certain font and a certain size and a certain color note, you can **set a default** so all your notes look like that without having to select your favorite specifications for every note. Just set up one note the way you like it, then go to the Note menu and choose "Use as Default."

- If you want your Stickie notes to **automatically open** and appear every time you turn on your computer, add Stickies to the Login Items for your user account (see page 333).

- To print a note, from the File menu, choose "Print...." Set your print options as you would with any other document. If you want to print multiple notes at once, you can copy and paste them into a single note, then print.

Photo Booth

Photo Booth

Photo Booth is a convenient and fun way to take snapshots or movies of yourself for use as an iChat buddy picture or as your user account picture. You can email the photos or movie clips to friends, upload them to web pages, open in Preview to save in other formats, or view as a slideshow.

Take a still picture

1   Open Photo Booth (it's in your Applications folder).

2   Click the still picture button (the first button in the row of three).

3   Then click the red camera button.

A red timer replaces the toolbar (below-right) and starts a countdown, including audible beeps. Your screen flashes when the picture is taken, and a thumbnail version of the picture is placed at the bottom of the window. You can take several pictures and they'll all line up in that thumbnail strip.

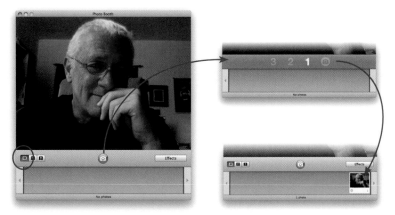

4   Click a thumbnail to display it in the main window. As soon as you do this, a new toolbar replaces the first one, as shown below. Click an icon in this toolbar to send the photo in an email message, place it in iPhoto, set it as your user Account photo, or use it as an iChat buddy picture.

To delete a snapshot, click the circled **X** on a thumbnail. Or select a thumbnail, then hit the Delete key.

Make a movie clip

1   Click the movie clip button (the film strip icon, highlighted to the right).

2   The camera button in the center of the toolbar changes to a red video button: Click it to begin recording.

While recording, the toolbar shows a timer and the red video button changes to a Stop Recording button (below). When you stop recording, a video thumbnail appears at the bottom of the window.

3   When you've stopped recording, select the movie clip thumbnail that appears in the thumbnail strip, then use the toolbar to choose how to use the movie clip. You have the following options:

- ■ Click "Email" to attach a QuickTime version of the clip to a message in Mail. Movie files are large, about 1MB per second, so keep your clips short.

- ■ To save the clip locally as a QuickTime movie, drag the video thumbnail to your Desktop or to any folder on your computer.

- ■ To use a single frame of the movie clip for your user Account photo or Buddy photo, select the movie thumbnail. Next, use the scrubber bar under the video (shown below) to select the frame you want, then click "Account Picture" or "Buddy Picture" in the toolbar. Move your pointer on top of the large video preview pane to make the scrubber bar appear.

This is the scrubber bar. Drag this diamond-shaped playhead back and forth to view individual frames of your movie.

This thumbnail strip holds both still photos and movie clips. Movie clips have a tiny camera icon in the bottom-left corner.

231

Add effects to snapshots

Photo Booth includes a gallery of special effects that you can apply *as you take a snapshot or record a movie clip.* That is, you can't apply these effects after you've taken the photo—you have to choose an effect before you snap the photo.

1 Click the Effects button (circled, below-right) to show a pane of effects (below-left). The center image always shows a Normal preview (no effects) that you can select to remove all effects and return the image to normal.

2 Click the arrows on either side of the Effects button to see all of the possibilities.

3 Click the effect you want. A full-size preview displays in the window (below-right).

4 Click one of the snapshot buttons to choose the type of snapshot you want (still picture, 4-up, or movie clip), then click the red camera button. The special effect snapshot appears in the row of thumbnails.

   The 4-up option makes one JPEG file of four grouped photos. To convert the JPEG into an animated GIF, select it, then from the File menu choose "Export."

5 Select the image in the thumbnail strip, then use the tools in the toolbar to share it (as explained on the previous pages).

 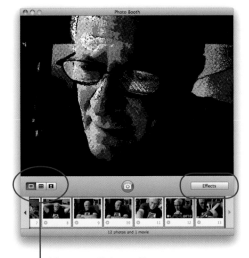

Click one of the four gray squares to jump to another pane of effects.

Or click the arrows on either side of the Effects button to cycle through the panes.

After you click an effect thumbnail, click one of these snapshot buttons.

Create a special effects backdrop

In the gallery of special effects (opposite page), the last pane is empty. In the empty spaces on that pane, you can add your own photos or movie clips to be used as a special effects backdrop for other still photos or movie clips.

To take a photo or movie using your own special backdrop:

1 In the toolbar, click the extreme-right gray square to show the pane of blank spaces.

2 Drag your own photos or movies into one or more of the blank spaces.

3 Select the image you want to use as a special effects backdrop.

4 Take a snapshot or start recording a movie. A message appears and instructs you to move out of the view so Photo Booth can patch the special backdrop into the background.
   So move out of the way for a few seconds.

5 A second message appears and telsl you the background has been detected and it's okay to move back into the frame. Move back in and click the red camera button to take a photo or record video.

TIP ——— To **preview** all of your snapshots that are lined up in the thumbnail strip, go to the View menu and choose "Start Slideshow." Press the Escape key to exit the slideshow.

QuickTime Player

QuickTime X (pronounced "ten") is multimedia software that you can use to play, and edit, movie and audio files. When you double-click a QuickTime file, it could open in either iTunes, or in the QuickTime Player, depending on the file's format—.mov (QuickTime movie), .m4a (MPEG4 audio), .m4v (MPEG4 video), .dv (Digital Video), etc.

If the multimedia file you double-click is an older one, created or saved with QuickTime 7, you may get a message with a download link that tells you to download QuickTime Player 7 in order to play the file.

While playing a movie in iTunes is OK, playing it in QuickTime Player X is a much more aesthetically pleasing visual experience. Plus, the QuickTime Player provides controls to trim files (edit a file's duration), and menu options that can automatically send a movie to iTunes, your online MobileMe Gallery (if you've purchased a MobileMe account), or YouTube (if you have a free YouTube account). You can also use QuickTime Player to create a new movie recording, a new audio recording, or a new screen recording (capture a movie of whatever is happening on your screen).

Play a movie or audio file

1 Click the QuickTime icon in the Dock to open QuickTime Player. If the QuickTime icon is not in the Dock, go to the Applications menu and double-click "QuickTime Player.app."

2 From the File menu, choose "Open File…" then select the movie (or audio) file you want to play. The movie opens in QuickTime's elegant movie window, with a playback control bar visible (shown on the following page). An Audio file opens as a small window with playback controls (below).

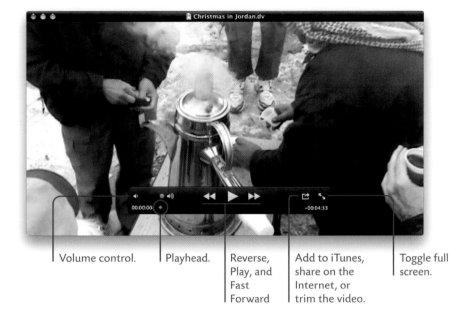

Volume control.   Playhead.   Reverse, Play, and Fast Forward   Add to iTunes, share on the Internet, or trim the video.   Toggle full screen.

3 Click the Play button. When you move the pointer off of the window, the title bar and control bar disappear to present the movie in an uncluttered window (shown below). To show the controls again, move the pointer over the window.

Share a movie

QuickTime can quickly and easily send movies to your MobileMe Gallery page, YouTube, or iTunes.

1   Open a movie file in QuickTime (as explained on page 234, "Play a movie or audio file").

2   Click the sharing icon (circled below) in the playback control bar, then from the pop-up menu, choose one of the options: save your movie to iTunes, MobileMe Gallery (a MobileMe paid membership is required), or YouTube (a free YouTube account is required). You can also go to the Share menu, then choose "iTunes…," MobileMe Gallery…," or "YouTube…."

Trim a movie or audio file

QuickTime makes it very easy to save or share just a partial selection of a movie or audio file.

1   Open a movie file in QuickTime (as explained on page 234, "Play a movie or audio file").

2   Click the sharing icon (circled below) in the playback control bar, then from the pop-up menu, choose "Trim…." You can also go to the Edit menu and choose "Trim…."

A thumbnail movie timeline appears at the bottom of the movie window, highlighted in yellow (shown at the top of the following page).

3   Drag the left and right sides of the yellow border to select the section of video
you want. After you make a selection, the dark gray "Trim" button highlights in
yellow (shown in the bottom example). Click "Trim."

The movie can now be saved to a location on your computer. Or, from the
Share menu, you can save the movie to iTunes, MobileMe Gallery, or YouTube.

4   To trim an audio file, open it in QuickTime, then from the Edit menu, choose
"Trim." An audio waveform bar appears on the file's window, highlighted with
a yellow border. Drag the ends of the highlighted
border to select the section of the file you want,
then click the "Trim" button. Now you can save
or share the audio file.

Make a new movie recording

If you have a built-in iSight camera, or have a video camera attached to your Mac, you can record a movie using QuickTime, then share it with others as explained on the previous pages.

1 Open QuickTime, then from the File menu, choose "New Movie Recording."

2 Click the red Record button on the Control bar. If you don't see a Control bar, hover your pointer over the movie window. The Control bar disappears when you move your pointer away from the window.

3 Click the red Record button again to stop recording. The Control bar changes to a playback control, so you can play the new movie.

4 To save the movie, go to the File menu, then choose "Save As…." If you close the movie window (click the red button in the top-left corner) without saving, the movie is automatically saved in the Movies folder in your Home folder.

Click here to set some preferences, such as choosing camera and microphone, quality settings, and where to save.

Make a new audio recording

If you have a built-in microphone, or have an external mic connected to your Mac, you can make audio recordings with QuickTime.

1 Open QuickTime, then from the File menu, choose "New Audio Recording."

2 Click the red Record button in the "Audio Recording" window.

3 To stop recording, click the Record button again.

Make a new screen recording

If you want to record the activity on your screen—for instructional purposes, or perhaps to record a streaming event on the Internet, or for any other reason—use QuickTime to make a screen recording.

1   Open QuickTime, then from the File menu, choose "New Screen Recording."

2   In the "Screen Recording" window that opens (below-left), click the red Record button. A dialog sheet drops down to confirm your request (below-right).

3   Click "Start Recording." To stop recording, click the "Stop Recording" button that appears in the menu bar (click "Show Me," circled below-right, to highlight the button in the menu bar). Or, press the Command Control Escape keys to stop recording.

If you don't manually choose a Save option from the File menu, or a Share option from the Share menu, your movie is automatically saved as "Screen Recording" in the Movies folder of your Home folder.

To save or export your movie in a format optimized for viewing on various devices or on the Internet:

From the File menu, choose "Save As…." A dialog opens (right) to name the movie and choose a location to save it. Click the "Format" pop-up window (circled) and select one of the format options. Each option is optimized for a size and quality that's best suited for different devices. The "iPhone" option saves a movie that's high quality and fits an iPhone screen. The "iPhone (Cellular)" option creates a movie that fits the iPhone screen, but is of much lower quality—and therefore a much smaller file size for sending over a wireless broadband network.

Also from the File menu you can choose "Save for Web…." From the Share menu you can send the movie to iTunes, your MobileMe Gallery (paid MobileMe membership required), or to YouTube (free YouTube account required.)

13

GOALS

Learn to use the tools that all Apple applications share:

Spell checker and grammar checker

Fonts panel

Special characters

Colors panel

Speech

Dictionary

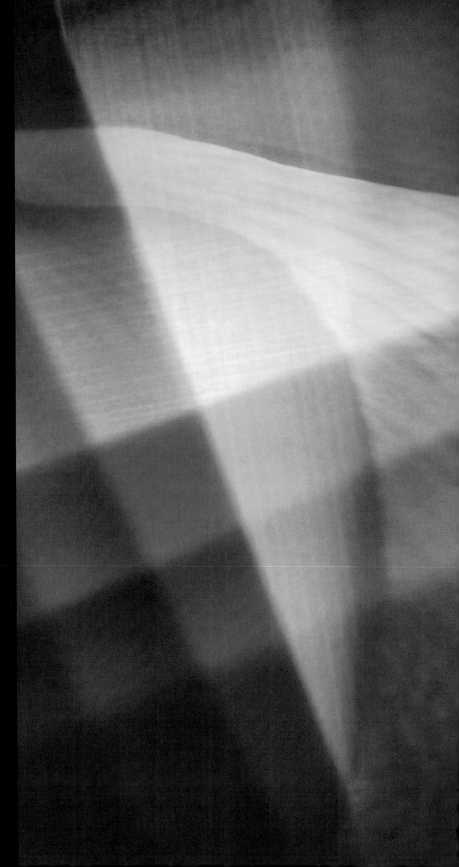

Common Tools in Mac OS X Applications

Every Apple application that comes on your Mac uses certain tools—the spelling and grammar checker, the Colors panel, the Fonts panel, the Dictionary, and a few others. Rather than tell you how to use each one within a certain application, included here are explanations of how to use each tool regardless of which application you're using it in.

Many applications from other vendors also take advantage of these Apple tools, so look for them—they will make your computing life easier and more fun.

Spell Checker

Options for the spell checker are found at the bottom of the Edit menu in Apple applications. You have several choices, each of which are explained here.

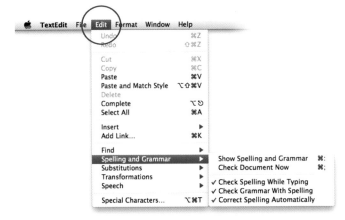

Show Spelling and Grammar

This brings up the dialog box shown below. This spell checker runs through your entire document and gives you options for each word it thinks is misspelled.

If you want the spell checker to also alert you to possible grammar mistakes, click the box in the bottom-right corner to "Check grammar."

Double-click the correct spelling.

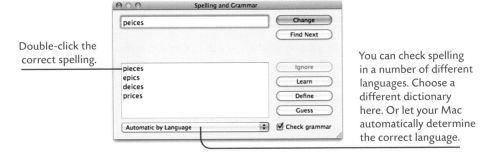

You can check spelling in a number of different languages. Choose a different dictionary here. Or let your Mac automatically determine the correct language.

To replace a misspelled word with an alternative, find the word you think is correct in the lower pane, then double-click it. *Or* you can type the correct spelling yourself in the top edit box, then click the "Change" button.

Ignore the spelling temporarily. If the spell checker keeps telling you the same word is misspelled, but you like the word spelled the way it is, click the "Ignore" button when that word is highlighted by the spell checker. The spell checker will ignore it for this document, but will correct you again in the next document.

Teach your spell checker new words. Spell checkers typically don't recognize most people's names, as shown below, or jargon specific to different specialities. If you often use a particular word that the spell checker thinks is a mistake (because it's not in the dictionary it's using), click the "Learn" button in the dialog box and the word gets added to the current dictionary. It will never bother you again.

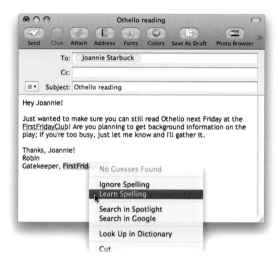

Or if you're not using the spell checker dialog box at the moment, Control-click (or right-click) a word that the spell checker thinks is a mistake (it probably has little red dots under it). In the contextual menu that pops up, click the "Learn Spelling" option while the word is selected. The spell checker will add that word to its dictionary and not whine about it being misspelled again. If the word is misspelled, spelling suggestions will appear at the top of the contextual menu.

—continued

More useful commands for spelling and grammar

The following useful commands are also found in the Edit menu, under "Spelling and Grammar."

Check Document Now

Choose this command to check the document for mispelling and grammar mistakes. *Or* use this keyboard shortcut (Command ;) to skim through the spelling in your document without opening the "Spelling and Grammmar" dialog box. It will stop at each word it thinks is misspelled. Well, the dictionary might think it's misspelled, but it might be your Grandmother's name that you don't want to change.

Check Spelling While Typing

This marks words that are misspelled as you type them—little red dots appear beneath words it thinks are misspelled. Any words not in its dictionary are considered misspelled, such as many names of people or towns and most specialized jargon.

Check Grammar With Spelling

Choosing this option automatically selects the checkbox in the dialog box, "Check grammar." It does what it says it does—applies standard grammatical rules to your text and lets you know if you're breaking any of those rules.

Instead of red dots that indicate a misspelled word, the grammar checker puts green dots under a word or phrase. Mouse over the word, pause to the count of three, and you will see a tool tip appear that tells you what the problem is. It's up to you to fix it.

He go to the store. What is.

The word 'go' may not agree with the rest of the sentence.

To change a misspelled word quickly without bringing up a dialog box:

1 Control-click (or right-click) a misspelled word (you don't need to highlight the word first).

2 A contextual menu appears, as shown below. At the top of this menu is a short list of alternative spellings for the word you clicked on.

3 Just single-click the correct spelling in the menu—the word is instantly corrected and the menu automatically disappears.

If the correct word is not offered, you can either type the correction yourself, or slide down to "Spelling and Grammar" in this menu and then choose "Check Document Now" from the sub-menu to run a spell check.

Even if the spell checker thinks it's misspelled, use your own judgment when deciding what to change. In some cases, such as an Elizabethan English sonnet or the use of an uncommon name, you should ignore unusual spellings.

Fonts Panel

Press Command T in any Mac OS X application and the Fonts panel appears, as shown below. If yours doesn't look like the one below, it might be because the Preview or the Effects are not showing.

Preview

■ **To display the Preview and/or the Effects** if they're not already visible, single-click the Action menu button (circled, below). Choose "Show Preview." Click the menu again and choose "Show Effects."

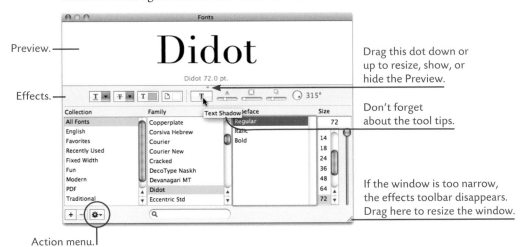

Preview.

Effects.

Drag this dot down or up to resize, show, or hide the Preview.

Don't forget about the tool tips.

If the window is too narrow, the effects toolbar disappears. Drag here to resize the window.

Action menu.

In any Apple application, open this Fonts panel to choose the typeface family, the particular style (called "Typeface," above, hidden beneath the tool tip), and the size of type. Whatever you choose here will change the *selected* characters in your document. Note that you must **first select the text** you want to change, *then* choose the font and size. *Or* position the insertion point (the flashing bar in the text) where you want to start typing, then select the font and size right *before* you start typing.

Preview your changes

Make a selection of text in a document, then make changes in this Fonts panel. You'll immediately see the changes take place in your document.

Effects

You can apply **shadow effects** to selected text with these five controls, as shown below. Select text on the page, click the "Text Shadow" button (the button with the T), then drag the sliders of the other four tools (Opacity, Blur, Offset, and Angle).

When this button is blue, that's a visual clue that the *selected* text has a shadow effect applied to it.

Collections

The Fonts panel has a number of **collections,** which are simply sub-groups of fonts from the main list. Making a collection does not disable or enable any fonts, it just makes it easier for you to choose a typeface—you don't have to scroll through a long list of fonts you don't care for.

To create a Collection, single-click the plus sign at the bottom of the Collection pane. Rename the Collection. Drag font families from the "Family" pane into the new collection—drop the family name directly on the collection name.

Favorites

If you find you often use a particular family, typeface, point size, and color, turn that combination into a Favorite and keep it in the Favorites collection for easy access. Just select the text on the page that is formatted as you like it, or choose your favorite combination in the Fonts panel. Then go to the Action button and choose "Add to Favorites."

When you want to use that typeface, single-click the collection called Favorites to display the combination. Select your text, then choose your favorite.

Action button options

Color: See page 250.
Characters: This displays the Character Palette; see pages 248–249.
Typography: Choose sophisticated options for certain typefaces.
Edit Sizes: Customize how font sizes are displayed in the Fonts panel.
Manage Fonts: This opens the Font Book; see pages 226–227.

Character Palette

Many fonts have a lot of characters you don't know about but might like to use if you did. And different fonts have different sorts of **extra characters.**

For instance, these are the ampersands available in the font Zapfino:

How do you know which characters are available? Use the **Characters palette.**

At the bottom of most Edit menus is an option called "Special Characters...." This displays the Characters palette, as shown on the opposite page.

Add special characters to your document:

1   Open TextEdit (it's in the Applications folder). A new, blank document appears on your screen. You'll see the insertion point flashing—that's where new characters will appear. Type what you need until you get to a point where you want to enter a special character.

2   From the Edit menu, choose "Special Characters...."

3   From the "View" menu on the palette (circled on the opposite page), choose "Glyph."

4   Make sure the "Glyph Catalog" tab is selected.

5   From the two "Font" menus, choose the typeface family and the individual style that you want to look at. In the example on the opposite page, you see the font "Skia." (Later, experiment with Zapfino!)

6   Scroll through the character pane to find the glyph you want. ("Glyph" refers to any individual variation of any character. For instance, above you see seven different *glyphs* for the ampersand *character.*)

7   Double-click the glyph you want to see on your page.

TIP ———— To reduce the Character Palette to a tiny box that is out of the way, but accessible, click its green Zoom button.

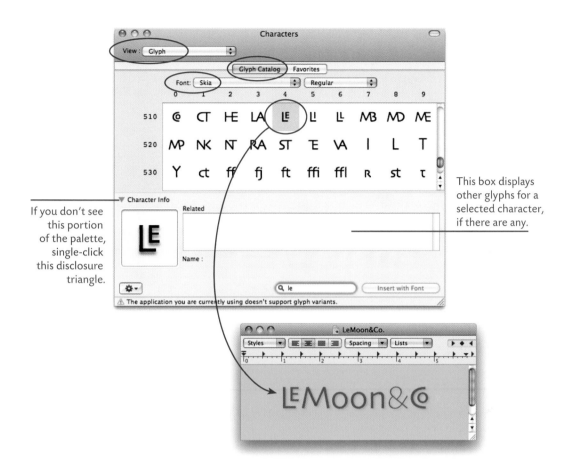

If you don't see this portion of the palette, single-click this disclosure triangle.

This box displays other glyphs for a selected character, if there are any.

Hoefler Text Regular   Hoefler Text Italic   Hoefler Text Ornaments

Colors Panel

When you click one of the color buttons (as shown directly below) in the Fonts panel or the "Colors" icon in a toolbar, you get a deceptively simple Colors panel. Select text in Mail, TextEdit, and other Apple applications, then choose a color.

Text color. | | Paper color behind the text.

- Click one of the icons across the top of the panel to choose a color mode.

- Click the magnifying glass and your pointer turns into a magnifying glass. Drag it around the screen and when you find a color you want to "pick up," click it and that color is added to the panel.

- In the "Color Wheel" mode, drag the dot around the circle to choose a color, and drag the slider up and down to change the color shade.

- In the "Image Palettes" mode, shown below-right, click the "Palette" menu, choose "New from File...," then choose a graphic or photo. You can also drag any image from the Finder and drop it on this palette. Move the cursor around the photo to pick up colors you need.

To save a color, drag it from here and drop it in one of the squares at the bottom.

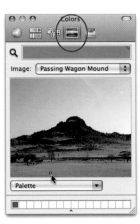

Experiment with the different ways you can select colors.

Speech

In many applications where there is typically a lot of text, **your Mac can read selected text to you.** Most Mac applications have this ability, and some third party applications do too, such as Adobe InDesign. Depending on the application, you will find the "Speech" menu and the "Start Reading" command either in the Edit menu, or in the "Services" menu, which is found in the Application menu (next to the black apple icon in the menu bar). Another way to access speech options is to Control-click (or right-click) selected text, then from the "Speech" option, choose "Start Reading."

Try this cool feature in iChat, Safari, Mail, TextEdit, Address Book, or even iCal. Besides just reading text aloud, you'll see other options in the Services menu that can be very useful, such as "Add to iTunes as a Spoken Track." This adds the selected text to the iTunes "Music" collection as an audio file named "Text to Speech." Double-click the name and rename it whatever you like.

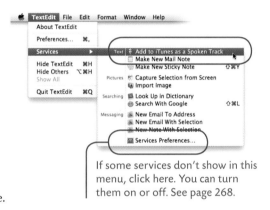

If some services don't show in this menu, click here. You can turn them on or off. See page 268.

Some applications, such as Mail, don't require that you select text before having it read aloud. Other applications don't show any available services in the "Services" menu unless something in the document is selected.

Have your email read out loud

1 Open an email message in Mail.

2 Click in the main body of text.

3 Go to the Edit menu, slide down to "Speech…," and choose "Start Speaking."

4 The entire text message will be read aloud to you.

 If you want just a portion read out loud, select that portion before you go to the Edit menu.

5 The voice that's used is the one selected in the "Speech" preferences.

To use the Services menu, first *select the text* in an application, or on a web page in Safari, then go to the application menu and choose the Services option.

Preview your Page before Printing

You can **preview** any page that you create or plan to print. Just open the document and choose to print (press Command P, or choose "Print" from the File menu).

If a small print dialog appears, as shown below, click the "Preview" button. Your Mac will create a preview of the document, open the application called Preview (see Lesson 11), and display the document. You can then print directly from the Preview application.

If you see an expanded print dialog (click the disclosure triangle circled below to show it) that shows more options, the Preview button won't be visible because the expanded dialog displays a preview right there.

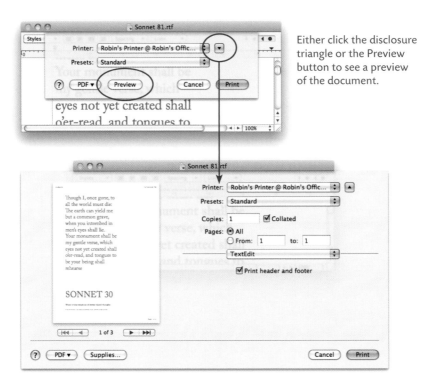

Either click the disclosure triangle or the Preview button to see a preview of the document.

Make a PDF of a Page or Document

Notice in the Print dialog above, there is a button labeled "PDF." Click that button to see many options for creating a PDF of the open document. See page 223.

Dictionary Panel

Dictionary

I keep the Dictionary application in my Dock because I use it so often. It's not only a **dictionary,** but also a **thesaurus,** an **Apple** resource, and it links directly to **Wikipedia** (if you're connected to the Internet). The Dictionary is in your Applications folder, and if you want it in your Dock so it's always accessible with the click of a button, just drag its icon from the Applications folder and drop it in the Dock.

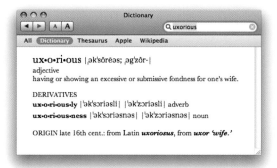

But this Dictionary has a special little feature that extends its use out to all other Apple applications. Go to its Preferences (from the Dictionary menu when it's open) and check the button to "Opens Dictionary panel" (circled, below-left)

Now in every other Apple application (and those that follow Apple standards), Control-click (or right-click) a word you want to look up in the Dictionary.

When you Control-click a word, you'll see this menu.

The Dictionary panel appears right on the document page. You can use the tiny menu (circled, left) to switch to the Thesaurus.

Click "More..." to open the Dictionary.

14

GOALS

Switch between open
applications with
a keyboard shortcut

Quit or hide applications
with keyboard shortcuts

Discover Spaces
to organize lots
of open windows

Drag-and-drop text or files
between applications

Take advantage
of the page proxy

Use Services to work
quickly and efficiently

Working between Mac OS X Applications

Now that you've had an overview of the main applications that come with Mac OS X and how they are all integrated, let's carry it one step further and work *between* all the applications—pop between windows, drag-and-drop content and files, take advantage of the Spaces feature, use the Services, and more.

Once you realize how easy it is to move data between applications and windows, you'll find more and more uses for it. Plus you'll feel like a Power User.

Snow Leopard's Services feature not only makes it possible to perform certain tasks and commands from within one application that would ordinarily require opening another application, it takes the concept to a new level. Services enables actions such as opening a web page from within a TextEdit document, or using selected text in Safari to create a new Note in Mail.

Work with Multiple Applications at Once

In Mac OS X, you can keep lots of applications and windows open at once so they're always accessible. You can just single-click an application icon in the Dock to switch to it, but there are also a couple of great shortcuts to switch between multiple applications quickly and easily.

Switch between all applications

No matter which application you are currently using, you can bring up a floating palette like the one shown below, then select the application you want to switch to—without ever having to reach for the mouse.

To get the Application Switcher that displays icons for all the *open* applications, press and *hold down* the Command key, then hit the Tab key once. Keep the Command key down. You'll see something like this:

> **To cycle through the icons** from left to right, tap the Tab key (or the Left/ Right Arrow keys) while you keep the Command key held down.
>
> **To cycle through the icons in the other direction,** right to left, keep the Command key down, but also hold down the Shift key while you tap the Tab key.
>
> **Or** press Command Tab to display the Application Switcher, then use the mouse to select an icon (just hover over it to highlight it).

However you choose to select an icon, when the application icon you want is high-lighted in the palette, **let go of the keys** and that application will come forward as the active program.

If there is no window open in that particular application, it might look like nothing happened—always check the application menu (see page 4) to see which one is currently active! You might need to hit Command N to open a window in that application once it's active.

Switch back and forth between two applications

Most of us probably spend the greater part of our time between our two favorite applications. There's a shortcut that will switch you back and forth between just those two, instead of having to bring up the Application Switcher.

While in one of your favorite applications, switch to another one using the method on the previous page, or just click its icon in the Dock. Now press Command Tab **to switch between those two applications.** I know it sounds too similar to the shortcut for switching between all applications, but the trick is to hold down the Command key, hit the Tab key *just once,* then let go of both keys right away.

Quit or hide applications

Use the keyboard shortcut Command H to **hide** all of the windows of the active application, and Command Q to **quit** the active application. Use these shortcuts in combination with the switching shortcut (above) to quit or hide selected (active) applications.

To hide all other applications except the one you're currently using, press Command Option H.

To switch to another application and hide the windows of the current one, hold down the Option key when you click the other application icon in the Dock.

Keyboard Shortcuts

Command Tab Tab Tab . . .	Select the open applications
Command Tab	Switch between two open applications
Command H	Hide the currently active application
Command Option H	Hide all the other applications *except* the active one
Command Q	Quit the active application

Spaces

Spaces

And here's yet another way to hide and show different applications if the Command Tab shortcut (page 256) and Exposé (explained on pages 42–45) aren't enough! Spaces gives you up to 16 separate Desktops. You can keep all the windows for one project open in one Space, perhaps your Mail application open in another, and iChat and Safari windows in another. You can work on different projects without having to move windows around and out of the way—just switch to different project space and unrelated items disappear. Yet everything is still accessible.

Exposé &
Spaces

You must first **set up Spaces.** If the Spaces icon is in the Dock, just click it. A message pops up to say "Spaces is not set up." Click the "Set Up Spaces" button to open the "Exposé & Spaces" system preferences, shown below. In the "Spaces" pane, checkmark "Enable Spaces." Also checkmark "Show Spaces in menu bar" so you can keep track of which space you're in at the moment.

If the Spaces icon is not in the Dock, go to the Utilities folder (it's in the Applications folder) and double-click the Spaces icon to set up Spaces. If you want to put the Spaces icon in the Dock, drag it from the Utilities folder to the Dock. When you click the Spaces icon in the Dock, your entire screen shows all the Spaces you've created. Click a Space to select it. You can also select a Space (by number) from the Spaces menu in the menu bar, but you won't see a preview of all Spaces. To save room in the Dock *and* see a preview of all Spaces (see the next page), press F8.

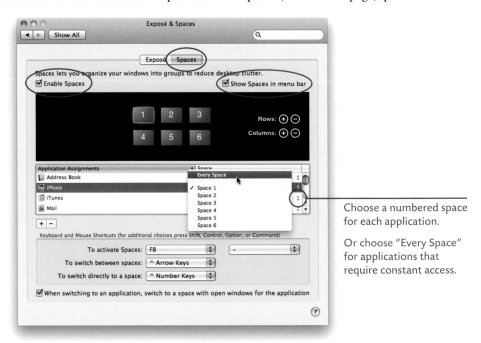

Choose a numbered space for each application.

Or choose "Every Space" for applications that require constant access.

To create or delete spaces, just click the **+** or **–** buttons for "Rows" or "Columns." Even though you can have up to 24 spaces, you might want to start with just four or six until you get used to working this way.

To assign applications to specific spaces, click the **+** button under the "Application Assignments" pane. In the pop-up menu, choose "Other," then choose the Applications folder. **To select more than one application,** hold down the Command key and click the ones you want to assign. Finally, click "Add."

To choose the specific space in which you want an application to appear, use the menus on the right side of that pane, as shown on the previous page.

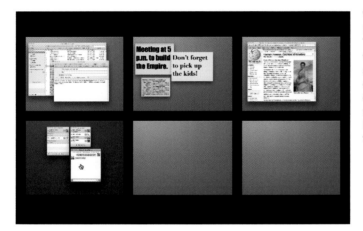

While in Spaces, tap F8 to activate Exposé. The documents and windows in each space that are stacked on top of each other will resize and rearrange so you can identify and select the one you want.

Once you have Spaces set up, it might be a little confusing at first, but you'll find that you get used to it and wonder how you did without it. There are several **shortcuts** for getting back and forth between spaces:

- **To display all your spaces,** as shown above, press F8 (you might need to press fn F8). Single-click the space you want to bring forward.

- **To cycle through the actual spaces** (instead of a picture of them all, as above), hold down the Control key and hit the left and right arrow keys.

- **To go directly to a specific space,** press Control *Number,* where *"Number"* is the number of the space you want to go to, such as Control 2.

- If you checked the box to "Show Spaces in menu bar," you'll see a Spaces icon and number in the right-hand side of the **menu bar.** Click this number and you'll get a menu of all the spaces you have set up. Select the one you want.

—continued

You can drag and drop items from one space to another. Even if you can't see the application to which you want to drag something, drag it to the Dock and drop it on that application's icon. That space will appear.

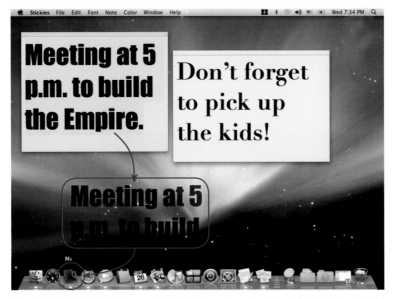

Here I selected the Stickies note text and am dropping it on the Mail icon in the Dock. It will immediately switch to that space, create a new email message, and put that text in the message.

You can drag items from one space to another while viewing all the spaces at once, as shown on the previous page.

And take advantage of the Services options in every application menu to work between applications, even while they're in different spaces. See page 268 for information about Services.

TIP —— The Fkeys provide useful shortcuts, such as tapping F8 to show Spaces. If the Fkey shortcuts don't seem to be working, it's probably because of a setting in System Preferences. Go to System Preferences and choose "Keyboard." Put a checkmark next to **"Use all F1, F2, etc. keys as standard function keys."** You can still access the **special feature** functions marked on the Fkeys (Volume Up, Volume Down, Brightness, etc.) by holding down the **fn key** (the Function key) and tapping an Fkey. When you uncheck this item, the opposite is true: tapping an Fkey **enables** the **special feature** marked on the key; to access the **standard** key functions (Show Spaces, Show Desktop, Exposé, etc.), hold down the fn key while tapping an Fkey.

Simplify your Work with Drag-and-Drop

You probably have lots of applications open on your Mac. Often you'll need to move data from one open application to another. Your Mac makes this so easy with **drag-and-drop:** Drag the information you want from one application and drop it into the other application. Below are some examples. Experiment with these, and then try dragging and dropping in all sorts of other ways! If it doesn't work, nothing bad will happen—it just won't work.

Move text around in a document window

In TextEdit or Mail messages, you don't have to cut-and-paste to move text, you can simply drag-and-drop it.

1   First select the text you want to move: With your mouse, press-and-drag over the text so it is highlighted. Let go of the mouse button.

2   Once the text is highlighted, press anywhere in the selected text and hold it for a second or two, then drag.

3   Watch for the insertion point! It's that thin, flashing, vertical bar. As you move the mouse and pointer, the insertion point moves too. When the insertion point is positioned where you want the new text to appear, let go of the mouse button. *Text will aways drop in or paste in at the flashing insertion point!*

Don't forget to use that great option in the Edit menu to "Paste and Match Style," as explained on page 65.

To move a *copy* of the selected text to somewhere else in the same document (and leave the original text in its place), press the Option key and hold it down while you drag the text.

If you drag text from one document window to another, you don't need to hold down the Option key because it will automatically make a copy.

TIP —— Often you'll find it works best to select the text or items, then ***press and hold and count to three*** before you drag.

Move text from one application to another

Not only can you drag-and-drop within one application, you can drag text from one application window and drop it in another. Let's say you wrote a nice essay in TextEdit—select it and drag it into an email message in Mail.

This automatically makes a *copy* of the text (instead of deleting it from the first application), so you don't need to hold down the Option key.

Make a text clipping on the Desktop

Have you ever wanted to save a quote from a web page or a statement from an email message? Just select the text, then drag-and-drop it onto the Desktop or into any folder or window. This makes a small file with an extension called "*filename*.textClipping" (if extensions are set to be visible; see pages 48 and 438).

The clipping names itself with the first few words of the text.

The lights burn blue.textClipping

Anytime you want to see what the text clipping says, just double-click on it. And you can drag-and-drop that clipping file into most text windows, such as TextEdit or a Mail message, and the actual text will drop onto the page.

Add email addresses to a Mail message

Drag a person's name from the Address Book or the Address Panel and drop it into any of the "To" fields in an email message to automatically address a message. You can drag addresses from one field to another.

To add more than one name at a time, select more than one name in the Address Book or Panel: Hold down the Command key and click the names you want to add. Then let go of the Command key and drag *one* of the names to the email "To" field— *all* of the selected names will come along.

To add a Group name, drag the Group name and drop it into one of the "To" fields.

Send contact information through email

You can send a person's Address Book data (his card information) to anyone who uses Mac OS X. Drag a person's name from the Address Book or Address Panel and drop it into the body of a Mail message. You'll see a "vCard" icon, as shown below.

Denise Kusel.vcf

The recipient can then drag the vCard to her Address Book where it will be added automatically. *Or* she can double-click the icon in the email message and all of the Address Book data will be added to her Address Book.

Make a web location file

In Safari, you can make a web location file that will take you to a specific web page. There is a tiny icon that appears in the location field (called a "fav icon"), directly to the left of the web address, shown circled, below. Drag that tiny icon and drop it in the Dock (on the right side of the dividing bar), onto the Desktop, or into any folder. This creates a web location file, shown below. It has two different appearances, depending on where you drop it.

If you drop the icon in the Dock (shown below-left), it looks like a spring. You can single-click it to open Safari and that web page.

If you drop the icon in the Finder, it looks like a document file (below-right). Double-click the icon, or drag-and-drop it into the middle of any open web page (don't drop it in the location field—drop it in the middle of the open page). *Or* drop it on top of the Safari icon in the Dock.

A web location file as it appears in the Dock.

A web location file as it appears on the Desktop, in a window, or folder.

Send a file to a Buddy

Drag a document to a Buddy name in the Buddy List of iChat and drop it. Hit Return or Enter and the file will go straight to that person. This is a great way to quickly send a photo or a document.

You can also use your iChat instant message window—just drag the file into the text field where you type your message. Hit Return and both your text message and the file will go to your Buddy. All he needs to do is click the link in the iChat window and the file downloads to his Desktop.

Also send Address Book data this way—to send the information from a person's card, drag his name from your Address Book and drop it on the Buddy List name or in the message field (see the previous page for more Address Book information).

Invite people to an iCal event

Drag a person's name from the Address panel or Address Book (from the Window menu) to an iCal event to automatically add that person as an "attendee." Be sure to drop it in the "attendees" field in the Info pane. You can drag a Group name as well. Once you have the names in here, you can click the "Send" button at the bottom of the Info drawer to send everyone on the list an email update of the event.

Drag addresses or files and drop them into these iCal fields.

Save into a particular folder

When you are saving a file, drag a folder from the Finder and drop it in the window of the Save As dialog box. Your Mac will save the document into that particular folder.

Take advantage of the page proxy

You may not have noticed the tiny page icon that is in the title bar of every document you create (it appears after you save the document). It's called the "page proxy." You can do a lot with this tiny icon.

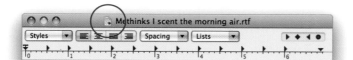

Make sure the document has been saved recently before you experiment with any of the following techniques. If there is a dark dot in the red button or if the page proxy is gray, that means you need to save the document first.

To create an alias of the document on the Desktop or in any folder or window, drag the page proxy and drop it on the Desktop, on top of any folder icon, or directly into any window. You'll see the telltale sign of an alias's tiny curved arrow as you drag the page proxy. (See page 435 about aliases.)

This tiny arrow indicates this icon is an alias. When you double-click it, it will go open the real file.

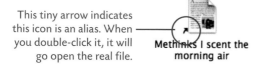

Methinks I scent the morning air

To create a copy of the document, hold down the Option key and drag the proxy. Drop it on the Desktop, on top of any folder icon, or directly into any window. You'll see a plus sign as you drag, indicating your Mac is making a *copy* of the document.

To send the document through iChat or Bonjour, drag the page proxy and drop it on a Buddy name in your iChat Buddy List or on any name in your Bonjour list.

Or drag the page proxy into the text field of an iChat instant message. The recipient will get a message with a button to "Save File."

To email the document, drag the page proxy to an email message and drop it anywhere in the body of the message.

To drop the entire document into another application, drag the page proxy and drop it into the window of the other app. For instance, you can drag a Microsoft Word page proxy into a TextEdit page or onto a web page. Remember to watch for the insertion point (well, not on a web page)—that's where the new text will drop in.

Open documents in other applications

Drag documents (or page proxies, as explained above) onto application icons in the Finder or Dock to open those documents in the targeted applications; if an application is capable of opening the document, the application icon will highlight. This is great for when you want to open a document in something other than the document's default application.

For instance, **open Microsoft Word files in TextEdit—**just drag and drop the file onto the TextEdit icon, either in the Dock or in the Applications folder.

Or **drag a PDF** and drop it in the middle of a Safari window or directly on the Safari icon and Safari will open and display the PDF.

Take advantage of spring-loaded folders

Combine drag-and-drop with spring-loaded folders to organize the Finder. A spring-loaded folder opens as you hover your mouse over it. You can use this technique to dig down into folders with a file you are dragging: Hover over a folder, its window pops open, hover over the next folder, its window pops open, etc. As soon as you drop the file, all of the previous folder windows close.

You can set the parameters for how long you have to hover the mouse to open a spring-loaded folder—use the Finder preferences (in the Finder menu). Or you can always use the Spacebar instead, even if the option for spring-loaded folders is unchecked: Whenever you want a folder to open instantly, hover over the folder as you drag a file and hit the Spacebar.

Drag content, images, or files between applications

Try dragging anything and everything!

Drag an image from the web onto a TextEdit page or an email message.

Drag a graphic file from the Desktop or a folder and drop it into the text area of your application. This works in lots of other applications, not just the ones from Apple. For instance, I'm using Adobe InDesign to create this book—I dragged the image you see below from the Finder and dropped it on this page (and it's linked):

Mac
Booda
Dakota
Jane
Reilly
Maximus

Drag text content and/or images from any application and drop them into other applications. Not everything will work, or it might work but not quite as you expect, but you will discover some wonderfully useful ways for working in your favorite applications.

You don't even have to open the other application first if you want to drag text from one place into a *new* file in another application. For instance, you can select and drag text from a web page and drop it on the Mail icon in the Dock—Mail will open a new message window with that text pasted in the message area. Or drag text and drop it on the TextEdit icon (which I keep in the Dock)—TextEdit will open a new window with that text in it. Or drag text from Mail and drop it on the Safari icon— Google will immediately do a search on the text and display the results. Amazing.

Take Advantage of Services

Every application, in its application menu, has an item called "Services." Exactly which services are available at any moment depends on which application you have open and what you have selected within that application, if anything.

Services also show up in contextual menus. Control-click in a window, or on a selected item in a window (text or image) to see a pop-up menu of items. The items at the bottom of the contextual menu are Services, such as "Add to iTunes as a Spoken Track," "Make New Mail Note," "New Email With Selection," etc.

Services enable you to use features of one application while you work in another application. For instance, you can be browsing in Safari and make a new note in Mail from selected text on a web page: Select text on a web page, right-click the selection, then from the contextual menu, choose "Make New Mail Note."

Because Services are *contextual,* only services that are relevant to the application you're using or the content you're viewing will show up in a Services menu (in both the application menu, and the contextual menu that pops up when you Control-click on a selection).

You can configure the Services menus to show, or hide, the services available. Open System Preferences and choose "Keyboard." Click the "Keyboard Shortcuts" tab, then select the "Services" item in the left pane. In the pane on the right that lists services that are available, put a checkmark next to the ones you want to be visible in menus, and uncheck the ones you want to hide.

If you the menu above is open, you can just click the "Services Preferences..." item at the bottom of the menu (shown circled).

Make it **Your Own Mac**

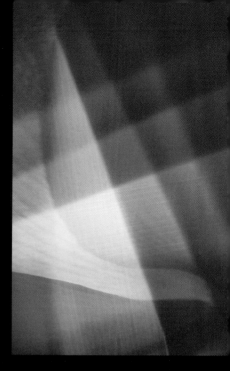

15

GOALS

Customize your Dock

Set up your Finder
windows to the way
you like to work

Use spring-loaded folders

Color-code your files
with labels

Customize your
Sidebar and Desktop

Learn to use the
System Preferences to
customize many features
of your Mac

Personalize your Mac to Meet your Needs

Now that you've learned all the basics of the various applications and system settings on your Mac, discover how to customize them to suit your particular way of working. Would you prefer to have your Dock on the side of the screen instead of at the bottom? Do you like a brightly colored Desktop? Do you want to customize the insides of certain windows? Color-code your files? Make the icons and text bigger? It's all do-able—and more.

Customize the Dock

When you first turn on your Mac, the **Dock** is sitting along the bottom at a certain size. But like everything else on the Mac, you can customize it to suit yourself. Would you prefer the Dock along the side of your screen? Would you like it to disappear altogether and only appear when you need it? Are the icons too small or too big? You can adjust everything.

There are three ways to customize the Dock: You can use the System Preferences, the Dock options in the Apple menu, or the secret pop-up menu in the Dock itself.

Customize the Dock using the System Preferences

1   Single-click the System Preferences icon in the Dock (left), or go to the Apple menu and choose "System Preferences...."

2   Single-click the Dock icon (below-left). You'll get the Dock preferences.

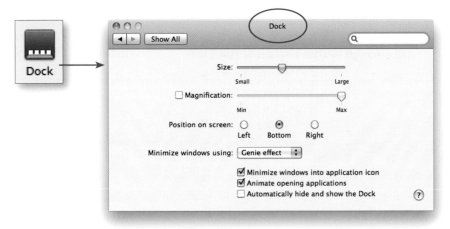

3   Here you can resize the Dock, turn "Magnification" on or off (see the example on the next page), adjust the size of the magnification, reposition the Dock, and other options.

Magnification

If you turn on "Magnification," the icons in the Dock will enlarge as you hover your mouse over them, as shown at the top of the next page. Just how big they enlarge is up to you—move the slider (above) to "Max," then hover your mouse over the Dock (don't click) and see how big the icons get.

Minimize using

Choose between Genie Effect and Scale Effect to visually change how windows float down into the Dock when you click the yellow Minimize button in a window. Hold the Shift key down when you click the yellow button to see the effect in slow motion.

Minimize windows into application icon

This option sends minimized windows behind their application icon in the Dock, instead of taking up space in the Dock. To show minimized windows, press on the application's Dock icon. See pages 44–45 for more information about this feature, called Dock Exposé.

Animate opening applications

This is what makes the icons in the Dock bounce up and down when you click to open them. You can turn it off.

Automatically hide and show the Dock

Click this and the Dock disappears. It reappears whenever you move your mouse into that edge where it disappeared. As long as your mouse is hovering over the Dock, it stays visible. Move your mouse away, and the Dock hides itself again.

Resize the icons and the whole Dock

- Press-and-drag the white striped dividing line in the Dock (shown below).

Customize the Dock with the Apple menu or Dock menu

- **From the Apple menu,** select "Dock," then choose your options.

- **In the Dock itself,** Control-click the dividing line (circled, below-right). From the menu that pops up, choose how you want the Dock to appear (and behave).

Customize the Finder

There are a number of features you can customize in the **Finder.** You might expect to find these in the System Preferences, but because the Finder is actually an application (it runs the Desktop), its preferences are in the Finder application menu.

Customize the General preferences

1   From the Finder menu, choose "Preferences…." Click the "General" icon.

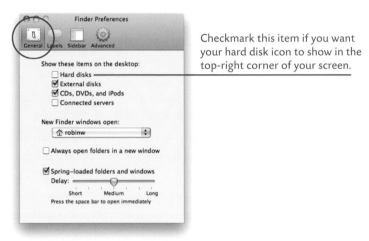

Checkmark this item if you want your hard disk icon to show in the top-right corner of your screen.

2   Because your Finder window can display the hard disk icons, removable disc icons, and servers in the top portion of the Sidebar, you can choose that these items do *not* also **show up on the Desktop.** Or if it makes you feel better to see the CD icons on the Desktop, you can choose to show only those. Whatever makes you happy.

3   Every time you open a **new Finder window,** it starts over—that is, it doesn't remember the last window you opened. From this menu, choose the window you want to see whenever you click the Finder icon in the Dock or press Command N to get a new window. For instance, I want to see my Home window every time I open a new Finder window. You might prefer to see your Hard Disk, the Documents folder, or perhaps a project folder.

4 If it bothers you to have only one Finder window open to work in, you can choose to have a **new window open** every time you double-click a folder icon.

Don't forget that you can always open a separate window for any individual folder: Command–double-click it.

5 If you turn on **spring-loaded folders and windows,** then a folder will automatically pop its window open as you hover a file over that folder. That is, just *hold* the file on top of the folder but don't click (just hover); the folder will "spring" open. This is great when you are dragging a file somewhere—you don't have to put it down to open the folder. And when you let go of the file to put it in the window, the Mac immediately takes you back to where you started.

The "Delay" slider sets how long your mouse has to hover over a folder before it pops open. If you find folders popping open when you least expect it, make the delay longer.

Even if you turn off spring-loaded folders, you can always hit the Spacebar to make a folder pop open, as long as your mouse is holding a file over that folder.

Create labels for files and folders

Labels are colors that you can apply to any file or folder or application as a tool for organizing and searching.

1 From the Finder menu, choose "Preferences…." Click the "Labels" icon.

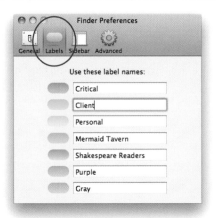

2 Change the label names for any color label you want. You don't need to use them all.

3 **To apply the labels,** select a file, then go to the File menu and at the very bottom choose a "Label" color. As you mouse over the color dot, a tool tip appears to tell you the label name.

Or Control-click (or right click) a file of any sort. From the contextual menu that pops up, choose a color label; choose the **x** to remove a label.

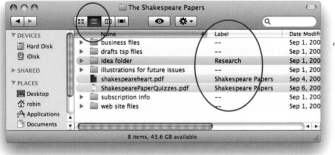

To add the "Label" column to your List View windows, see page 274.

Choose what appears in your Finder window Sidebar

1 From the Finder menu, choose "Preferences...." Click the "Sidebar" icon.

2 Check the items you want to see in the Sidebar of your Finder windows, and uncheck the items you don't want to see. Coordinate this with the "General" Finder preferences shown on page 274—you don't want to eliminate the hard disk icon, for instance, from both the Desktop *and* the Sidebar!

Choose file extensions and turn off the Trash warning

1 From the Finder menu, choose "Preferences...." Click the "Advanced" icon.

2 **File extensions** are those three- or four-letter abbreviations at the ends of file names; see pages 48 and 436. When this box is checked, you will not see the option to "Hide Extensions" in Save As dialog boxes.

3 If that **warning** you see whenever you **empty the Trash** makes you crazy, turn it off here.

4 **Empty Trash securely** overwrites the disk space of files in the Trash in a way that can't ever be read or recovered.

Choose "Search This Mac" to search your Mac and all connected external disks.

Customize the Inside of Finder Windows

Are the icons too big? The text labels too small? Do you want more columns of information available? Fewer columns? In the List View, would you like to rearrange the columns? In the Column View, do you want to turn off the preview column? You can do anything you want.

Customize the Icon View

1   Open a Finder window. Click the "Icon View" button, as circled below.

2   From the View menu, choose "Show View Options." The options panel shown below-left opens.

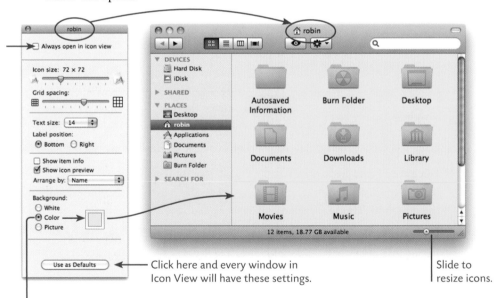

Click here and every window in Icon View will have these settings.

Slide to resize icons.

Click here, then click the color swatch to customize the background color.

3   Choose whether you want *this particular window* to **always open in icon view.**

Notice the title bar of the preferences pane (above-left) shows you the name of the currently active window, the one to which these changes will apply.

4 Experiment with these options.

- Use the sliders to change the **size of the icons** and how far apart they will be spaced (the **grid spacing**).

> **TIP** —— If you hold down the Command key as you move an icon in a window, it will snap to the nearest spot on this grid. Whenever you go to the View menu and choose "Clean up," the icons get arranged in this grid.

- Use the **Text size** menu to change the size of the text that labels each file.

- And use **Label position** to position the labels (file names) on the left or right side of the icons (they're generally on the "Bottom").

5 **Show item info:** This displays information about some icons. For instance, the window will display how many items are in each folder. It will also display the size (in pixels) of graphic files.

Show icon preview: This displays tiny thumbnail versions of the actual images for graphic files and photos, and even for documents.

Arrange by: You can choose *two* options from this list. To make every icon in the window snap into that underlying grid, choose "Snap to Grid."

Then, open this menu again and choose an arrangement for all those items. For instance, choose "Name" and any file you drag or save into this window will automatically snap to the underlying grid *and* alphabetize itself. Choose "Kind" and all items will be grouped by what kinds of files they are—applications, folders, text files, etc. "Label" is also an option, but in this case it refers to the colored labels, as explained on page 270, not the labels (file names) mentioned in Step 4!

> **TIP** —— With "Snap to Grid" chosen, you can't reposition icons—they will always jump to the nearest spot in the grid. To override this, hold down the Command key as you drag an icon.

6 **Background:** Click the "Color" button to make a tiny color swatch box appear; click the color box to get the Colors Panel and choose a background color for the window, as shown on the opposite page.

Click the "Picture" button to select a graphic image for the background.

Click "White" to remove all color and images from the window background.

Customize the List View

1   Open a Finder window. Click the "List View" button, as circled below.

2   From the View menu, choose "Show View Options." The options panel shown below-left opens.

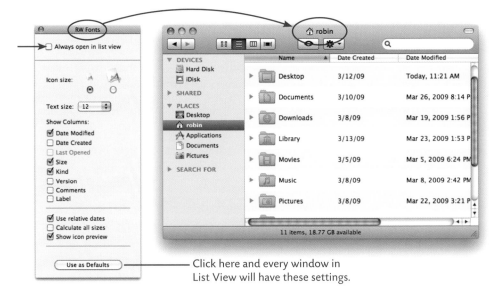

Click here and every window in List View will have these settings.

3   Choose whether you want this particular folder (my Home folder, in the example above) to always open in List View.

4   Choose the **icon size** you want, the **text size** for the labels, and which **columns** you want visible. This is where you can choose to display the "Label" column if you like to use labels (see page 276).

See the next page for the option to show "Comments."

5   **Use relative dates:** Under the "Date Modified" and "Date Created" columns, you will see "Today" or "Yesterday" instead of the actual date.

Calculate all sizes: With NO checkmark in this box, the Size column will display the file sizes of documents and graphic images, but NOT folders. Calculating the sizes of very large folders can take a lot of extra time.

Add comments and show the Comments column

This is a great feature that not many people take advantage of because they don't know it exists. In the List View options, shown on the opposite page, you see that you can choose to show the Comments column. But where are those comments?

You can add comments to the Info window of any file, shown below-left. You might add notes to someone who will be receiving this file, or notes to yourself, or details about the file, or a reminder about what to do with it. This is the same field in which you can add keywords for Spotlight to find, as mentioned on page 353.

To open the Info window and add comments, select a file and press Command I (I for Info). **Or** Control-click or right-click a file and choose "Get Info" from the contextual menu that appears. Add whatever text you want in the "Spotlight Comments" field, as shown below-left.

Once you do that, those Comments will appear in the Comments column in the List View, as shown below.

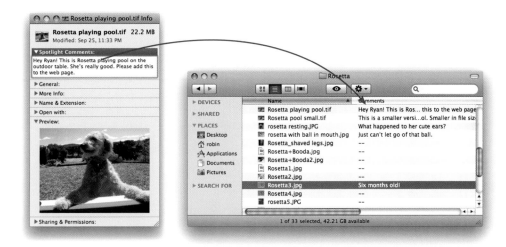

TIP —— If you want to add comments to more than one file, you don't have to select them one at a time to open their individual Info windows. Do this: Select one file, but instead of pressing Command I to open the Info window, press **Command Option I.** This opens the "Inspector" window. Now when you click on any other file, that file's info automatically appears in the already-open Info/Inspector window.

TIP —— If you like to use the contextual menus, Control-click a file, then hold down the Option key; "Show Info" changes to "Show Inspector."

Organize the columns in List View

1 **To organize the items in your list** by any column, just click a column heading to organize everything by that. For instance, if you want all the different sorts of files grouped together so you can clearly see which ones are, say, Photoshop files, organize by the "Kind" column.

   The selected column heading under which everything is organized is the blue one. In the example below, the items are organized by "Name."

2 **To alphabetize, or sort,** the items in the list backwards or forwards, click the heading triangle. That is, perhaps you want the items in the "Name" column to be listed alphabetically backwards: First click on the "Name" column heading. Then single-click the tiny triangle (the "sort" triangle, or arrow) you see on the right side of the column heading.

   If you would like your items to be sorted by "Size" in ascending or descending order, first click the "Size" column heading. Then, if necessary, single-click the tiny sort arrow to reverse the current order.

3 **To horizontally rearrange the order** of the columns (except the "Name" column), *press* any column heading (except "Name") and drag it to the right or left. You will see the other columns move over to make room. Drop the column (let go of the mouse button) when it's positioned where you want it.

4 **To resize the width of the columns,** just *press* the dividing line between any column; the pointer changes to a double-headed arrow. Drag the double-headed arrow to the left or right.

Customize the Column View

1   Open a Finder window. Click the "Column View" button, as circled below.

2   From the View menu, choose "Show View Options." The options panel shown below-left opens.

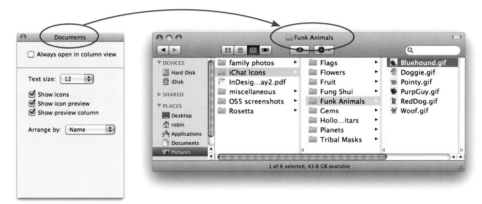

3   Choose the **text size** of the labels.

You can choose **not to show icons at all**—just a nice, clean list of items. Uncheck the box to remove the icons. (But keep in mind that the icon can tell you a lot about a file! If you can't see it, you'll miss its visual clues. This might not matter in a folder that contains nothing but photographs or nothing but text documents.)

If you uncheck **Show preview column,** the last column will NOT display a preview image of the selected file, such as a photograph.

Customize the Cover Flow View

1   Open a Finder window. Click the "Cover Flow View" button, as circled below.

2   From the View menu, choose "Show View Options."

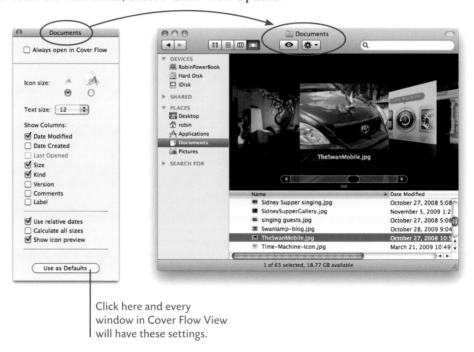

Click here and every
window in Cover Flow View
will have these settings.

3   You can't change the actual view of the covers. But you can choose the
text size of the labels.

You can choose **not to show the icon preview** in the list part of the window.
You'll still see icons, but graphic image icons will just display a document icon,
not a preview of the actual image.

Customize the Desktop View

1   Click a blank spot on the Desktop to make sure no Finder window
    (or any other window or icon) is selected.

2   From the View menu, choose "Show View Options."

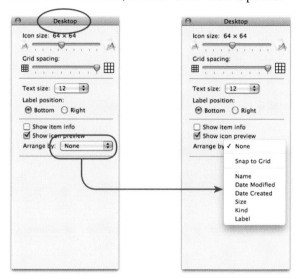

You can resize the icons or the text labels, reposition the labels, show extra file
information, display an icon preview, snap the icons to a grid, or always keep
the icons arranged by your chosen criteria, such as alphabetized ("Name"),
Kind, Label, etc.

Take Advantage of the System Preferences

The System Preferences control dozens of features on your Mac. Don't like the picture on your Desktop? Do you want your Mac to go to sleep sooner or later or never? Do you need to change the time because you moved? Would you like a whiny voice to yell at you every time you make a mistake? You can customize these and many other things through System Preferences. (Remember, every *application* has its own preferences, as explained on page 57.)

To open System Preferences, click on its icon in the Dock. **Or** go to the Apple menu and choose "System Preferences...."

This is the System Preferences icon.

If you would rather see these preferences in alphabetical order (as shown below) instead of grouped in categories, go to the View menu and choose "Organize Alphabetically."

Global versus user-specific preferences

If you have set up more than one user, as explained in Lesson 18, individual users will discover there are some preferences they can't change because they will affect other users; these preferences are "global" and only the master administrator can change them. Individual users can change the preferences that are "user-specific" because they affect only that one user. So if you run across a System Preference that you can't change, it's probably because you are not the main administrator (please see Lesson 18 for details about users and administrators).

How to use the System Preferences

Once you open the System Preferences pane, single-click an icon to display those particular preferences. Most things are self-explanatory—poke around and see what your options are. We'll look at a couple of examples.

Keyboard

1   Open System Preferences as described on the previous page. Single-click the **Keyboard** icon, shown to the left.

2   In the Keyboard preferences pane, shown below, single-click the "Keyboard" tab to see the settngs for that feature.

3   You can adjust how fast any **key repeats** across the page as you press it down.

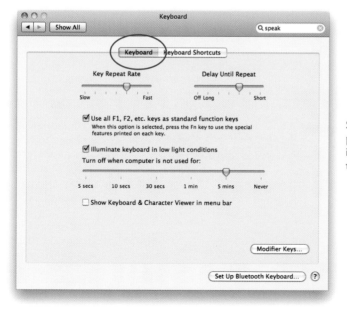

See the following page for more information about these options.

—continued

The **Delay Until Repeat** refers to how long your fingers can linger on the keys before they start repeating. If you find you type lots of double letters or spaces, choose a longer delay here. If your fingers are really heavy on the keys, slide the blue slider all the way to "Off" and the keys will never repeat automatically.

4 **Use all F1, F2, etc. keys as standard function keys** lets you set the F keys as standard function or special feature keys. Standard functions are default commands assigned to F keys. For instance, tapping F11 usually shows the Desktop. "Special features" are the command symbols printed on F keys, such as the "Exposé" symbol on the F3 key (seen on newer keyboards, but not all). If you *uncheck* "Use all F1, F2, etc. as standard function keys…," you can simply tap an F key to activate the special feature control printed on the key, such as the volume or brightness controls. *Checkmark* this item and the F key becomes a standard function key that activates whatever command is assigned to it by default (F11 shows the Desktop). The bottom line is, use the Fn key if an F key isn't acting like you think it's supposed to.

Now click the **Keyboard Shortcuts** tab to see (or customize) the default shortcuts for many of the commands in Snow Leopard.

1 Select a category in the left pane. Checkmark shortcuts in the right pane to turn them on; uncheck to turn them off.

2 To change a shortcut, double-click it, then hold down the keys you want to use.

3 To delete a shortcut: select it, then click the Minus (–) button.

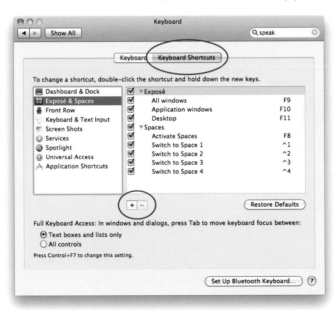

This pane shows you the default keyboard shortcuts for the categories listed on the left.

To add shortcuts of your own, choose a category on the left, then click the Plus button (circled on the left).

Mouse

In the System Preferences main window, single-click the **Mouse** icon to the mouse settings you can change (shown below). Most of these controls are self-explanatory. **Tracking Speed** determines how far the pointer moves across the screen when you move your mouse. **Scrolling Speed** sets the speed for the scroll wheel on your mouse. **Primary mouse button** lets you set which mouse button to use as the primary button for clicking. When you checkmark the **Zoom** option, and set a modifier key from the pop-up menu, you can use the scroll wheel on your mouse to zoom in (to magnify your screen view) and zoom out (to return to normal view).

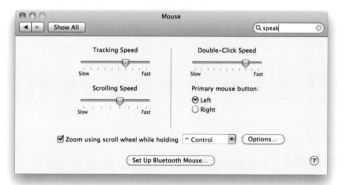

The faster the tracking speed, the less distance you have to move the mouse to cover a specific distance. Set a fast tracking speed to easily move the mouse around the screen with minimal effort.

Desktop & Screen Saver

This is another fun and useful System Preference—use it to **change the color or image on your Desktop.**

1   Open System Preferences and single-click the "Desktop & Screen Saver" icon, then single-click the "Desktop" tab, circled below.

2   In the list on the left, select a folder to its contents displayed on the right.

4   Single-click any image on the right to immediately view it on your Desktop.

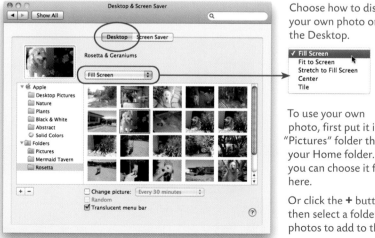

Choose how to display your own photo on the Desktop.

To use your own photo, first put it in the "Pictures" folder that's in your Home folder. Then you can choose it from here.

Or click the **+** button, then select a folder of photos to add to this list.

289

Correct the **date and time** on your Mac, change it when you go to a different time zone, show the date, day of the week, and date in the menu bar, and more.

1   Open System Preference, then single-click the "Date & Time" icon. **Or** if the System Preferences are already open, go to the View menu at the top of the screen and choose "Date & Time."

2   Click the "Date & Time" tab to set the date and time. Click the "Clock" tab to choose other options, such as "Show the day of the week" in the menu bar.

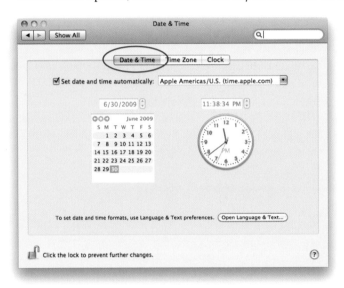

The option to "Set date & time automatically" is useful if you have a full-time broadband connection (don't bother if your connection to the Internet is a dial-up). This keeps your Mac in touch with a satellite so your time is always correct—it will even switch to daylight savings time for you.

The "Time Zone" tab opens a world map where you set a Time Zone. Your Mac can detect your general location and set this for you. The polar ice cap rendering changes with the seasons.

A selected time zone.

Find the right System Preferences for your task

Sometimes you know you need a System Preference to customize a particular Mac feature, but you're not sure which one has the option you need. That's where the Mac's Spotlight feature can help.

Just type what you're hoping to find in the System Preferences search field. As you type, you'll see certain System Preference icons highlight, and you'll see a list of possible options. The more you type, the more specific the results will be.

Try the example shown below. I was looking for all the preferences that give me an option to speak or use sound.

Choose an option in the list, and the appropriate System Preference will flash twice at you and then open.

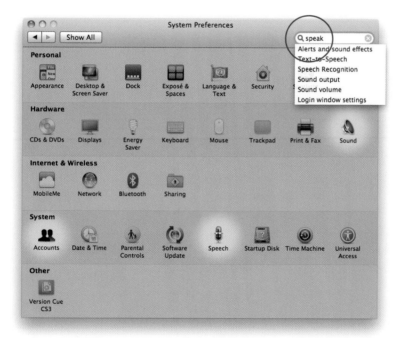

And don't forget about other features on your Mac that let you customize and personalize your machine! Check out Exposé & Spaces, plus all the individual application preferences. This is *your* Mac!

16

GOALS

Learn about the different kinds of widgets available

Show and hide the widgets

Display the widgets you want to have available

Remove a widget from your display or from the widgets bar

Flip widgets over and customize them

Display more than one of any widget

Change the keyboard shortcut that displays your widgets

Get more widgets

Dashboard—Important Information at your Fingertips

Ever want to know what time it is right now in London? Or what the weather is like where you mother lives? Do you need to track the plane your daughter is taking to Istanbul—including whether it's going to leave on time and from what terminal—and then follow the flight path across the world in real time?

These are just a few of the many things you can do with literally the click of one button, using Dashboard. The information appears to you in the form of widgets. Some widgets are already on your Mac, but many others are being created by creative developers. Oh, the things we will see!

Take a Look at Dashboard

Dashboard provides quick access to information customized just for you, displayed in the form of **widgets.** Dashboard pops up in a split second, but only when you want it. With the click of a button, it goes away just as quickly. Below is an example of my **Dashboard,** with the **Widget Bar** showing (the Widget Bar doesn't appear until you ask for it; see page 296).

When you activate Dashboard, the widgets instantly appear on top of a gray overlay on the Desktop, on top of any windows or applications you have open. Do what you need, then click in any blank area to send them all away. Use the Widget Bar to add and delete items, as explained on page 296.

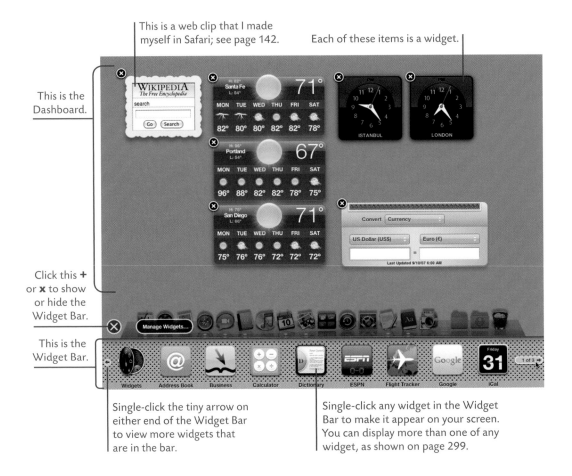

This is a web clip that I made myself in Safari; see page 142.

Each of these items is a widget.

This is the Dashboard.

Click this **+** or **x** to show or hide the Widget Bar.

This is the Widget Bar.

Single-click the tiny arrow on either end of the Widget Bar to view more widgets that are in the bar.

Single-click any widget in the Widget Bar to make it appear on your screen. You can display more than one of any widget, as shown on page 299.

Discover Different Kinds of Widgets

There are three different kinds of widgets, although they are all so interesting and easy to work with, you won't really care which is which!

- **Information widgets** work with data from the Internet. You can check external events such as the weather anywhere in the world, the flight status of any plane, or current prices of your favorite stocks. You must be connected to the Internet to get the information for these widgets.

- **Application widgets** work with applications on your Mac. They typically provide a small and easy way of displaying the critical features of the main application. For instance, the iTunes widget is a small controller that gives you buttons—start, stop, play songs, and more—to listen to your Playlists or Internet radio without having the iTunes interface take up your whole screen. If the main application requires the Internet to function, so will its widget.

- **Accessory widgets** are self-contained little utilities that provide a variety of features. Widgets such as clocks, calculators, notes, or timers are accessories. Some of these do need Internet access, but they are not dependent on any application on your Mac.

Activate Dashboard and the Widgets

Dashboard is built into your Mac—just single-click the Dashboard icon in your Dock to **make it appear,** or press the F12 key.

 If you're using a **laptop,** you might not have an F12 key, or it might be used for something else. You can change Dashboard's keyboard shortcut; see page 300.

Add Widgets to Your Dashboard

 To add widgets to your onscreen Dashboard, first open Dashboard and bring up the **Widget Bar:** Single-click the plus sign you see in the bottom-left of your screen. (The plus sign then turns into an **X** to **close** the Widgets Bar; see page 294.)

> **To add a widget,** single-click on it. The widget appears on your screen.
>
> **To see other widgets** that are already installed, single-click one of the tiny arrows that appear at either end of the Widget Bar.

Organize widgets on the screen in any arrangement you like—simply press anywhere in a widget and drag it around. They will stay where you put them, even after you put away Dashboard.

Remove Widgets from Your Dashboard

Hold down the Option key and click the **X** that appears on the upper-left of the widget.

Or remove widgets from the Dashboard when the Widget Bar is visible. First display the Widget Bar: Single-click the plus sign shown above. Now you see an **X** in the upper-left corner of each widget. **To remove a widget,** click that **X**. It stays in your Widget Bar until you want it again.

Put Dashboard Away

To put Dashboard away, single-click outside of any widget, *or* press your keyboard shortcut again (probably F12). When you reopen Dashboard, your widgets are right where you left them.

Work with Widgets

Different kinds of widgets have different kinds of features. Experiment with them all! For instance, open the Unit Converter and check all the different types of conversions you can make.

Many widgets (not all) have a tiny *i* in a corner, the **info button.** It's not in the same corner for all widgets, and it won't even appear until your pointer gets close to it. So hover over the corners of a widget to see if an *i* appears, then click it—the widget turns over so you can change preferences.

Single-click the *info* button to flip the widget.

On the back side of many widgets are preferences for that particular item. For example, this information tells the Phone Book widget where to look.

Enter information into a field, then be sure to hit the Enter key to enter that data.

Click "Done" to flip the widget back over.

Experiment with Your Widgets!

Lots of different people create widgets and I can't explain here all the different things they will do. So be sure to pay attention to the sometimes-subtle visual clues that are built into widgets.

In the iTunes widget shown below, notice the tiny dot in the outer circle. That's a clue! Drag that tiny dot around to change the volume.

Notice the info button that appears (the *i*)—click on it to flip the widget and see what options are available on the other side. In this case, you can choose which iTunes Playlist to listen to.

In the Dictionary widget below, there are several visual clues, as shown.

The double-arrows are a clue that there is a menu hidden here. Click on it to see the options.

Back and forward arrows indicate you can return to panes you previously viewed.

Now "Thesaurus" is the visible menu option, indicating you are looking at the thesaurus entry.

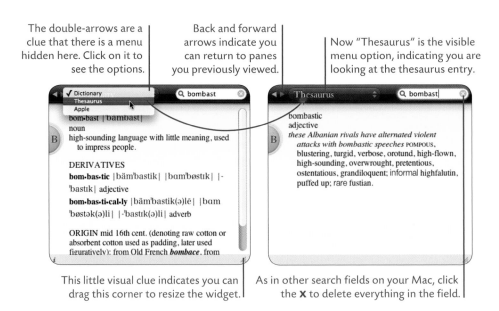

This little visual clue indicates you can drag this corner to resize the widget.

As in other search fields on your Mac, click the **X** to delete everything in the field.

Display More than One of a Widget

You can display multiple copies of any kind of widget. For instance, you might like to know the weather in several different places, view the flight paths of a number of different flights, open several different dictionary widgets to compare words, or view a number of different conversions at the same time.

To display more than one of any kind of widget, open the Widget Bar (when Dashboard is showing, click the **+** sign in the bottom-left corner of your screen). Then just single-click the widget as many times as you want, one for each instance on your screen. Each new widget shows up in the center of the screen. Just drag it to any position and it will stay there.

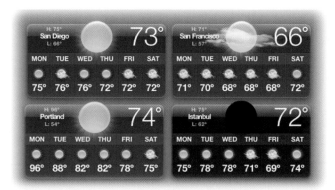

Here I can see at a glance what the weather is like (and whether it's day or night) in the different cities where my kids live.

TIP ——— To change the picture in the tile puzzle widget, do this: When Dashboard is open, put the tile puzzle on your screen. Close Dashboard.

In the Finder, find the picture you want to use in the tile puzzle. Start dragging it to nowhere in particular. While you are dragging (don't let go of the mouse), press F12 (or whatever your shortcut is, if you've changed it) to open Dashboard. Drop the picture you're dragging onto the tile puzzle.

So now my dog Rosetta is in the puzzle.

Change Dashboard's Keyboard Shortcut

If you don't like the default shortcut that opens Dashboard, you can change it.

1   At the Finder, when Dashboard is *not* active, go to the Apple menu and choose "System Preferences…."

2   Single-click "Exposé & Spaces."

3   In the preferences pane, as shown below, make sure the "Exposé" tab is selected (it will be blue; if not, click it).

Choose an Fkey from the "Hide and show" menu (circled, below) to use as your shortcut.

To add one or more of the modifier keys to your shortcut, just press that key(s) while the menu is open. The menu will change to reflect the key combination you are pressing. For instance, you might want to use Control F1 to activate Dashboard. So hold down the Control key, click the Dashboard pop-up menu, then choose this option in the menu: **^F1** (**^** indicates the Control key).

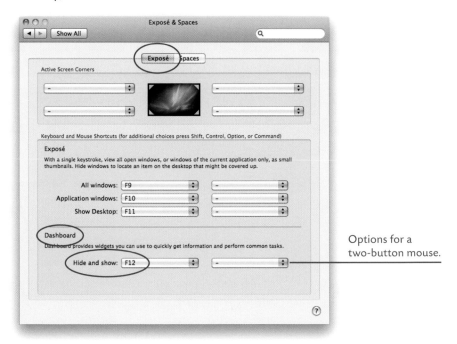

Options for a two-button mouse.

If you have a **two-button mouse** attached to your Mac, you will see a second column of menus, as shown above.

You can choose to assign the Secondary or Middle mouse button (in combination with an F key) to activate Dashboard. Or, you can disable the F key in the left pop-up menu (choose the dash symbol from the pop-up menu) and choose just the Secondary or Middle mouse button from the pop-up menu on the right. With the Secondary or Middle mouse button assigned to Dashboard, I can click once (using just one hand) and Dashboard instantly appears.

Manage your Widgets

If you become a Widget junkie and start collecting lots of them, you'll want some way to get rid of the ones you don't want anymore, or at least remove them from the Widget Bar. Widgets that come pre-installed by Apple can't be deleted, just removed from the Widget Bar. Click the **Widget Manager** button that appears when you click the Plus sign to show the Widgets Bar (below-left). In the Widget Manager panel (below-right) uncheck the Widgets you want to hide from view in the Widget Bar. Third-party Widgets have a red minus (–) symbol to their right. You hide third-party Widgets, or click the red minus symbol to delete them.

Both the button and the icon open the Widget Manager, shown to the right.

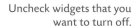

Uncheck widgets that you want to turn off.

To retrieve Widgets you've hidden, open the Widget Manager and checkmark them.

To get more widgets, click the "More Widgets..." button in the Widget Manager, shown above. This takes you to the Apple web site where you can download lots of free widgets that do cool things.

To make your own Web Clip widgets from Safari web pages, see page 142.

17

GOALS

Set Up Printing and Faxing

Printing gets easier and more reliable with every new operating system. The Mac recognizes and automatically sets up more printers, individual applications can apply more special parameters to your print jobs, and sharing one printer with many computers gets easier all the time. Now Snow Leopard automates one of the most troublesome aspects of using a printer: When you connect a new printer, Snow Leopard checks to see if the proper printer driver is installed. If not, it automatically goes online, finds the latest up-to-date version, and installs the driver software for you. Snow Leopard even periodically checks to ensure it has the latest version of the printer driver and automatically downloads new versions through your built-in Software Update application (found in System Preferences).

Set Up your Printers

If you're already printing to your printer, then skip a couple of pages and go straight to the section about accessing special features of your printer, just in case you're not familiar with what it can do.

If your Print dialog box says, "No Printer Selected," see "Add a printer," below.

Be sure to install the software

If you bought a fancy printer of some sort, meaning it cost more than a hundred dollars, be sure to install the software that it came with. What you particularly need to install is the latest "printer driver." In the past, if you didn't have the software driver for your printer, you would go to the manufacturer's web site and download the latest version of the driver software. But now your Mac does that for you. When you print a job, your Mac automatically checks for the appropriate software, and, if necessary, downloads and installs it for you.

You can often print pages without the latest driver, but the more expensive your printer is, the more important it is that you have the proper driver. If not, you will lose some of the most valuable features of the printer. For many printers, the drivers that Apple included with Snow Leopard will probably work just fine. Try printing and see what happens.

Add a printer

Your Mac automatically detects printers that are directly connected to the computer or that are on your local network. If you've installed the software for your expensive printer or if you have an inexpensive printer, the process is generally really easy.

Try to print something for the first time (press Command P, *or* go to the File menu and choose "Print"). If you see your printer listed in the menu in the Print dialog (shown on the next page), then you're all set up.

Often, however, the first time you try to print, the Print dialog box tells you there is "No Printer Selected," as shown below. Your Mac just needs to be told to go find the printer and add it to its list. So:

1 Make sure the printer is connected to your Mac, that all the cables are secure, and that the printer is turned on.

2 Press the pop-up menu that says "No Printer Selected" and choose "Add Printer...."

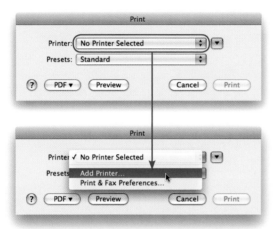

3 This brings up a window listing all of the printers your Mac can find, shown below. If everything is connected properly and the printer is on, you should see the name of the printer in the pane. Single-click its name.

4 When the name of the printer appears in the bottom portion of the pane, all is well. Click the "Add" button. The Print dialog box, shown above, reappears and you can carry on.

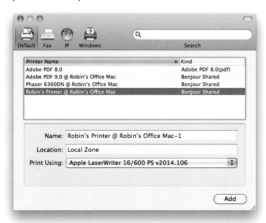

Use the Print & Fax Preferences

Print & Fax

Usually the steps on the previous pages to add a printer work just fine. But sometimes you might want to **set up printers** here in the Print & Fax system preferences, or you might need to use this pane to troubleshoot printing problems.

1   Make sure your printer is turned on and tightly connected to your Mac with the proper cables.

2   Go to the Apple menu and choose "System Preferences...."

3   Single-click the "Print & Fax" icon to get the pane shown below.

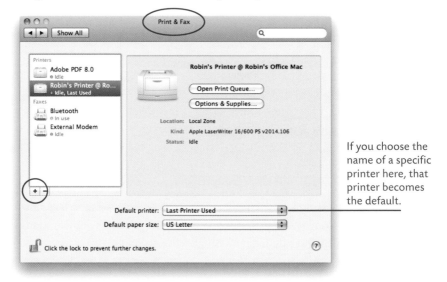

If you choose the name of a specific printer here, that printer becomes the default.

4   If you don't see the name of your printer in the list on the left, click the **+** button. (Also check again to make sure the cable between the Mac and the printer is snug on both ends, and that the printer is turned on.)

When you click the **+**, a printer browser window opens, shown on the opposite page, that lists every printer that your Mac recognizes.
If you see your printer listed, single-click its name to select it, then click the "Add" button.

If you *don't* see your printer listed, it has most likely lost its connection. If you're sure it's plugged in properly, then you might want to try a different cable—they can go bad all by themselves. Another possibility is that you didn't install the printer software that came with the printer. Install it now, then try these steps again.

Click the **+** button shown on the opposite page to open this printer browser window. Select a printer in the list, then click the "Add" button.

To add a fax device open System Preferences, then select the Print & Fax icon to open the window shown below. The list in the left pane shows faxes devices that are automatically detected (listed under "Faxes"). If you don't see your device in the list, click the Plus button (**+**), then select a device that's connected via cable or Bluetooth. Type the fax number to which you want to send a document in the "Fax Number" field.

In the example below, the selected device "External Modem" is a USB modem that's connected to my laptop computer. If your computer has an internal modem, it will appear in the list as "Internal Modem."

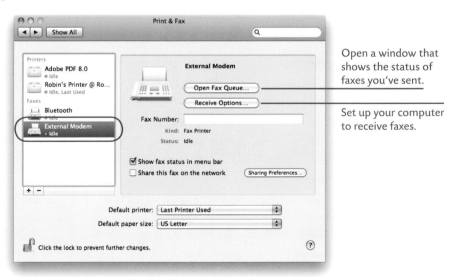

Open a window that shows the status of faxes you've sent.

Set up your computer to receive faxes.

Access the Special Features of your Printer

If you installed the software that came with your printer, then you probably have special features that allow you to choose the correct paper, the quality settings, adjust the colors, and more. The quality difference in output between a setting for inkjet paper as opposed to glossy photo paper is quite amazing.

To access the specific printer settings:

1 Start to print the job (press Command P).

2 If you see a small Print dialog box as shown on page 305, click the blue disclosure button (see below) to reveal an expanded dialog.

3 In the expanded Print dialog box, click the menu circled below.

Depending on the printer you have selected, you'll see such labels as "Print Settings" or "Image Quality." Here you will have lots of options, different options for each printer you choose, and for some printers you can select specific paper/media (of course, you should have that particular paper loaded in your printer).

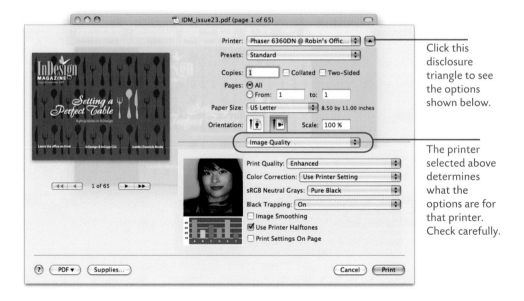

Click this disclosure triangle to see the options shown below.

The printer selected above determines what the options are for that printer. Check carefully.

Access the Special Features of your Software

Not only does your printer offer special printing features, but most software applications also have special features.

In the Print dialog box, be sure to check the pop-up menu (circled below and on the opposite page) to see if there is an option for the particular software you're using.

Below you see the print settings for Keynote, which is software from Apple for creating multimedia presentations.

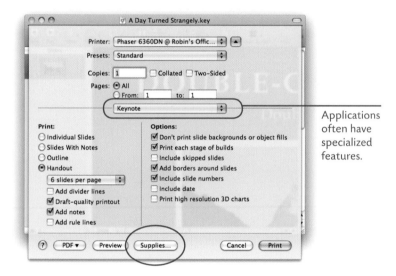

Applications often have specialized features.

Buy ink cartridges for your printer

Apple makes it very easy to buy new ink cartridges for most printers and to buy them from Apple. Just single-click the "Supplies…" button you see at the bottom of the Print dialog box (shown above). This takes you to an Apple web site where you can buy the cartridges for your specific printer.

You can do the same thing in the "Print & Fax" preferences pane shown on page 300: Single-click the button called "Options & Supplies…."

Having Trouble Printing?

Print & Fax

1 If the printer has been chosen but isn't responding when you try to print, open the "Print & Fax" pane: Go to the Apple menu, choose "System Preferences...," then single-click the "Print & Fax" icon.

2 Make sure you choose the correct printer to print to; its name should be highlighted on the left.

3 On the right side of the pane, click the button to "Open Print Queue...." This brings up the list of jobs waiting to be printed, as shown below. These are the jobs that are lined up to print to that particular printer.

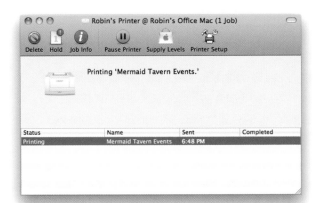

You can also get to this print queue by clicking on the printer's icon that appears in the Dock when you print. I like to keep that icon in my Dock at all times.

4 Check to make sure the jobs are not on hold or paused. The buttons should look like the ones above. When you click the "Pause Printer" button to pause a print job, the button changes to say "Resume Printer."

If a job is paused, select the job in the list and click "Resume Printer" to start the printing process. *Or* select a job and click "Delete" to get rid of it.

TIP —— If you send a job to print and nothing happens, often your initial reaction is to send it again. And again. And again. Then when you remember to look at the Print Queue, you notice there are a dozen copies of the same job lined up waiting to print because the printer's been on hold. So just remember, if you send a job to print and it doesn't come out, do not send it again! Go to the Print Queue and see what the problem is! If you have a dozen of the same jobs lined up to print, select each one and delete it.

Share your Printer with Other Macs

Any printer can be set up to share, meaning any other computer in your office or home network can print to it without having to be directly plugged in to the printer. This is great because until Mac OS X came along, you had to buy a special networkable printer. Now you can have one printer in your office and everyone can print to it.

If the printer you want to share is plugged directly into the router or switch for your network, anyone can print to it no matter which other computers are turned on. Typically, that means it's an Ethernet printer, probably a laser printer.

If the printer is plugged directly into a particular computer, that computer must be turned on for others to print to its connected printer.

To share a printer:

1   Turn on the printer that you want to share. The computer it's directly connected to must also be on, of course.

2   On the Mac that is directly connected to the printer, go to the Apple menu and choose "System Preferences…."

3   Click the "Sharing" icon.

4   In the pane on the left, check the box for "Printer Sharing." Then you should see the printer that is connected to your computer in the box on the right. Make sure there's a checkmark next to the printer you want to share.

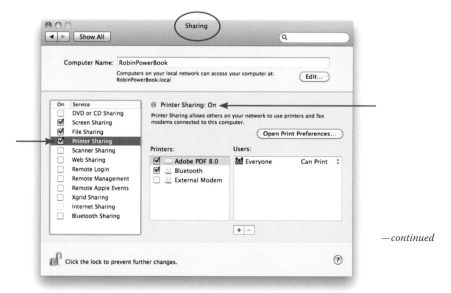

—continued

5 On the right side of the Sharing pane (shown on the previous page), click the "Open Print Preferences..." button.

6 In the "Print & Fax" preferences, shown below, select the printer in the pane on the left, and then in the pane on the right you should see a checkmark next to "Share this printer on the network." All is well.

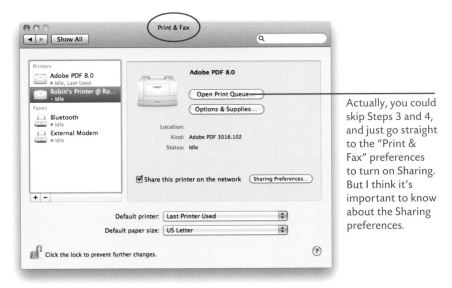

Actually, you could skip Steps 3 and 4, and just go straight to the "Print & Fax" preferences to turn on Sharing. But I think it's important to know about the Sharing preferences.

To print to a shared printer:

1 The Mac that is directly connected to the shared printer must be turned on. That computer must have chosen to share the printer, as explained on the previous page. The printer must be turned on.

2 On your other Mac, open your document. Press Command P to get the Print dialog box.

3 In the "Printer" pop-up menu, the shared printer's name should appear and you can print to it. If the printer's name is not in the menu list, see below.

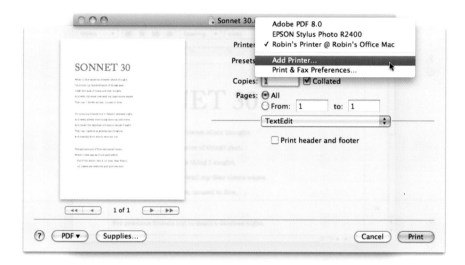

If you don't see the printer in that list, click the "Add Printer…" option in the menu and add the shared printer just as you would add any other printer, as explained on pages 304–305.

If you don't have an "Add Printer…" option in the menu, go to the "Print & Fax" preferences as explained on the previous pages and add the shared printer. You might have to quit the application you're trying to print from and open it again to see the added printer.

Once you have added it, that printer will be in your Print dialog box whenever that printer and its connected Mac are turned on.

4 After you choose the shared printer, click the "Print" button.

Fax From and To your Mac

If your Mac has a modem built in or attached to it, you can fax from any application and you can receive faxes. But many Macs today do not have modems built in!

If you use a dial-up modem with a phone cable to connect to the Internet, then you are all ready to fax, as explained below.

But if you have a broadband connection to the Internet, you must first get a phone cable (a standard RJ11 phone cable like you use for your telephone). Plug it into the phone port on your Mac (if you have one!) and into a phone jack in the wall—you cannot fax through an Internet connection, only through an old-fashioned phone line. If your Mac doesn't have an RJ11 port, get a USB-to-RJ11 adapter. Connect it to a USB port, then connect a phone line to the other end.

Or you can get a USB modem. One end of the USB modem plugs into a USB port on your computer. Plug your RJ11 phone line into the other end (an RJ11 port).

Send a fax from your Mac

1   Make sure you have a telephone cable connecting your Mac to a working phone outlet. (This assumes you have a modem built in to your Mac.)

2   Open the document you want to fax.

3   From the File menu, choose "Print...."

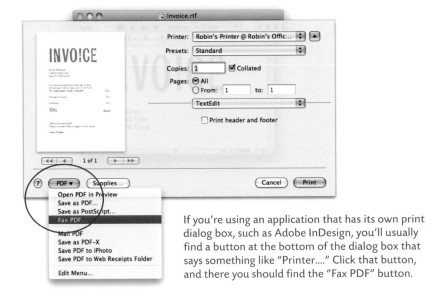

If you're using an application that has its own print dialog box, such as Adobe InDesign, you'll usually find a button at the bottom of the dialog box that says something like "Printer...." Click that button, and there you should find the "Fax PDF" button.

4 In the standard Apple dialog box, click the "PDF" button in the bottom-left corner and choose "Fax PDF...."

5 A dialog sheet appears (shown below) where you enter the person you want to send the fax to. As you type, your Address Book is searched for a match.

If necessary, the "Dialing Prefix" is where you enter any number that gets you "out" of the office building. Typically it's 9. If you need to create a pause after the 9 (for time to access an outside line) before the phone starts dialing, put one or two commas after the 9. Each comma makes the Mac wait two seconds.

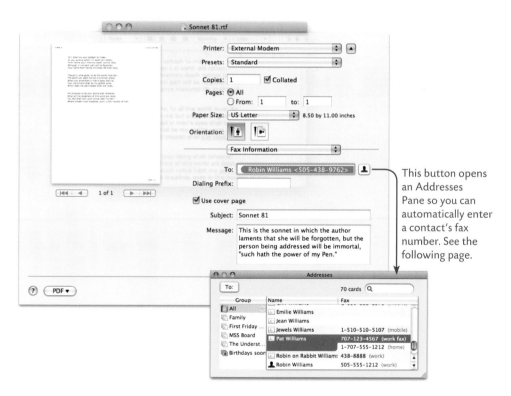

This button opens an Addresses Pane so you can automatically enter a contact's fax number. See the following page.

6 If you want a cover page, check the box to "Use Cover Page," then enter the subject and message. The preview pane on the left displays what you're sending.

7 Click "Fax" and off goes your page. You'll see the Fax icon in the Dock.

TIP ———— If you and the person you're faxing have Internet connections, consider emailing a PDF instead of sending a fax. The document will be of higher quality, it can be in full color, and, if necessary, the recipient can print the PDF in reasonably high quality.

Enter fax numbers in your Address Book

You must **enter the fax number into your Address Book** properly before the Address Pane shown on the previous page can supply it for you.

To enter a fax number into your Address Book:

1 Open your Address Book.

2 Find the person whose fax number you want to enter.

3 Single-click the "Edit" button at the bottom of the pane, shown below.

4 There are two fields at the top of the card, both pre-programmed for phone numbers. This is where you will enter the fax number. If both phone number fields are being used, click the green Plus sign to add another field.

5 Single-click the tiny arrow next to the field where you will enter (or have already entered) the fax number.

6 In the menu that pops up, choose "home fax" or "work fax."

7 Click the Edit button again to set your changes. Now when you click the little Address Pane icon when faxing, as shown on the previous page, this fax number will appear in the pane.

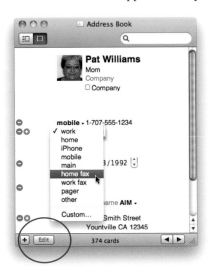

Receive a fax on your Mac

Set up your Mac to **receive faxes** using the "Print & Fax" pane in System Preferences, as shown below.

Select your modem in the left pane, then enter your fax number. Click "Receive Options…," then check the box to "Receive faxes on this computer" in the sheet that opens (shown at the bottom of the page). Choose the actions your Mac should take when you receive a fax, then click OK.

Remember, you'll need to connect a phone line to your Mac before you can send or receive a fax.

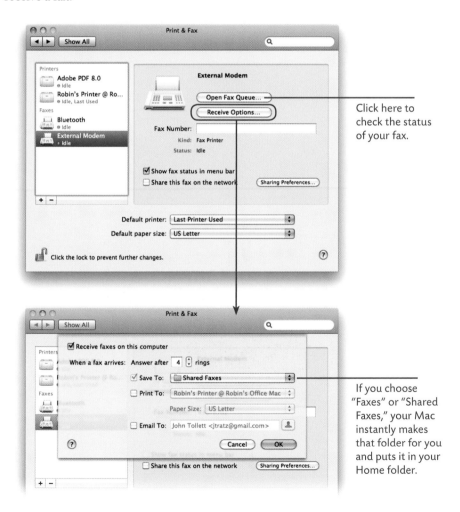

Click here to check the status of your fax.

If you choose "Faxes" or "Shared Faxes," your Mac instantly makes that folder for you and puts it in your Home folder.

18

GOALS

Understand why it's useful to have multiple users for one Mac

Learn to create new users

Learn how to log out and log in

Enable fast user switching

Allow other users to be Administrators

Teach users to adjust some of their own settings

Learn to share files with other users on one Mac

Apply parental controls from mild to stringent

Share One Mac with Multiple Users

Mac OS X is specifically built for what's called a **multiple user environment;** that is, Apple *expects* that more than one person is probably using the same computer, whether it's in a school, office, or home. You can set up another user so no one else can access your personal letters, change your sound level, poke around in your financial files, put up a dorky picture as the Desktop background, or change any of your settings.

If you are the only user who ever has or ever will use this Mac, you can skip this lesson altogether. But are you really the only user? Perhaps your grandkids come over and want to use your computer. Or maybe your husband uses your machine from time to time. Or sometimes you have relatives staying for a week who just want to use your Mac to get their email. Or you're a teacher who wants a place on your computer safe from your students. If so, set up another user.

Overview of Multiple Users

First, let me explain the **concept and advantages of having multiple users** on your Mac so you can decide if you need or want to create other users.

You already have one user, **you,** which was automatically created when you first turned on your Mac and went through the setup process. You are the main user known as the **Administrator.** The password you set up when you first turned on your new Mac or installed Leopard is your **Admin password.**

You might not have noticed that you are a "user" because Apple sets a default so when you turn on your Mac, you are automatically "logged in" without having to type in a password. Once you have other users set up, you can change this default so everyone must log in with a password. If others use your Mac only occasionally, like your grandkids, you can leave it set to automatically let you in daily; then when the kids come over, you go to the Apple menu and **log out,** which means they must then **log in** with their own settings and yours will be protected.

One user, the first one (which was you, if it's your own Mac), is automatically created as the original, main **Administrator (Admin)** of the computer. If you are the *only* user, you are still the Administrator.

Limitations of other users

So you are the **Admin** and other people are either **standard users** or **managed users.** All other users are limited in certain ways:

- Applications can be made available to everyone, *or* limited to specific users. This means you could install a game in your child's Home folder and it won't clutter up your own Applications folder. If the game has to change the resolution of the monitor and the number of colors and your child cranks the volume way up, it won't affect what you see and hear when you log back in. You can install your financial program in your own Home folder so others cannot use it or access your files.

  You can create managed users for young kids and grandkids, where you can customize their Docks so they only have access to certain programs. You can seriously limit with whom they chat and email and which web sites they visit.

- Even if an application is available to everyone who uses the machine, an individual user can set his own preferences because the preferences are stored in the user's personal Library folder.

- Every user can customize the Mail program, and all of a user's email is privately stored in each user's personal Library folder.

- Every user can set up her own screen effects. Fonts, window and Desktop backgrounds, Sidebar, Dock placement, Spaces, and preferences are individually customizable. Preferences are also individual for the keyboard, mouse, web browser bookmarks, international keyboard settings, applications that start up on login, and QuickTime.

- The features that make the Mac easier to use for people with challenges can be customized by each user. This includes the Universal Access settings, full keyboard access, Speech preferences, VoiceOver (having your Mac talk you through doing things), etc.

- Users who need international settings for such things as date, time, numbers, or for typing other languages, etc., can customize the Mac without bothering other users. If you have a laptop that you travel with, you can set up yourself as another user, such as "Carmen in Paris," and customize those settings for that country without affecting all your settings for home.

- **Standard users cannot** change the date or time (except for the menu bar settings), nor can they change the preferences for energy saving, file sharing, networking, or the startup disk. They cannot add new users nor can they change certain parts of the login process. And they cannot install software.

- **Managed users** have all of the above limitations, *plus* they have parental controls applied. You can severely limit a managed user, as explained on pages 336–341.

- The **Guest account** is a special and very temporary account. Everything a Guest user does on the Mac while logged in completely disappears as soon as he logs out. This is great for someone who says, "Can I use your Mac to check my web mail?" He can log in as Guest, use Safari to check his mail, and leave no trace.

More than one Admin

As the Administrator, you can **assign Admin status to any other user** (see page 325). When that Admin user logs in, he can make system-wide changes that standard users cannot; he can create and delete other users, and do most of the things you can do. But your personal Home files are still protected from everyone else, including other Admins.

Guest Account Is Already Created

Apple has already created a special Guest account for you. This is a very temporary account! It's for those times when someone comes over to your house and wants to use your Mac to check their mail or write a quick TextEdit report. As soon as this person logs out, everything they did on the computer is completely erased.

There is no password for a Guest user. As soon as you **enable login** (explained below), anyone can log in as Guest, but they have no access to any of your files.

To log in as Guest, from the Apple menu, log yourself out. The login window that appears has a "Guest Account" option. Just click it once.

To log out as Guest user, go to the Apple menu and choose "Log Out Guest Account." There will be a warning that all files that have been created will be deleted.

1. Click the lock to allow you to enable login for the Guest Account. If you don't, a Guest can use the network to share public files, but cannot log in to your Mac.

2. Click "Guest Account" in the left pane, to see the dialog shown to the right. Checkmark "Allow Guests to log into this computer."

3. Click the lock again.

Create New Users

If you are the Admin (as explained on pages 320–321), you can create standard or managed users (also explained on the previous pages). You'll create the user in the "Accounts" pane of System Preferences, plus you'll assign a password and a login picture. In the "Login Options" pane (click the house icon that you see just above the lock icon), you can make adjustments to the login window.

To create a new user:

1 Go to the Apple menu and choose "System Preferences…."

2 In the System Preferences pane, single-click "Accounts." You'll get the dialog box shown below, except it probably has only two users listed, you and Guest Account. Your user account is also the **Admin.**

3 Click the lock icon in the bottom-left corner. In the dialog that appears after you click the lock, enter the Admin password (the one you chose when you set up your Mac), then click OK. The lock in the bottom-left corner is now open, as shown below.

4 To add a new user, click the "plus" button. This makes a sheet drop down (as shown on the following page) where you will add new user information.

—continued

5 Type the full name (or any descriptive phrase) in the "Full Name" text field. A short name is automatically created for you, but you can edit it. *You will never be able to change the short name after you leave this pane!* The only way to "change" it is to delete the entire user and make a new one.

The short name should be short, you can't use spaces, and you should avoid non-alphabet characters (like * ! ? or /).

Mac OS X can use either the short name or long name. But the short name is sometimes necessary if you use FTP, Telnet, or other applications that let you log in to your Mac from some other location.

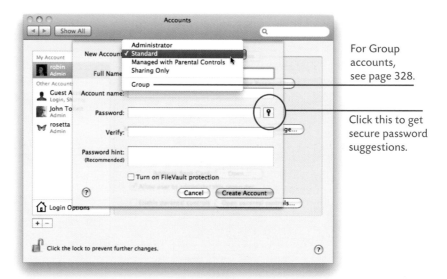

For Group accounts, see page 328.

Click this to get secure password suggestions.

6 Enter a **password** for the user. **Write this down somewhere.** As you've probably seen before, you need to type in the password twice to make sure you've spelled it right, since you can't see it. If you like, click that tiny key icon to get some suggestions for passwords that are very secure.

Passwords are "case sensitive." That means capital or lowercase letters change the password: "ChoCho" is not the same password as "chocho." So be darn sure when you write down your password somewhere that you make note of any capital letters used.

It is possible to leave the password blank, but that makes the entire computer easier to get into. If privacy is an issue, be sure to assign a password.

You can, if you like, enter a **password hint.** On login, if a user enters the wrong password three times, a message appears with this hint (see the following pages to make sure the box is checked to make the hint appear).

7   If you know how to use **File Vault,** click that option. Don't click it if you don't know how it works! (See Lesson 23).

8   Click the "Create Account" button. You will be asked about Automatic Login, which lets you turn on your computer and automatically logs you in without a password. If you have security issues with your Mac, turn off Automatic Login.

9   **To choose a login picture,** do one of the following:

   - Single-click the existing picture you see in the window and choose another from the collection that appears.

   - **Or** do the step above (click the picture), then choose "Edit Picture...." Then skip to "Edit the image," below.

   - **Or** drag a photo or other image from a Finder window and drop it on top of the existing picture.

   - **Edit the image:** Resize, reframe, take a new photo, or choose a different image. You can edit this at any time in the future as well.

10   Enter the user's MobileMe account name if she has one.

Click here to show a selecion of recent pictures.

Press-and-drag this image to position it within the frame.

If you have a camera attached, click this button to take your photo.

To resize the image, drag the blue slider.

To choose another image from your Mac, click here.

When you're happy with the image, click "Set."

—continued

11 If you want to allow this user administration privileges so she can change preferences, install software, etc., check that box.

If you want to enable parental controls, check the box, then click the button to "Open parental controls" (see pages 336–341).

12 In the Accounts window, single-click **Login Options** to assign a user the ability to automatically log in, as shown below. This pane is available only to Administrators (that is, standard and managed users will not be able to change anything on this pane).

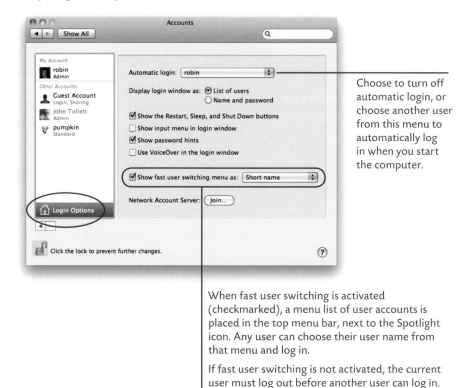

Choose to turn off automatic login, or choose another user from this menu to automatically log in when you start the computer.

When fast user switching is activated (checkmarked), a menu list of user accounts is placed in the top menu bar, next to the Spotlight icon. Any user can choose their user name from that menu and log in.

If fast user switching is not activated, the current user must log out before another user can log in. See page 330.

I set up several new users, but my Mac will **automatically log in** to "robin," meaning I do not have to go through the login screen and enter a password whenever the Mac starts or restarts. This is good for me on my big tower Mac in my office because I work by myself; for my laptop that I travel with, I **disable** automatic login.

Only one user can be assigned the automatic login. At any time, click the Login Options button (shown on the previous page), then choose another user from the "Automatic login" pop-up menu to give automatic login privilege to.

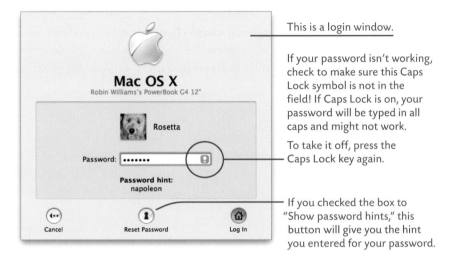

This is a login window.

If your password isn't working, check to make sure this Caps Lock symbol is not in the field! If Caps Lock is on, your password will be typed in all caps and might not work.

To take it off, press the Caps Lock key again.

If you checked the box to "Show password hints," this button will give you the hint you entered for your password.

Display login window as: The "List of users" displays a list of all accounts, including the picture that were chosen for each account. At login, click a picture, then type the password. (If you have a very young user who can't type and you feel your Mac is safe from strangers walking by, do not assign a password; she can just click her picture to log in.)

The "Name and password" option (see the previous page) displays a small log in window with two edit boxes, one for the user name and one for the password. A user will have to type in both name and password. This makes it one step more secure.

Show the Restart, Sleep, and Shut Down buttons: This adds a wee bit more security to your Mac. You see, when you log out, your computer does not turn off. It sits there with a little window where you can log back in again, and there are buttons in the window to "Sleep," "Restart," or "Shut Down." If your Mac is set to automatically log you in on startup, then an unauthorized user can walk by after you have logged out, click the Restart button, and your Mac will restart and automatically log you in. Or, someone could shut down your Mac, insert an OS X DVD, boot up the Mac, and get access to your whole computer. By disabling these buttons, your Mac is at least one step closer to being protected.

—continued

However, there is nothing to prevent anyone from pushing the Restart button on the Mac, so if you really don't want people getting into your Mac, do not enable automatic log in, and do not leave the original install disk laying around.

Show Input menu in login window: This gives you access to the language options that you may have set up in the International system preferences.

Show password hints: If a user enters the wrong password three times, the hint that was provided in the password pane when the user was created is displayed. Or you can click the button (shown on the previous page) to provide the hint immediately.

Use VoiceOver in the login window: This turns on Apple's built-in spoken user interface so a visually impaired person can log in. It reads everything on the login screen out loud to you and tells you what is highlighted so you know where to type your name and password. To disable VoiceOver, make sure this checkbox in *not* checked.

Show fast user switching menu as: This is so cool—it allows multiple users to stay logged in at the same time without having to close files or quit applications (see page 330). The fast user pop-up menu lets you choose how a user is shown in the menu at the top of the screen: as a full name, short name, or icon.

13 **To limit** what the new user can access, see pages 336–341.

To choose login items that automatically open, see page 333.

When done, close the Accounts preferences pane. You can always make changes at any time. To make changes to other users, they must be logged out.

Create a Group

You can create a Group account that consists of individual users. This makes it even easier to share files with a group of people who are all using the same network, such as students or co-workers.

Simply choose the "Group" option from the "New Account" pop-up menu when making a new user account (see page 323). After you name the group, you'll get a pane in which you can add existing users to this Group.

To maximize the file sharing capabilities, use the Sharing preferences to turn on various sharing possibilities, then add this Group to the list of sharing users.

Log Out and Log In

Automatic login allows *one* selected user to use the Mac without having to enter a password. If automatic login is enabled (page 326), then you must make sure to **Log Out** (*not* restart or shut down) before another user can log in. This is because the computer will automatically log you in again when it starts up.

If automatic login is *not* enabled, then it doesn't matter how you turn off the Mac—it will always display a **Log In** screen where every user, even Admins, will have to enter a password.

When you log out, all of your documents will close and your applications will quit. If this is inconvenient, read about "fast user switching" on the next page.

To log out, go to the Apple menu and choose "Log Out *User...*," where *"User"* is the name of the currently active user. All applications will quit, the current screen will disappear, and the login window will appear, waiting for the next user to log in.

To log in, click your name and then type your password. If the password is incorrect, the login window shakes back and forth, as if it's saying "No! No! No!" After three wrong passwords, it will show you the hint you assigned (see page 327). Or you can click the "Forgot Password" button and it will provide the clue immediately.

Switch Users with a Click

The Mac has a feature called **fast user switching** that allows multiple users to stay logged in at the same time without having to close files or quit applications. You didn't have to close your documents and quit your applications to log out.

When fast user switching is turned on, all users are listed in the top-right corner of your screen, next to the menu clock. The currently active user's name appears in the menu bar.

To see other user names and to see which ones are logged in, single-click the current user name in the menu; a menu drops down showing all users. Users in the list that have a checkmark next to them are already logged in. The currently active user is grayed-out.

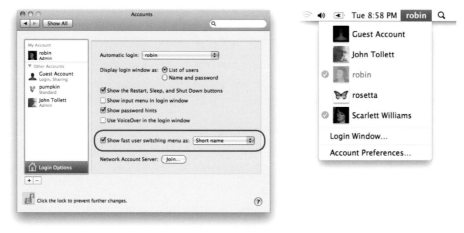

To enable fast user switching, click the checkbox "Show fast user switching menu as:" in the "Login Options" pane of the Accounts system preferences (shown above-left). See page 326 for more about fast user switching.

To switch to another user, choose one from the user menu (above-right). If you (the Admin) assigned a password to the chosen user, a login window opens so the user can type a password. Enter the correct password and the user's own personal Desktop environment opens.

If a password was not assigned to a user, that user's Desktop opens immediately, without a password-protected login window. Actually, it doesn't just open like some ordinary computer; the entire Desktop rotates like a cube to the new user space.

To open the main login window, choose "Login Window..." from the user's list in the menu bar, as shown on the previous page. This is a convenient way to leave the screen if you have multiple users. The next user that sits down at the Mac just clicks her name to log in and start work (or play).

TIP —— If the rotating-cube effect isn't happening for you during fast user switching, the graphics card installed on your Mac might not be able to handle the intense processing that this effect requires. Fast user switching will still take place–it's just not quite as sexy.

Allow Other Users to be Admins

An Admin can select another user and give that user Administrator privileges. In the Accounts preferences, select the user in the left panel, then click the button to "Allow user to administer this computer" (circled below).

A standard user can give himself Admin privileges if he knows the name and password of an Administrator. All he needs to do is click the lock icon and enter the correct information.

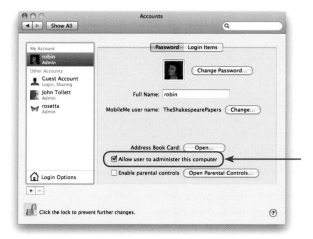

Adjust User Settings

You, as Admin, cannot make changes to another user if that user is already logged in. So if you try to make changes and it won't let you, log out that user.

Let Users Adjust their own Settings

Once a **standard user** is *logged in,* she can adjust some of the login settings, even if she's not the Administrator. She can change her password (she has to know the current password before she can assign a new one). She can change the login picture, and choose which applications open automatically when she logs in.

Below you see the applications that Scarlett likes to have open automatically when she comes to visit and uses my Mac. See the opposite page for details about assigning Login Items.

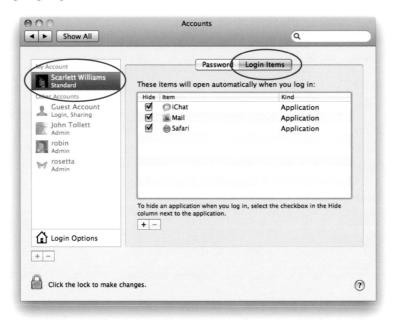

Set Up Login Items

In the **Login Items pane,** any standard or Admin user (including yourself) can choose to have certain items automatically open during the login process. You can open your favorite applications, utilities, documents, even movies or music. If you choose to have a document open, the application it was created in will have to open as well, even if you don't have it in the list.

This pane applies only to the user who is currently logged in! No other user even has access to the Login Items pane for someone else.

To add items to the Login Items list, click the "plus" button circled below. A dialog box opens to let you choose any file or application to add to the Login Items. To add more items, click the "plus" button again.

The files will **open in the order in which they are listed.** Drag any file in the list up or down to change the order.

If you don't want to see a certain application right away every time you turn on your Mac, click in the checkbox to **hide** it. It will still open, but its windows won't be visible on the screen. The application icon in the Dock will have the blue bubble under it, though, so you know it's open and you can access it at any time.

The current user is always at the top of this list.

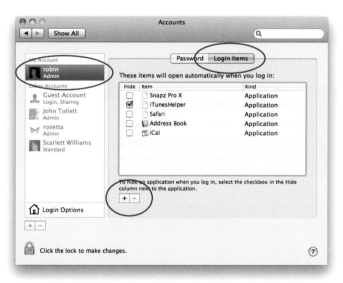

Another way to add items to this list (or remove items): Press an icon in the Dock. Choose "Options," then choose "Open at Login" to place a checkmark next to the item.

To remove the item from this Login Items list, repeat the above procedure to remove the checkmark next to "Open at Login."

To delete items from the Login Items list, first select the item, then click the "minus" button.

Share Files with Other Users

Once users are set up, other users can only access each other's Public folders, the Drop Boxes inside the Public folders, and the Sites folders. But the Shared folder (which is in the Users folder, which is on your main hard disk) is available to everyone who uses the Mac. Here's how it works:

- Put files in your own **Public folder** that you want others to be able to read, copy, or print. They have to open your Public folder to do so.

- Other users can put files *for you* into your **Drop Box,** which is located inside of your Public folder. They cannot *open* your Drop Box, not even to see if their file successfully transferred.

- Put files in the **Shared folder** that you want everyone who uses the Mac to be able to access. This is a good way to distribute something to everyone on the Mac without having to copy it to each individual's Drop Box.

- The **Sites folder** is where you can store a web site or files that you want people to access through the Internet.

You can also change the sharing "privileges" for any folder in your Home folder. That is, you can turn *off* the sharing privileges for the Public folder and the Drop Box so no one can access them, and you can also choose to share *any* or all of your other folders, with varying levels of access. Please see the following page for details.

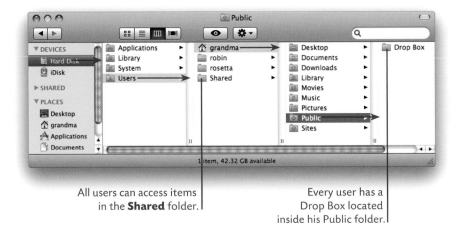

All users can access items in the **Shared** folder.

Every user has a Drop Box located inside his Public folder.

Set Permissions for Shared Files

Every file on your Mac has "permission" settings. Some of these permissions you can change, if you like. For instance, you might want to send a memo to all users of this Mac, but you don't want them to be able to edit it. So select that document and give the others a permission of "Read only." Or perhaps you don't want anyone to access your Sites folder; give it a permission of "No Access." Maybe you want to share your Movies folder so another user can drop movie files into it; select the folder and change its permission to "Read & Write" or "Write only" (which means they can put files *into* your folder but can't take them out).

To change permissions on a file or folder:

1 Single-click a file or folder to select it.

2 Press Command I to display the Info window, as shown below.

3 Click the disclosure triangle next to "Sharing & Permissions."

4 Click the lock icon in the bottom-right corner and enter your Admin password. Click OK.

5 Click the "Privilege" menu next to user names to change the permissions.

6 When you're finished, just close the Info window.

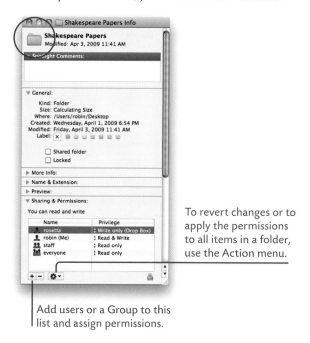

To revert changes or to apply the permissions to all items in a folder, use the Action menu.

Add users or a Group to this list and assign permissions.

Parental
Controls

Apply Parental Controls

There are several levels of limited user access you can create. Once you apply any of these parental controls, the user changes from a "Standard" user to a "Managed with Parental Controls" user. Choose the level of access you want to control. Each of these options is explained on the following pages. Only an Admin can apply or change parental controls. You can even manage these controls from another computer.

You can limit the applications to which a user has access, the content of the Dictionary and web sites, whether or not a user can burn CDs or modify their Dock, and more. You can set time limits and check logs to see where a user has been.

The **Simple Finder** is the most serious limitation. This is appropriate for very young children who want to use their educational software and games on your Mac and really don't know how to surf or chat anyway. It makes the Mac very easy for them to use and they can't do any damage.

Set limitations on a user

1   Set up a new user, as explained on pages 323–328, if you haven't already.

2   Make sure that the user is not logged in. If he is, log him out.

3   Go to the Apple menu and choose "System Preferences...."
    Single-click on the "Accounts" icon.

4   If the lock icon in the bottom-left corner is locked, single-click on it
    and enter the Admin name and password. Click OK.

5   Select the user in the left-hand pane.

6   Check the box to "Enable Parental Controls."

7   Click the button to "Open parental controls...."

8   You'll see the window at the top of the next page. Make sure the account to
    which you want to apply parental controls is selected on the left.

9   The rest of the process is pretty self-explanatory. Go through the next few pages
    for some clarification. Essentially, you're going to choose what you want to
    limit. Don't choose the **Simple Finder** until you read page 340.

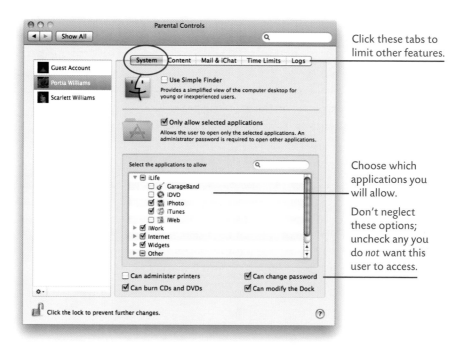

Click these tabs to limit other features.

Choose which applications you will allow.

Don't neglect these options; uncheck any you do *not* want this user to access.

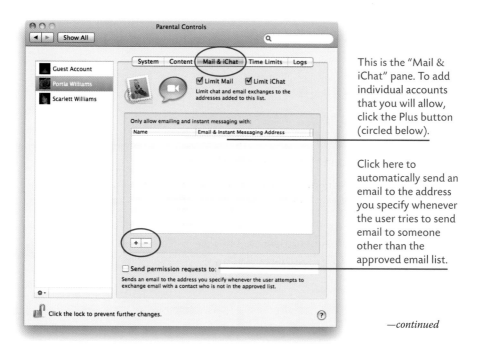

This is the "Mail & iChat" pane. To add individual accounts that you will allow, click the Plus button (circled below).

Click here to automatically send an email to the address you specify whenever the user tries to send email to someone other than the approved email list.

—continued

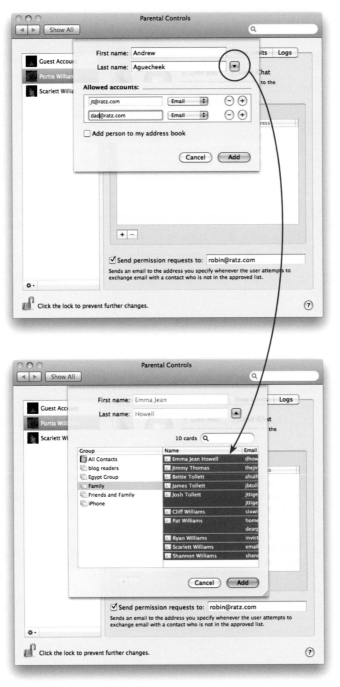

This is the "Mail & iChat" pane. You can add the individual accounts that you will allow, or click the disclosure button (cirlced) to access your Address Book (below) and choose allowed accounts from there.

This is the "Content" pane where you can hide naughty words in the Dictionary and limit access to the web.

This is the "Logs" pane where you can keep track of every web page this user has visited, as well as with whom they've chatted and what applications they've used. Wow.

Be sure to check the 'Time Limits" pane where you can limit the amount of time the user can use the computer, and turn it off at a certain bedtime.

—continued

Simple Finder

The Simple Finder is the most serious limitation. The illustration below shows what a user logged in using **Simple Finder** might see.

- The Applications and Utilities are limited to what you allow.

- The user has no access to a Desktop, hard disk, or other partitions.

- The user cannot move files from one folder to another.

- The user has three folders in her Dock: My Applications, Documents, and Shared. The Shared folder contains items placed in it by other users of the computer, as explained on page 334. Anything anyone puts into the Shared folder (shown in the Dock) will be available even to users running Simple Finder.

- The Finder windows have no Sidebars or Toolbars.

My Applications folder.

Shared folder.

Documents folder; all saved documents will be in this folder.

In Simple Finder, click an icon just once to open it.

To set up a user with Simple Finder:

1 Follow the steps to create a new user (see page 323), up through Step 9.

2 Click the button to "Use Simple Finder."

3 In the list of applications, uncheck the boxes to deselect applications.
   Every checked item will be available to the user in Simple Finder.

   The applications list in the Parental Controls window (below) are shown in groups. Click the disclosure triangle next to an application checkbox to hide or show the individual applications in that group.

Disable the Simple Finder

To disable the Simple Finder in a user account, the managed user must be logged out (from the Apple menu, choose "Log Out *user name*." An Admin user (or anyone with an Admin name and password) can then go to the System Preferences select "Accounts," then click the padlock in the bottom left corner. A dialog opens that requires an Admin name and password. The Admin user can then select a managed account in the "My Account" sidebar list, then uncheck the "Enable parental controls" item. If you want to manage parental controls on one computer from another computer, click the "Open Parental Controls..." button, then checkmark "Manage parental controls from another computer."

Delete a User

Any Admin can delete a user. You have three choices about what to do with all of the files that belong to a user when you delete her account:

Save the home folder in a disk image. The contents of the user's Home folder will be compressed as a disk image format (.dmg) and saved into a "Deleted Users" folder located in the Users folder. This is a nice safety net in case you need to access that user's files later—just double-click the .dmg file, it opens to a hard disk icon (as shown on the opposite page), and all the files are restored in that hard disk icon.

Do not change the home folder. This stores the entire Home folder and all its contents in a folder called "*username* (Deleted)." All of the folders except Public and Sites are locked. However, you, as Admin, can open a folder's Info window and change the permissions to give you access to it, as shown on page 335.

Delete the home folder. Choose this if you're certain you don't need anything the deleted user may have in her Home folder. The user account and all of the files in the user's Home folder will immediately disappear.

To delete a user:

1 From the Apple menu, choose "System Preferences…," then click the "Accounts" icon.

2 If the lock icon in the bottom-left corner is locked, single-click it and enter the Admin name and password. Click OK.

3 Click once on the name of the user you want to delete. If the user name is gray and you can't select it, that means that user is logged in. She must log out before you can delete the account.

4 After you select the user, click the "minus" button at the bottom of the user list8 pane.

5 A sheet drops down, shown at the top of the next page, asking what you want to do with the files belonging to this user. Make your choice based on the information above.

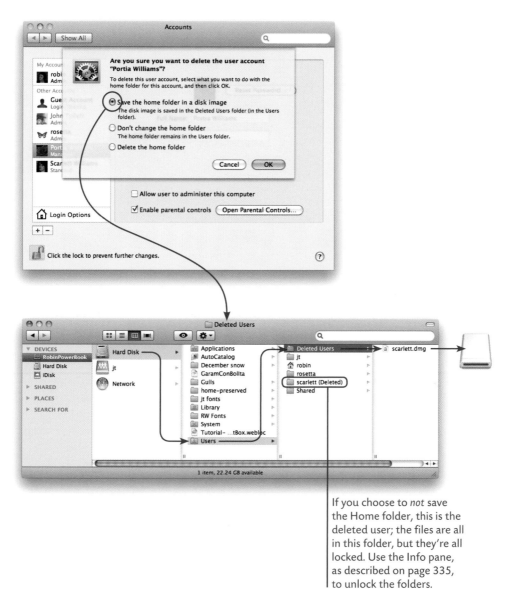

If you choose to *not* save the Home folder, this is the deleted user; the files are all in this folder, but they're all locked. Use the Info pane, as described on page 335, to unlock the folders.

To access the saved user files later, double-click the .dmg file. It will open to a hard disk icon (shown above-right). Open the hard disk icon (double-click it) and you'll find all the files.

19

GOALS

Understand the different ways to access Spotlight and search your Mac

Choose or change the categories for searching

Prevent selected folders from being searched

Expand the search with metadata

Add searchable keywords to files

Create Smart Folders

Take advantage of Spotlight in other applications

Find What You Want, Fast—with Spotlight

Spotlight is not just a search feature, it's a way of working with your Mac. Once you get accustomed to its speed, versatility, and usefulness, you'll find yourself using Spotlight regularly instead of opening and closing folders and windows.

If you find you perform a certain search often, save it as a Smart Folder. Files that match the search criteria are automatically listed in the Smart Folder and the folder updates itself every time a matching file is created or changed.

The Many Faces of Spotlight

Spotlight really has **five** different ways of working. You'll find yourself using them in different ways at different times. Experiment with each one so you'll know which is the most appropriate for what you need to do. Details for each option are on the following pages.

1. Spotlight menu

Click the Spotlight icon in the upper-right of the menu bar, **or** use the keyboard shortcut, Command Spacebar.

Type your query into the field that appears and Spotlight instantly starts presenting results. As you type more letters, the search narrows and updates.

Access to the Spotlight menu is available no matter which application you're using—you don't have to go to the Finder to run a search. See pages 354–355 for all the details.

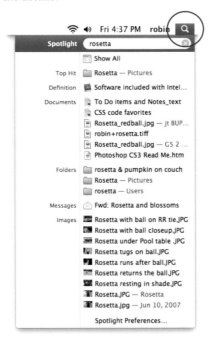

2. Spotlight window

To get the Spotlight window shown below that displays more information:

Either click the option to "Show All" at the top of the Spotlight menu after you've made a search, as shown on the previous page.

Or use a keyboard shortcut:

If you're in the Finder, press Command F.

If you're in an application, press Command Option Spacebar.

See pages 356–357 for details.

3. Spotlight-powered search in the Finder

When you type into the Search field in a Finder window, Spotlight instantly kicks in and shows you simple results directly in that window. It automatically looks in the last "location" that was chosen ("This Mac" in the example below). See page 356 for more details.

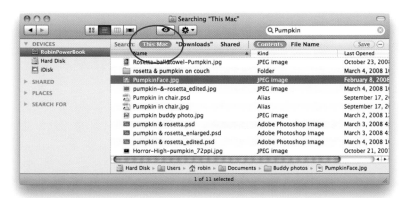

4. Quick "Search For"

There is a section in the Finder window sidebar called "Search For." Apple has created several pre-defined searches for you. If you're looking, for instance, for a file you used yesterday but you can't remember what you called it, check the "Yesterday" search and see if it jumps out at you.

You can't change these search parameters, but you can get take them out of your sidebar if you're not using them. Just drag them off to the side and let go—they'll go up in a puff of smoke. If you want them back, use the Finder preferences: Go to the Finder menu, choose "Preferences...," and click the "Sidebar" tab. Then checkmark the items you want to put back in the sidebar.

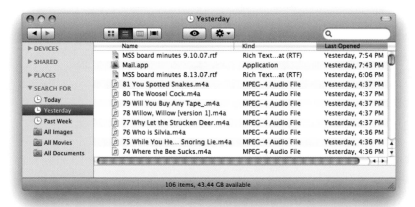

5. Spotlight-powered search in many applications

You can find Spotlight-enabled searches in many other applications. Some applications also let you create other forms of Smart Folders.

- Mail and Smart Mailboxes, pages 94–97.

- Address Book and Smart Groups, pages 122–123.

- Spotlight in text, page 362.

- System Preferences, page 291.

- Open and Save As dialog boxes, page 363.

- Safari, page 362.

But Before You Begin

There are several things you might want to know before you start using Spotlight. In the Spotlight preferences, you can choose which **categories** of items you want Spotlight to search through. You can also choose certain disks and folders that you (or anyone using your machine) *cannot* search through, giving you some extra **privacy.** And on the following pages are some tips to help you make your searches more productive.

Choose the categories for searching

1 From the Apple menu, choose "System Preferences...."

2 Single-click the "Spotlight" icon.

3 Click the "Search Results" tab if it isn't already highlighted.

Click the "Privacy" tab to designate locations that you don't want Spotlight to search.

4 *Uncheck* boxes for categories you *don't want* Spotlight to search.

5 Drag the category items to change the order in which results appear in Spotlight

Create some privacy

1 If you haven't already, open the Spotlight preferences, as explained on the previous page.

2 Click the "Privacy" tab.

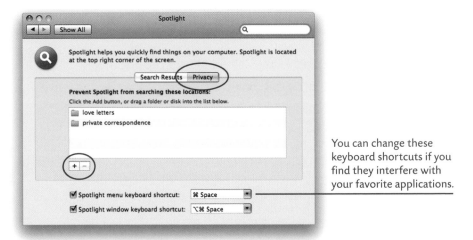

You can change these keyboard shortcuts if you find they interfere with your favorite applications.

3 Click the **+** sign to open a dialog box where you can choose any folder or disk on your Mac that you don't want Spotlight to search.

Or drag any folder or disk icon from the Finder and drop it into this pane.

Note: This isn't a very *safe* privacy feature because anyone using your computer can just open the preferences and remove these items.

Keyboard shortcuts to open Spotlight

Notice in the illustration above that these preferences also include options for you to change the existing keyboard shortcuts or to turn them off altogether (uncheck the boxes). Some applications might use those same shortcuts; Spotlight will override the applications' shortcuts, so if it creates a problem for you, go to the preferences above and change them.

Don't search just file names

Spotlight doesn't just search file names. It searches the contents of email messages; it knows who sent you email; it can look through the contact information in your Address Book, images and graphics, calendars and events and to-do lists, System Preferences, PDF text, the contents of TextEdit pages (but not text clippings), even iChat logs (if you previously chose to log them).

Expand your repertoire of searchable items

You're not limited to searching just for *words* that might be found in a file. In the Finder Spotlight search, you can use the existing parameters to find particular categories of files. For instance, you can look for "music" to find all your music files, or choose "Image" in the pop-up menu and select "Today" in the sidebar to find all the images you have opened or added today.

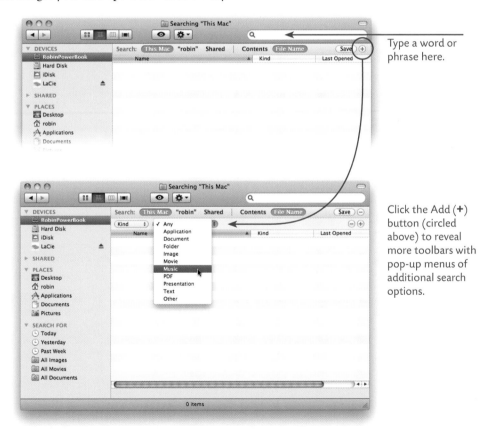

Type a word or phrase here.

Click the Add (**+**) button (circled above) to reveal more toolbars with pop-up menus of additional search options.

Expand the search with metadata

Spotlight also looks in the **metadata** that every file contains. Metadata includes information about who created the file, when it was created and modified, the copyright date, the file type, the color space for a photo or image, even what kind of camera a particular photo was taken with. Different kinds of files have different kinds of metadata associated with them.

To make a metadata attribute appear in the parameter pop-up menus, click the pop-up menu, then choose "Other...." In the sheet that opens, find an attribute you want included in the pop-up menu, then checkmark its box in the column labeled "In Menu."

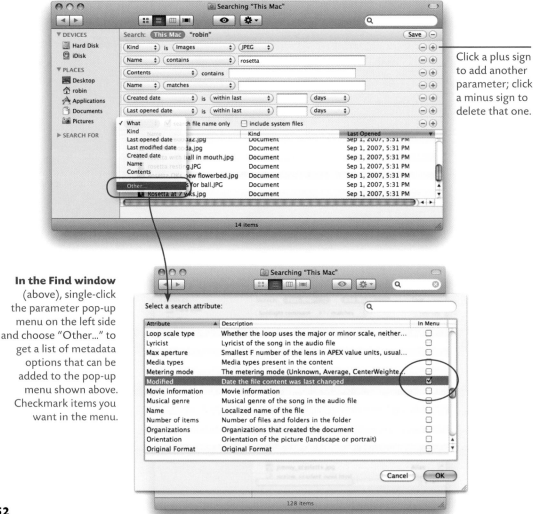

Click a plus sign to add another parameter; click a minus sign to delete that one.

In the Find window (above), single-click the parameter pop-up menu on the left side and choose "Other..." to get a list of metadata options that can be added to the pop-up menu shown above. Checkmark items you want in the menu.

Add keywords to files

There are some files that, even with all the options in Spotlight, still won't be found because there is nothing associated with them that Spotlight can decipher. For these files, you can add your own **keywords.** For instance, the example below is a music file of an Elizabethan song written in the 16th century. I can search for "music," "Hecate," and other data, but if I search for "elizabethan," this piece of music won't be found. So I added a number of keywords that I might use in a search to the Get Info window for this file and for all the other Elizabethan music I have on my Mac. Now Spotlight can find them.

To add a keyword to a file:

1 Single-click a file to select it.

2 Then press Command I to open the Get Info window.

3 Type your keywords into the "Spotlight Comments" area.

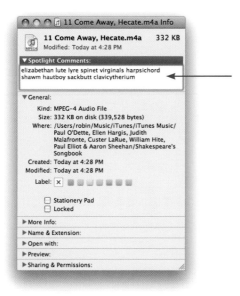

If you have more than one file to which you want to add keywords, select one file, then press Command *Option* I. Now as you select other files, this Get Info window automatically displays the information for the currently selected file.

Spotlight Menu

The Spotlight menu is available no matter which application you are using at the moment (although this is *not* the tool to use to search within your application, such as searching the text on a visible web page or in your word processor).

To open the Spotlight menu:

1   Simply click the Spotlight icon in the upper-right of the menu bar, **or** press Command Spacebar to open it.

2   A small field appears. Start typing in it.

Results appear instantly in the Spotlight menu, as shown below. The more letters you type, the narrower the search becomes.

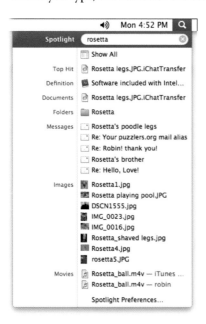

To use the Spotlight menu:

Below are callouts of the various parts of the Spotlight menu. Use the Spotlight menu for a quick search for something you think can be found easily.

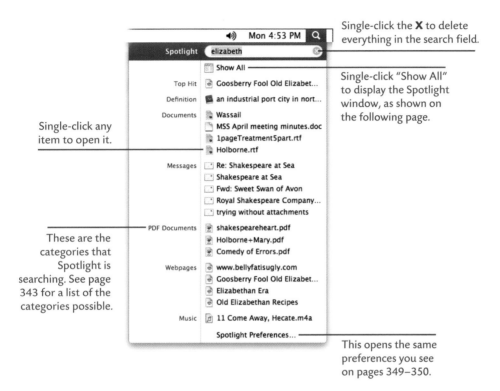

Single-click the **X** to delete everything in the search field.

Single-click "Show All" to display the Spotlight window, as shown on the following page.

Single-click any item to open it.

These are the categories that Spotlight is searching. See page 343 for a list of the categories possible.

This opens the same preferences you see on pages 349–350.

Spotlight in the Finder

There are two ways to use Spotlight in the Finder, both of which use your Finder window. You can do a **quick search** by simply typing in the search field that appears in the upper-right corner of every Finder window, as described below. *Or* press Command F to go straight to a more **specific search** window with options to narrow your search, as described on the following pages.

Quick search in a Finder window

Below are the **results** of a quick search for "death." As soon as you start typing in the search field, results appear. Also, a bar appears that tells you where Spotlight looked. In the example below, it searched the *contents* of "This Mac" (the dark gray highlight).

In this window, you can easily choose another location for Spotlight to search— just single-click one of the locations in the bar ("This Mac" or whatever specific location is listed, such as "robin," as shown below). If you select an item in the sidebar before you begin the search, it will limit the search to that location.

You can also click the **+** button that now appears (circled, below) to add more parameters for narrowing your search, as shown on the opposite page, and page 352.

To see where a file is located, single-click any result; the path to that file (the folders within folders) appears in a horizontal list at the bottom of the window.

To open the folder that holds the selected file, press Command R (or Control-click, right-click, or use the Action menu to choose, "Open Enclosing Folder").

To open that file, double-click it.

To quickly view the file, click the Quick Look button (the eyeball in the toolbar). Or press the Spacebar.

Specific search in a Finder window

On the Desktop, press Command F and the active window will switch to what you see below. If no window is open or active, a new one will open automatically. This window includes the search field, and the location bar is already visible.

The only difference between this window and the one on the opposite page is that this Find window automatically provides parameters for you to work with.

To add more parameters to narrow your search, click the plus sign; to delete a search parameter, click its minus sign.

To change the parameters, single-click a parameter menu to choose a different option. Start with the menu on the left, as shown below, which will change the specifics in the next menu to the right, which might then create a new field for you to enter a new parameter, shown circled below.

As in the example on the opposite page, you can choose to search the "Contents" or just the "File Name."

Choose a location to search and whether to search the contents or the file name.

You can narrow your search even further with Boolean operators, which are not as scary as they sound. See the next page.

Sortable search results

Sort search results by different criteria. Click the Action menu in the toolbar (the gear icon), choose "Arrange By," then choose on of the sort items (Name, Date Modified, Date Created, Size, Kind, or Label). If some of these options are not available, you can turn them on. From the Action menu, choose "Show View Options." Checkmark the options you want turned on.

Use a Boolean search

A Boolean search simply means that you limit the search by using the words AND, OR, and NOT. As you can see below, a search for "mabel" showed me three files. But a search for "mabel AND love" found exactly the one I was looking for, and only that one.

The Boolean operator (the AND, OR, or NOT word) *must* be typed in all caps or it won't work.

You can also use quotation marks, just as you probably do when searching the web. For instance, if you search for *knitting yarn* without quotes, you'll get every document that has the word knitting in it and every document that has the word yarn in it. But if you search for *"knitting yarn"* in quotes, you will only find pages with that exact phrase.

Smart Folders

Once you do a great search in the Finder via Spotlight, you might like to create a **Smart Folder** that automatically keeps track of every file that fits that search. This folder doesn't store the original files—the originals stay in their original folders, and the Smart Folder just keeps a list of everything so it's easily accessible to you.

For instance, you might want a Smart Folder that contains all the various presentations you've made so you don't have to go looking through numerous folders to find a particular one. If so, make a Smart Folder that just stores presentation files.

Or you might have used the Labels feature on your Mac (see page 276) to color-code all the files that belong to a certain project. For instance, your newsletter might include a **document** in the application Pages, **images** from the last event, **word processing files** your authors have sent you, and a **spreadsheet chart** from the Apple spreadsheet software called Numbers. And you used the Labels to give them each a label color of orange. Your Smart Folder can keep track of all the orange-labeled files in one place for you, even though the files themselves are organized into their own particular folders. The Smart Folder updates automatically as new files are labeled or old files are trashed.

To create a Smart Folder:

1 In the Finder, press Command F to open Spotlight in a Finder window.

2 Define your parameters. Below is a simple search of all files in my Home folder that are presentations. Notice there is *nothing* typed into the search field at the top of the window because I want to find *all* presentations regardless of their names.

The search field is empty, but a specific parameter of "Presentations" is chosen from the pop-up menu.

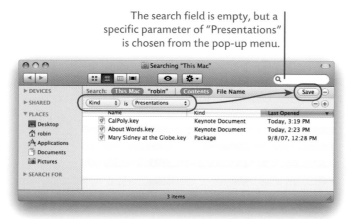

—continued

3   Click the "Save" button, which is just below the search field. You will be asked
    to **name** this Smart Folder and **where** to save it. In the example below, I saved
    this into my Documents folder.

    If you want this folder to be visible in your Sidebar, check the box to "Add To
    Sidebar." Click "Save."

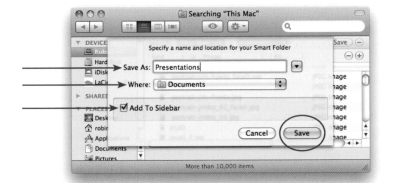

I saved this Smart
Folder into my
Documents folder
and added it to
my Sidebar.

4   Now that the Smart Folder is saved, all you need to do is double-click it
    and your Mac will display all the files that match the criteria you originally set.
    (If the Smart Folder is in the Sidebar, just single-click on it.)

To edit this Smart Folder search at any time, select it in the sidebar, Control-click it,
then choose "Show Search Criteria." Edit the search parameters that appear in the
window (as shown on page 352), then click the "Save" button in the top-right corner.

System Preferences

As explained in Lesson 15, Spotlight also works in System Preferences. This is great when you know you need a System Preference to do something in particular, but you're not sure *which* one you need.

To search in System Preferences, simply type into the search field. As you type, Spotlight highlights all the possible preferences that might help you.

When you click one of the options in the menu that appears, Spotlight highlights the best preference for that option in a bright white spotlight, as shown below, then opens it for you automatically.

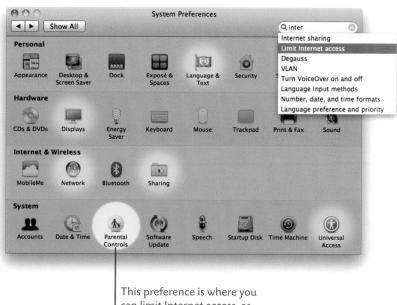

This preference is where you can limit Internet access, as selected in the menu above.

Spotlight Search in Time Machine

If you use Time Machine to automatically back up your files, you can use Spotlight searches within Time Machine and find files that may not still be on your computer. See page 372.

Spotlight Search in Text

In some applications on your Mac, you can select a word or phrase and let Spotlight find other occurrences of that word or phrase on your Mac. This might be useful when you're browsing the web and find the name of someone in the news and it makes you say, "Hmm, didn't she send me an email last month?" Or if you're in your word processor and you're writing an essay and you want to find the article you saved earlier on a topic that's mentioned.

For instance, try this in Safari or TextEdit:

1 On a web page, press-and-drag to select a word or phrase.

2 Control-click (or right-click) that selected word or phrase.

3 From the contextual menu that appears, choose "Search in Spotlight." Remember, Spotlight searches your Mac, not the Internet!

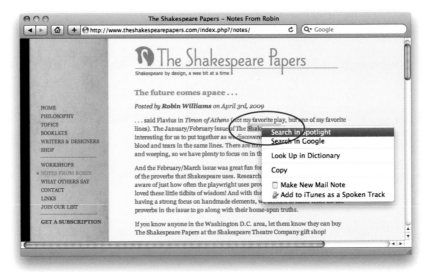

Spotlight Search in Mail

Type a search word or phrase in Mail's search field when you can't find a particular message in a large collection of emails. Choose a folder in the sidebar to search.

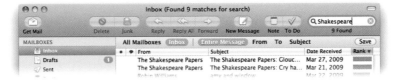

Spotlight Search in an "Open" Dialog

In any "Open" dialog, as shown below, you can search for a **file name.** Spotlight will locate all files that your open application thinks it can open and display, plus all folders with that search phrase in the name (it will also search contents of files). Any Smart Folders you have placed in the Sidebar will also appear here.

After you start typing in the search field, this bar appears.

Narrow or expand your search by clicking one of the locations listed in the bar.

Choose to search the contents of files or file names.

Spotlight Search in a "Save As" Dialog

You can do a search in the "Save As" dialog and Spotlight will find **folders** for you to save into. Any Smart Folders in the Sidebar will also appear here. Double-click the folder into which you want to save, then click "Save."

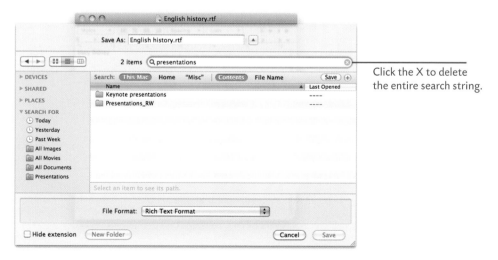

Click the X to delete the entire search string.

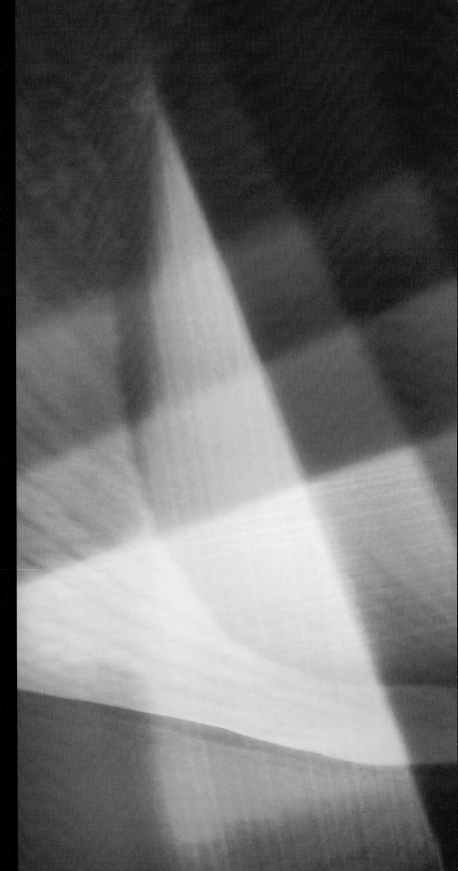

20

GOALS

Learn about
Time Machine

Create a backup of your
entire hard disk

Find and restore files

Search and switch
to Time Machine

Time Machine Backup

We know we should back up important files every day, but really, "It's just too much trouble." Surely everything will be okay for a couple of days until we have time to make backups. Months later we finally have some extra time and the files are nowhere to be found. Or the original version has been overwritten by a newer version with unwanted changes in it. Oh, if only we had a time machine that could go back in time and grab earlier versions of files. And wouldn't it be nice if the time machine did this without us doing anything—except maybe turning it on?

Wait . . . there *is* such a thing! And, amazingly, it's called . . . Time Machine!

About Time Machine

After you set up Time Machine, it backs up your computer regularly. For the initial backup, Time Machine backs up everything, including system files, applications, etc. After that, only files that have changed are backed up. Hourly backups are stored for 24 hours, daily backups are stored for a month, then weekly backups are stored until the backup disk is full. Because backups are stored by date, you can restore files or folders (or your entire system) exactly as they were at certain points in the past.

When the backup disk fills up, Time Machine deletes the oldest backups to make room for new ones. It could take a long time to reach this point, but be prepared to either replace the Time Machine disk with another one, or to let Time Machine delete older files when necessary.

While Time Machine is a good solution for temporary storage of backups and a great way to restore files that have been thrown away, lost, or changed, it isn't a final solution for creating permanent archives of your files. If you plan to keep using the same backup disk and let Time Machine delete the oldest files to make room for new backups, be sure to use other backup methods to create permanent backups of important files and folders (burn files to CDs or DVDs, copy items to your .Mac iDisk, or copy items to other external drives). Remember, it's safest to create *multiple* backups of items that you absolutely cannot afford to lose, and be sure to store those multiple copies in several different places—if your office burns down or floods, it won't matter if you had 16 backups in that office—they're all gone.

What kind of disk to use as backup

You must use a disk for Time Machine that is separate from the hard disk you work on. An extra internal hard disk is great, and external hard disks work fine too. The disk needs to be big enough to backup the drive it's assigned to. For best results, use a disk dedicated only to Time Machine backups. If you use this backup disk to also store other files, you lose that storage space for Time Machine backups.

Both FireWire and USB disks work with Time Machine, including most disks that might be available on your local network. Disks used for Time Machine backups must be formatted as Mac OS Extended (journaled), and have Access Control Lists (ACLs) enabled. Time Machine will erase and reformat the disk if necessary.

Create a Time Machine Backup

It's very easy to start the process. Make sure you have an appropriate disk connected.

To set up Time Machine backups:

1 Once you have an extra **internal** hard disk installed *or* you've connected an empty **external** hard disk, open the Time Machine system preferences: Click its icon in the Dock, then click "Set Up Time Machine," *or* go to the Apple menu, choose "System Preferences…," then click the "Time Machine" icon.

2 Click the "Select Backup Disk…" button. You'll get a list of possible drives that can be used; choose one and click "Use for Backup."

   If you have a single external disk attached, Time Machine will probably automatically ask if you want to use that disk for backup.

Click here to place a Time Machine icon in the menu bar that appears at the top of your screen.

Click the icon in the menu bar to access some helpful commands, such as "Back Up Now" and "Open Time Machine Preferences…."

3 Once a backup disk has been assigned, Time Machine automatically switches itself On and displays information about that disk, including when the first backup will start.

4 Click the Options button to display a sheet (shown on the next page) in which you can designate items you want to *exclude* from Time Machine backups.

See the next page.

—continued

5 To add items to the "Do not back up" list, click the plus (**+**) button, circled below.

Another sheet slides down from the title bar, covering up the one shown below. Select the items (drives, volumes, files, or folders) that you do NOT want Time Machine to back up. Click the "Exclude" button. This returns you to the first sheet, shown below.

To remove items from this list so that Time Machine *will* back them up, select them and click the minus (**−**) button on the sheet shown below.

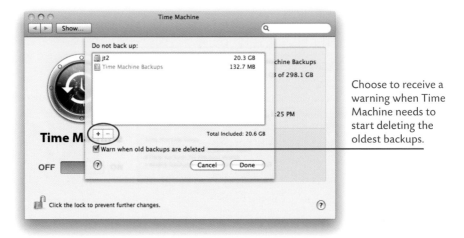

Choose to receive a warning when Time Machine needs to start deleting the oldest backups.

6 Click "Done."

Time Machine makes an initial backup that includes everything on your computer (shown in progress, below). This backup can be time consuming, depending on how many folders, files, and applications are on your Mac. Subsequent backups are faster since only changed files are backed up.

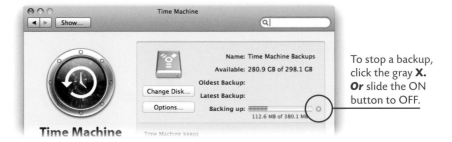

To stop a backup, click the gray **X.** *Or* slide the ON button to OFF.

Backup failed?

If a Time Machine message tells you the latest backup failed (see below), click
that red info button (*i*) for an explanation. The disk may be too small or perhaps
you're out of room on the chosen disk. Or maybe some minor little digital hiccup
happened, in which case it often works to click the Time Machine icon in the menu
bar at the top of the screen and choose "Back Up Now" from the pop-up menu,
shown below. See page 367 to learn how to add Time Machine to the menu bar.

To switch to another disk, click the "Change Disk…" button, then select another
connected disk.

If Time Machine alerts you that the new disk must be erased (shown at the bottom
of this page), click "Erase." This will of course destroy everything that's already on
that disk! If you don't want to lose information on that particular disk, connect
another hard disk and click "Choose Another Disk."

How to Use Time Machine

Once you've got Time Machine all set up, as explained on the previous pages, there are several different ways to use it to find earlier versions of files that have changed or to find missing files.

To find and restore a file:

1   On your Desktop, single-click a file or folder in a Finder window to select it.

2   Click the Time Machine icon in the Dock. The Time Machine universe is revealed in the background. It shows the current Finder window in the foreground, with earlier versions of that same window receding into the recent (or distant) past. The selected file is prominently displayed in Cover View and is also shown highlighted in the List View in the bottom section.

Notice that the bar at the bottom of the star field universe is labeled "Today (Now)." In other words, any files shown or accessed through this particular window are the most current versions.

3   To go back in time and find *previous* versions of the selected file, click the back-in-time arrow (called out, below). The star field zooms back in time through the floating windows until it reaches a window where an earlier version of the selected file exists.

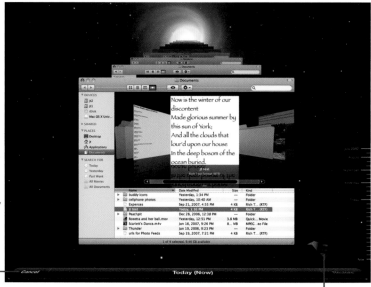

Click "Cancel" to exit Time Machine, or press Escape on your keyboard.

These are the back-in-time and forward-in-time arrows.

The file is selected and displayed, as shown below. Notice that the bar at the bottom of the window now says "Today at 8:50 AM," which is about twelve hours earlier than my current time. And you can see that the file had different formatting in this earlier version.

If this isn't the version of the file you're looking for, click the back-in-time arrow again to find earlier versions. *Or* drag your pointer over the vertical timeline on the right edge of the screen and select a backup time or date.

4 **To restore the version of the file** you want, first make sure it's selected. Then click the "Restore" button on the right side of the bar at the bottom.

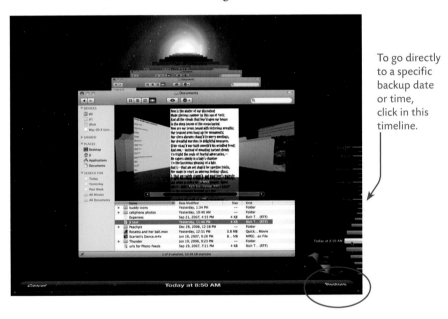

To go directly to a specific backup date or time, click in this timeline.

5 A message asks if you want to keep the original version of the file (instead of the backup), keep both files, *or* replace the original with the backup version.

If you choose "Keep Both," a restored copy of the backed-up file is made and put in its original location on your computer. The word "original" is added to the original file's name (right).

jt text

jt text (original)

Do a Spotlight Search in Time Machine

When you use Spotlight to search for items on your computer, the search naturally takes place in the "Now" time frame; in other words, it finds files in their current versions. But if you've lost or deleted files, Time Machine can zoom into the past and find the files in the various states in which they were saved.

Search, then switch to Time Machine:

1 Start a Spotlight search in the Finder (see Lesson 19). If Spotlight doesn't find the item you're looking for, click the Time Machine icon in the Dock.

   The Time Machine universe appears, with Finder windows receding into the past. The window in the foreground is labeled "Today (Now)." Your search term is in the Spotlight search field, circled below.

2 Click the back-in-time arrow. Time Machine zooms back in time until it finds the item. To look for an even earlier version of the item, click the back-in-time arrow again, *or* click in the timeline along the right edge of the screen. Notice that the time label in the bar at the bottom of the screen shows when the *selected* item was backed up.

3 When you find the item you want, click "Restore" on the right side of the bar at the bottom of the Time Machine screen (circled below).

You can also go straight to Time Machine (click Time Machine in the Dock) and initiate a Spotlight search—type a word in the foreground window's search field.

To show a Quick Look of the item, make sure the item is highlighted, then tap the Spacebar.

To close the Quick Look preview, tap the Spacebar again, or click the Close button (**x**) in the top-left corner of the Quick Look window.

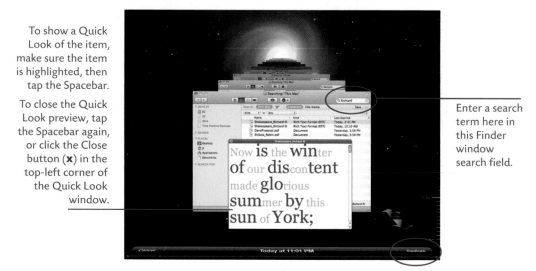

Enter a search term here in this Finder window search field.

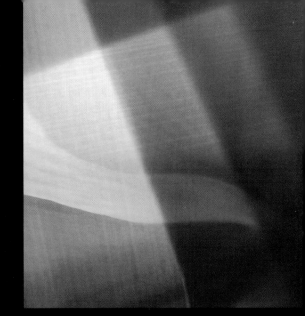

Tech Stuff

21

GOALS

Get Connected and Share Files

On a Mac, you have various ways to connect to the Internet. You might have a dial-up account that goes through your phone line, a cable modem, a DSL modem, a wireless connection, an Ethernet office connection that plugs into a broadband setup, or some other arrangement.

And you have various ways to connect your Macs together in a home or office. Once your computers are on a local network, you can transfer files between them and even access your own Mac from another computer.

The feature that most amazes me is screen sharing, where you can connect to someone else's computer and actually see her screen and use her computer!

How your Mac Connects to the Internet

When you first turned on your Mac and walked through the setup process, you probably filled in the information for your Internet connection. The Network preferences is where your Mac stored that information and where you can change it, adjust it, or troubleshoot it.

The Network preferences lists all of the ways that your Mac might be connected and displays the current status of each option. You can configure all interfaces for all your possible connections from this one window.

To open the Network preferences, go to the Apple menu and choose "System Preferences…." Single-click the "Network" icon.

When you first open the window, it probably looks something like the one below, showing you the status of any possible connections your Mac might have access to.

These are the available "network port configurations" on your Mac.

This pane shows you how you are connected to the Internet and to the other computers in your office.

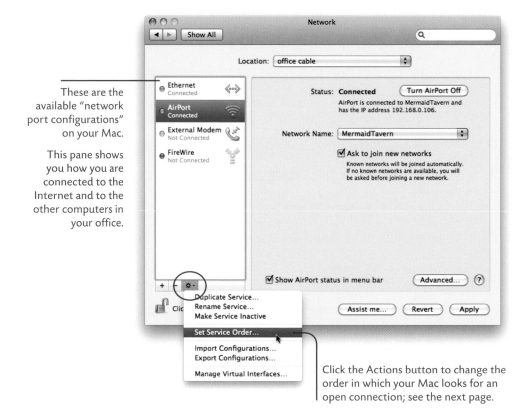

Click the Actions button to change the order in which your Mac looks for an open connection; see the next page.

Check the port configurations

You might have several options for connecting. For instance, your Mac might recognize a modem port, if you have one (whether or not you use it), and it might find a wireless card and an Ethernet port. Every possibility it finds is listed in the Network preferences, in that pane on the left side.

As you see on the opposite page, you can click the Actions button (shown circled) and choose to "Set Service Order...." This is the first place I go if there is a connection problem because the Mac goes down this list in order and chooses the first interface that works. **If you're having problems making a connection,** make sure your *preferred* connection is at the top of the list—just drag it to the top. Click OK, then click the "Apply" button to force the change.

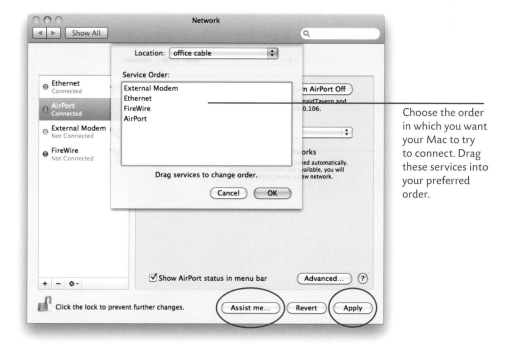

Choose the order in which you want your Mac to try to connect. Drag these services into your preferred order.

Establish a new connection

If you didn't set up your Internet connection when you first installed Snow Leopard, or turned on your brand-new Mac, you can always do it in this Network preferences pane. Just click "Assist me..." (circled above). A sheet drops down from the title bar (as shown on page 379). In that sheet, click the button labeled "Assistant...." It will walk you through the process.

Troubleshoot your Internet Connection

If your connection doesn't work when you first turn on your Mac, perhaps the information you entered in the setup process wasn't correct. Or if you changed Internet Service Providers or changed your connection process, you might need to change the information. Now, most of the information is supplied automatically, but if your provider says you need to change a setting, this is where you'll do it. There is also a little trick you can do here that sometimes kicks things into gear.

Network

1 From the Apple menu, choose "System Preferences…," then click the "Network" icon.

2 In the left-hand pane, you can instantly tell whether or not your Mac thinks your connection is working. (Sometimes the Mac swears it's working, but it isn't and you know it.) Choose the connection that you need to fix or change.

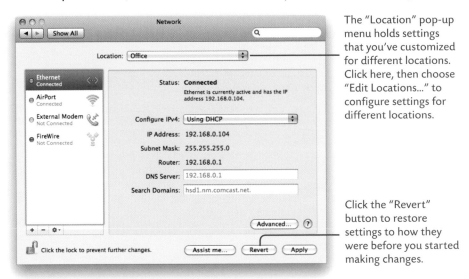

The "Location" pop-up menu holds settings that you've customized for different locations. Click here, then choose "Edit Locations…" to configure settings for different locations.

Click the "Revert" button to restore settings to how they were before you started making changes.

3 First, use the technique on the previous two pages to make sure the connection you want to choose is the first one in the list. Click "Apply." Wait a minute or two and see if your browser will connect to the Internet. If not . . .

4 This trick often works if all the settings are correct and there's no major problem with your modem or router (if you have one): Change any setting; for instance, if you see "Using DHCP," change it to "Manually." Then immediately switch it back. This makes the "Apply" button available. Click the Apply button. Sometimes all it needs is a kick in the pants to make it take effect.

5 If you think the settings need to change, do so here; you need to click the "Advanced..." button to get to the rest of the settings. If you're not sure what the appropriate settings are, you have two choices:

a Call your **ISP** (Internet Service Provider) and ask them what to enter in which panes. Your ISP is the company to whom you pay the monthly fee for your connection to the Internet. Although these windows look scary, there are only two or three settings you need. If you use cable or DSL with "DHCP," it probably sets it up for you automatically. Click "Apply."

To check, open Safari and see if it goes to a web page. If it does, you're done.

b Use the **Network Diagnostics tool,** as described in the following steps. This tool automatically appears when your connection goes down, but you can also call on it here whenever you need it.

6 Click the "Assist me..." button at the bottom of the Network pane. This drops down a sheet from the title bar, as shown below. For troubleshooting help, click the "Diagnostics..." button.

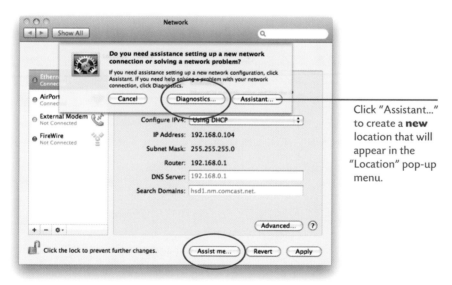

Click "Assistant..." to create a **new** location that will appear in the "Location" pop-up menu.

7 The diagnostics tool will check all the relevant settings on your Mac and ask you simple questions. If it can't fix the problem, it will at least pinpoint it so you can call your ISP with the specific issue.

Use the AirPort Utility

If your connection is through an AirPort wireless setup, use the AirPort Utility to see if you can figure out what's wrong. You'll find this tool in the Utilities folder, which is inside the Applications folder. Use the same trick as on the previous page—make a change that you don't need, immediately switch back to the one you know is correct, then click the "Apply" button.

Unplug everything and reboot

Your modem box, whether it's a dial-up, cable, or DSL, usually has a tiny **reset button.** It's often so tiny you need to poke it with a pin or paper clip. That can sometimes get things going again.

If not, do the unplug routine (I have to assume you've got all the wires in the right places). If you have a number of devices in your system, such as a switch, a router, and a modem box, unplug the items starting with the smallest one, the dumbest one. That would be the switch, if you have one. Next the router (which might be your AirPort Base Station). Last, unplug the modem itself. Let everything sit for at least a minute or two. It's not a bad idea to shut down your Mac as well.

Then plug everything back in again in the opposite order—start with the most important item first, the modem box. Let it get going and make sure all the lights are green. If the problem is in your modem box, call your provider.

Then plug in the router, if you're using one, and let it get going. Then the switch. Let everything get running, then turn your Mac back on. And pray.

Sometimes we go through all this and give up. Shortly thereafter it starts working again. Sheesh.

Talk to your ISP; check your cables

If everything seems okay on your end and you still can't get connected to the Internet, call a friend who uses the same ISP and see if she is connected (actually, we do this first). If her connection is down as well, then just let go and wait until they fix it. But if her connection is working, call the ISP. They can check your modem from their office and help pinpoint the cause. Also check your cables—they might have wiggled loose or one might have gone bad. They do that sometimes. If you're setting it up for the first time and using Ethernet cables, make sure they're the right kind; see page 384.

Troubleshoot your Mail Account

If you have problems getting your email, there are several things you can do. Make sure your Internet connection is working, of course (check by making sure your browser can get to the Internet.) Then check your account information in Mail (go to the Mail menu, choose "Preferences," and click the "Accounts" tab):

The **Description** is anything that will tell you which account this is.

The **Email Address** and **Full Name** describe your mail to those you send it to so they know who it's coming from.

- The **Incoming Mail Server** is information that you have to get from whoever hosts that particular email account. I have more than a dozen email accounts, not one of which is with my ISP. So I need to get the Incoming Mail Server of each of the hosts where I have the email *coming from.* Typically it's something like *mail.domain.com* or *pop.domain.com.* And as I mentioned in the Mail lesson, some providers don't allow you to get your email through a mail application like this; see page 82.

- Keep in mind that some ISPs have a different **User Name** and **Password** *for your account with them* than the user name and password to get your email. This is especially true if you've had the account for a long time. If your email account is not with your ISP, then of course the account information in your Mail window is definitely not the same as for your ISP. You might have to check their web site or call your email host and ask what to enter here.

—continued

■ The **Outgoing Mail Server (SMTP)** is always from your ISP, no matter where
your email account is located. Well, there are exceptions, like you *can* use
a me.com SMTP (if you have a MobileMe account), but in general, you are
always assured of being able to *send mail out* if you use your ISP's SMTP. If you
don't know what the SMTP is, call and ask them or check their web site—it
should be listed. For all 15 of my email accounts from a variety of servers, I use
the same Comcast SMTP because that's who connects me to the Internet.

To change your SMTP setting, click on the SMTP pop-up menu and select
"Edit Server List...." Click the **+** button to add an SMTP server. Double-click
the blue bar that appears to add the SMTP name. Make sure that is the *selected*
server (highlighted in blue), then click OK.

Some companies will not give you an SMTP address unless you pay an extra
fee. In this case, you cannot use the Mail application—you must go to the
company's web site and do all mail online.

■ If you have a POP email account set up, you can tell Mail to "Remove copy
from server after retrieving a message" (go to the Mail menu, choose
"Preferences...," click the "Accounts" button, then click the "Advanced" tab).
This prevents your POP server from running out of storage room over time.
However, sometimes it just doesn't work. If that happens, select the POP
Inbox in Mail's sidebar, then press Command I to open the "Account Info"
window. (The example at the bottom of the following page shows the Account
Info window, but with a MobileMe (IMAP) email account selected rather
than a POP account). With a POP account selected in Mail's sidebar, click the
"Messages on Server" tab to show the email messages that are on the POP mail
server. Select all (or some) of the messages shown in the window, then click
the "Remove from Server" button.

Reminder: where to get the information

Your email provider's web site should include the information for the *incoming* mail
server (also known as the POP address), user name, and password. Your ISP's web
site should provide the SMTP (*outgoing* mail server) address information.

If you have a **free webmail account** like Google, Yahoo, or Hotmail, you should be
able to set up Mail to check those mail accounts. If you have trouble setting up your
webmail account in Mac's Mail program, go to the service's web site and search for
webmail instructions. Or, go to Google and search for something like "Google POP
settings Mac," or "Yahoo SMTP settings Mac," etc.

Use the Mail Connection Doctor

If your account information is correct but email still isn't working, check this utility: In Mail, go to the Window menu and choose "Connection Doctor." You'll get the window shown below; it will automatically check your accounts. If it finds a problem, the dot is red; depending on the problem, you may be able to click the "Assist me…" button (page 379) to help pinpoint the issue further.

In this case, I had the wrong information in the Accounts pane.

Get Info About your Mail Accounts

Select a Mail account (a folder) in Mail's sidebar, then press Command I to open the Account Info window shown below. A MobileMe email account shows how much server storage space your different mail folders are using. The horizontal bar tells me that I have lots of available space for messages.

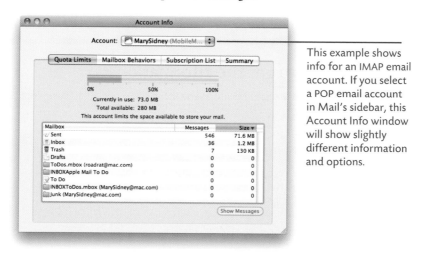

This example shows info for an IMAP email account. If you select a POP email account in Mail's sidebar, this Account Info window will show slightly different information and options.

Share Files on a Local Network

Sharing

File sharing on a local network is so great—as Apple says, your Mac just "discovers" other Macs. But it can't discover them unless the computers are connected in some way. So first, a wee bit about networking.

Simple networking

The Macs you want to share files between must be **networked** together—you must have some sort of cable connecting them to each other or both to the same printer, or AirPort cards installed so they can connect to each other wirelessly.

Networking can get very complex and specialized! I am only going to explain the simplest method to get a couple of Macs talking to each other.

Ethernet cables

You might have to buy Ethernet cables.

- If the cables are going from the computer into a hub, router, or switcher, or into a cable or DSL modem, you need **straight-through cables**—not *crossover* cables. Straight-through cables are the most common.

- If the cables go directly between two computers (or between any two Ethernet devices, like a Mac and a printer), you need **crossover cables** (see below).

To tell if an Ethernet cable is crossover or not, hold both ends up, facing the same direction, with the locking clips facing up. Look at the colored wires coming through the end.

- A straight-through cable has the colored wires in **exactly the same order.**
- A crossover cable does **not** have the colored wires in the same order.

Just two computers?

Two computers can be connected with one crossover Ethernet cable **or** a FireWire cable for easy and instant file sharing on two working Macs.

If you have one Mac that is having trouble and you want to copy files off of it onto a reliable machine, use a FireWire cable and Target Disk Mode, as explained on page 418. Target Disk Mode treats the target computer as an external hard disk, without having to get its operating system working.

What else you need

If you have a number of machines in your office, you will need something called an **Ethernet switch** that can connect all of your machines, including your modem. The switch will have a number of Ethernet ports; you connect each Mac *to that box* with straight (not crossover) Ethernet cables. (If you want to share printers, see pages 311–313; it's easy once you have your network working.)

If you have several computers in your office, a broadband connection, and all your Macs get on the Internet at the same time, you're probably using a **router**—you're already set up for networking. An AirPort base station can function as a router.

If the router doesn't have enough ports for the items in your office, buy the small **hub** or **switch** mentioned above and connect the router to it with an Ethernet cable.

Peer-to-peer network

This simple network in a small office is called a **peer-to-peer network,** where every computer is considered a "server," which is a computer that can "serve" files to others. This is different from a client-server network in a large corporation, where lots of computers connect to one huge, main server and everyone gets files from that main server, rather than from each other's computers.

Turn on Personal File Sharing

Now that your computers are connected, you need to tell them it's okay to share files. On each Mac, go to the Apple menu and choose "System Preferences…." Click the "Sharing" icon. Put a checkmark in "File Sharing."

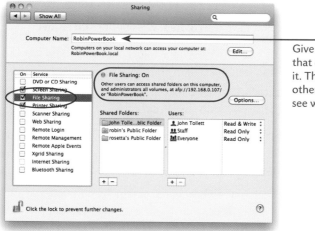

Give each Mac a name that clearly identifies it. This is the name that other computers will see when networking.

Connect to Another Mac

Once the Macs are connected in some way and you've turned on File Sharing in the Sharing preferences (as explained on the previous pages), you're ready to connect.

Make sure you are in the Finder (single-click any blank space on the Desktop). Then follow *either* Process **A** or **B**.

Process A, directly through the Finder window:

1 Open any Finder window. Click the Column View icon (circled below).

2 In the Sidebar, if your "SHARED" group is not visible, click its triangle to display the other computers on the network.

3 Single-click the name of the computer to which you want to connect.

Your connection status is shown here. Click "Connect As..." to connect as a registered user with more privileges.

You are automatically connected as a Guest. What you see in the window above is the Home folder and Public folder of a shared computer on the local network. As a Guest, you have access to the user-created folders. The default Mac-created folders are marked with red badges, and do not permit access. You can take copies of any folder in the Public folder, and you can select the "Public Folder" and put files into the shared computer's Drop Box.

4 To access the rest of this other computer, you need to know its name and password (the same name and password that the Admin uses to log in with). If you have them, click the "Connect As..." button and log in.

If there is more than one volume on that other computer, you can Command-click any of them that you want to access.

To keep straight which computer you're working on, or which computer you are viewing in a window, stay in Column View so you can see where a folder originates.

Process B, through the Go menu:

1 From the Go menu, choose "Connect to Server...." The window below appears.

If you connect to the same computer regularly, put it in the "Favorite Server" list (see page 389).

If you know the name of the Mac you want to connect to (as shown in the Sharing pane of the *other* Mac; see page 385), type it in the "Server Address" field, with ".local" after its name.

Or, what usually works more consistently, enter the afp:// number that you see circled on page 385.

2 Click the "Connect" button. You'll see this window:

To connect as a **Guest,** you don't need a name and password; see the previous page.

To connect as a **Registered User** so you will have access to the entire computer, you need to enter a name and password. **Important!** Even though this window shows up with *your* name in the field, it doesn't want *your* name and password! It's asking for the name (long or short) and password *of the computer you're trying to connect to!* Guess how long it took me to figure *that* out.

3 Enter the name and password of the other computer, then click "Connect."

—continued

4 The next window that appears lists the hard disk, the Home folder, any partitions or other hard disks attached to the other Mac, and any other volumes
   that are currently shared. Double-click the one you want to connect to.

   To have access to more than one of the partitions, hold down the Command key
   and click as many as you want to connect to, then let go of the Command key
   and click OK. You can also repeat this entire process if you decide later you
   need to connect to another volume.

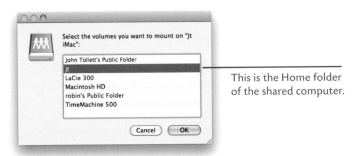

This is the Home folder
of the shared computer.

5 On the Desktop of the computer you're working on, you'll see a shared volume
   icon for the volume you're connected to, shown below-left. Double-click that
   icon to open a window to that drive, shown below-right.

A shared
volume icon
on your
Desktop.

It's not an easy task to keep track of which windows are on which machine since the
default folders (the folders that you *didn't* create) all have the same names! Don't
open any applications or documents from the window of the other Mac because you
will actually be working on the other machine at that point, which might affect the
person using it. It's best to drag the necessary documents to your own computer
before you open them.

Connect as a Guest

Follow Step 1 on page 387. When you get to the window shown in Step 2, click the "Guest" button. Then click "Connect."

The Mac opens the **Public folder** of the computer you are connecting to, shown below. The only things you will have access to on the other computer are the files that user has put in her Public folder for you. The only place you can move documents *to* on the connected Mac is the Drop Box, shown below.

Create Favorite Servers

In the "Connect to Server" window (choose it from the Go menu at the Finder), type the name of the computer you want to connect to. Click the **+** button to add that computer (server) to your favorites in the list below. Now you can just double-click a server name to connect to it.

Bonjour–Share Files Locally

Once your Mac is on a network of computers running OS X, version 10.2 or later, you can send files back and forth to everyone through Bonjour, which looks and acts just like iChat. In fact, it's a part of iChat.

Bonjour is very similar to iChat. But instead of using it to instant message someone over the Internet, it automatically detects other iChat-enabled computers on your local network and lets you communicate or share files with others on the network.

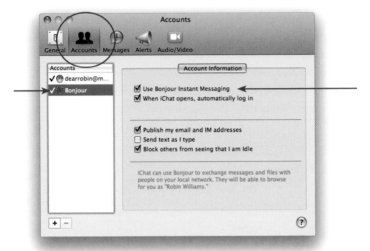

The iChat icon should be in your Dock; if not, it's in your Applications folder. See Lesson 9 for details about iChat and Bonjour.

If you didn't **turn on Bonjour** the first time you opened iChat, you can do it in the iChat preferences, in the Accounts pane:

But you can also turn it on with this shortcut:

1   Open iChat.

2   From the Window menu, choose "Bonjour List."
    If you're not already logged in, it will ask if you want to start it up.

3   Click "Login."

Now the Bonjour List window is open, as shown on the next page.

Send a file to someone on the network

This is so easy it will boggle your mind.

1   First open the Bonjour window, if it isn't already: Open iChat, then from the Window menu, choose "Bonjour List." Bonjour must be open on both computers.

2   Now drag a file and drop it on someone's name in that list. That person will get a message that she has an incoming file.

3   She clicks once on that message and has a choice to "Decline," in which case the message will disappear, or "Save File," which downloads the file to her Downloads folder.

Here's another way to send a file (this also works in iChat). Just open a chat with someone in either Bonjour or your Buddy List (double-click a *name*, not a phone or camera icon, to open a text chat). Drop a file in the text field and hit Return.

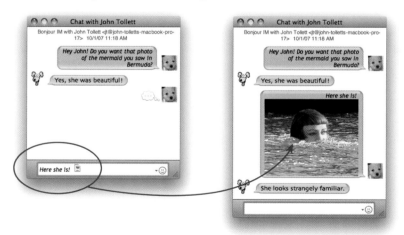

Even more amazing is the screen sharing feature accessed through iChat and Bonjour, explained on the following pages.

> **TIP** —— If you need to share files on a local network regularly, you can drag a folder from another computer and put it on your computer and even in your Sidebar. Then you can move and save files directly into that folder on the other computer. You don't even have to go through the connection process—as soon as you put something in that folder, it acts as an alias and makes the connection.

Screen Sharing

Screen Sharing enables you to share not only your screen but your entire computer either through your Finder on the local network, or through iChat with a buddy anywhere in the world. Through iChat, you can choose to either share your own screen (and computer) or share the buddy's screen (and computer).

This is great for anyone who has experienced the frustration of trying to give Mac support and instruction over the phone or through email. Now you can just activate Screen Sharing and watch as you give instructions. Or control the buddy's computer while she watches and listens. When Screen Sharing is activated through iChat, it automatically starts an audio chat so you can discuss whatever matter is at hand.

> You can screen share over a *local* network using Bonjour or the Go menu; if the other user is running 10.4 Tiger, tell him to go to his Sharing preferences and turn on "Apple Remote Desktop."

> You can use Screen Sharing over the *Internet* through iChat; both computers need to be running Mac OS 10.5 Leopard or later.

Set up screen sharing

Before you start Screen Sharing, make sure both computers have "Screen Sharing" selected in the Sharing pane of System Preferences:

1   From the Apple menu, choose "Preferences...." Click the "Sharing" icon.

2   Put a checkmark in the option called "Screen Sharing"; see the callout on the opposite page.

3   If you have other users on the network, you can choose to allow only certain ones: Check the button, "Only these users," then click the **+** button to add the ones you want.

4   Close the preferences and carry on.

Your computer's vnc number (circled) can be helpful. See the following page.

Check the network for local screen sharing options

Below is the simplest and fastest way to connect to another monitor in your home/ office to screen share and access the computer.

1 In your Sharing group, select another computer running Leopard on the network.

2 You will probably see a "Share Screen…" button, as shown here. Click it, and a Finder window opens displaying the other computer. Amazing.

3 To stop screen sharing, close the window that the other computer appears in.

Now, if you don't see the "Screen Sharing…" button, as shown above, don't despair. The process on the following page works very well.

Screen Share locally through the Go menu

This method is a quick and easy way to get to another user's screen who is on the same network. You can also use Bonjour, which looks a little different, as explained on the following pages. Using Bonjour, you'll be able to talk to each other as well.

1 First make sure you get the vnc address from the computer you want to connect to. This address appears in the Sharing preferences pane when you turn on Screen Sharing—you can see it circled on the previous page.

2 In the Finder, go to the Go menu and choose "Connect to Server...." You'll get the window shown below.

3 Type in the vnc address as shown below. Click the "Connect" button.

4 A window will appear on your Mac and inside that window is the other person's entire computer! You can open his iTunes and play a song for him, or open Sticky notes and leave a message. It's freaky.

5 **To turn off screen sharing,** close the window of the other computer.

If you need to go to this computer often, click the **+** button to make the address a favorite. It will appear in this pane under "Favorite Servers" whenever you open this window.

Screen Share globally through Bonjour and iChat

Of course, the buddy whose screen you want to share must have first turned on
Screen Sharing, as explained on the previous pages.

1   **To screen share through iChat,** open either your Buddy List to screen share
    with someone over the Internet, or open your Bonjour List to screen share
    with someone on your local network.

2   You can tell which buddies have turned on Screen Sharing: When you select
    a name in the list, the Screen Sharing button at the bottom of the Buddy List
    or Bonjour List is black (instead of gray) for those who have turned it on.

 This is the Screen Sharing button.

3   Click a buddy's name. Click that Screen Sharing button and choose
    "Share My Screen…" or "Share (Buddy Name's) Screen…."

In this example, the user
chooses to share his own screen
with his buddy instead of
sharing his buddy's screen.

4   When you receive and accept the invitation to share someone's screen, the
    other (remote) screen appears full-size on your screen, while your own
    Desktop appears as a miniature screen (see the next page). When you mouse
    over the miniature screen, a "Switch to My Computer" message pops up.

    To enlarge your own Desktop to full-size and miniaturize the remote screen,
    click anywhere on the miniature screen. Meanwhile, the buddy who initiated
    Screen Sharing doesn't see any change on his own screen, even though you
    can now control his computer, grab files, open applications, or do anything
    he can do.

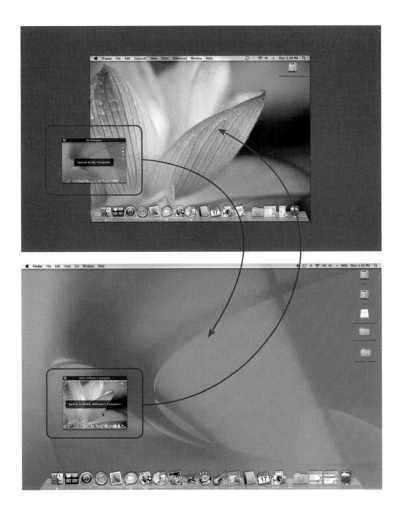

To copy files between computers: Simply drag a file from one screen to the other. If the file you want is on the miniature screen, just click the miniature screen and it will become large enough to find the file you need. Drag it to the [now] miniature other screen; as you drag, hover over the miniature screen for a few seconds until it enlarges to full-size, then drop the file wherever you want to place it.

To end a Screen Sharing session: Click the circle-**x** in the top-left corner of the miniaturized screen. **Or** go to the iChat icon in the menu bar and choose "End Screen Sharing."

Disconnect

Disconnect from any connected servers in the same way you disconnect from any other hard disk.

- ■ Click the Eject symbol next to the server name in the Sidebar.

- ■ **Or** if the server is visible on the Desktop, drag its icon to the Trash.

- ■ **Or** select the server icon. Go to the File menu and choose "Eject."

- ■ **Or** select the server icon and press Command E for Eject.

- ■ **Or** Control-click a server icon to get the contextual menu; choose "Eject *'disk'.*"

To hide or show the servers on the Desktop:

1   In the Finder, go to the Finder menu and choose "Preferences...."

2   Click the "General" tab, if it isn't already selected.

3   Check or uncheck the box to show "Connected servers." When it's unchecked, you won't see the server icons on the Desktop, but they will all be accessible in the Sidebar.

4   However, you can go to the Sidebar pane in those same preferences, (click the "Sidebar" icon in the toolbar) and choose to take server icons out of the Sidebar and leave them on the Desktop.

22

GOALS

Basic Troubleshooting

All computers, even Macs, act funny at times. Fortunately, it's often something that you can fix yourself. Try these troubleshooting techniques before you call tech support. Even if you're not having a computer problem at the moment, check out these tips so you'll know what to do if your Mac someday needs a hug.

Robin and John's Personal Troubleshooting

These are the steps we follow to fix troubles on our Macs. We keep going down the list until the problem is fixed (but also check this chapter for other problem-solving tips):

> Make sure we've got plenty of free space on the hard disk, at least a gigabyte of free space. If not, clear up space and restart.
>
> We quit and then restart the application that's causing trouble. If it's really having trouble, we might have to force quit the app (see page 400) and then relaunch it.
>
> We relaunch the Finder (see page 401) if it's a problem on the Desktop.
>
> We restart the computer (or we Shut Down for a more serious but still quick test, then reboot). See page 401.
>
> Then we repair permissions (see page 404) and see if that fixed things.
>
> We do a Safe Boot (see page 403) and restart and see if that fixed it.
>
> Then we throw away the preferences for the application that's giving us trouble (see page 402) and restart the computer.

In several years and on a number of Macs, we haven't had any issues that could not be resolved with the above steps. If you hear your hard disk make noise, however, stop everything and take it to the repair shop!

Force Quit an Application

Sometimes just one application has trouble and you need to force it to quit. There are two ways to **force quit** any application. This doesn't affect any other application or the system. If an application isn't responding to anything you ask it to do, if it's hung up and the wheel keeps spinning, or it won't let you quit, then force quit the app. After you've force quit an application, try restarting it. It should be fine.

- Hold down the Option key and **press** *(don't click)* on the application's icon in the Dock. A menu pops up with a choice to "Force Quit." Choose it.

- **Or** press Command Option Esc. The window called "Force Quit Applications" appears. From this window, select the application you want to force quit (if it isn't already selected), then click the "Force Quit" button.

Relaunch the Finder

You can't force quit the Finder, but you can **relaunch** it, which only takes a minute. If things are acting a little squirrely, try this. It doesn't hurt anything.

- Hold down the Option key and **press** *(don't click)* on the Finder icon in the Dock. A menu pops up with a choice to "Relaunch."

- **Or** press Command Option Escape (as explained on the opposite page) to open the "Force Quit Applications" window. Select the Finder in the list, and the "Force Quite" button changes to "Relaunch." Click it.

Restart

It's amazing what a simple **restart** will fix. Especially if you rarely turn off your Mac (like me), sometimes little things may start acting a bit quirky. Perhaps your Mac can't find the printer you've been using for months, or icons for new files don't appear. For little unexplainable things, restart.

- **To Restart,** go to the Apple menu and choose "Restart...."
- On most laptops, **press the Power button for one second** and you'll get a little message with a button to restart.

If you **can't restart,** then Shut Down; see below.

Shut Down

Sometimes shutting down fixes small problems that a restart doesn't fix. This is especially useful when you're having connection problems.

- **To Shut Down,** go to the Apple menu and choose "Shut Down...."
- Sometimes things are so bad you can't even get to the Apple menu. In that case, **hold down the Power button** (the one you push to turn on your Mac) for at least five seconds. This forces it to shut down.

Delete the Application Preference File

Another tip to troubleshoot an application that isn't acting right is to delete that application's **preference file.** This is perfectly safe—when the application opens up again, it will recreate a new preference file from scratch. You will lose any preferences you had personally changed in the application, but it can be worth it because this works pretty well to solve inexplicable annoyances in applications.

1 Quit the application.

2 Open a Finder window and view it by columns, as shown below.

3 Single-click your Home icon in the Sidebar.

4 In the column that appears to the right, single-click the "Library" folder.

5 In the next column to the right, single-click the "Preferences" folder.

6 In the next column to the right, find the ".plist" file for an application that's giving you trouble. That is the preferences file. Some vendors include their own preference files as well that might be named something else, as shown below.

7 Drag the application's preference file to the Trash. Empty the Trash.

8 Restart the application and hope it works better.

The preferences for Apple applications have an extension of .plist.

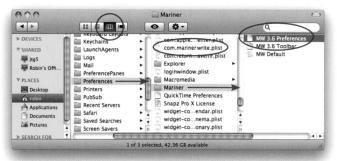

The preferences for non-Apple applications may also have their own names for their preferences. These are the prefs for the Mariner Write word processor.

Safe Boot

This is one of my favorite troubleshooting techniques. During a safe boot the Mac actually goes in and fixes little things, such as minor file corruptions that build up over time, eventually causing problems. If you've ever used the terminal commands to do the fsck technique, you'll be pleased to know the safe boot does the same thing. This is safe and easy and comfortable and fixes lots of mysterious problems.

1   Go to the Apple menu and choose to "Restart…." If you're having such problems that you can't even get to the Apple menu, hold down the Power key for five seconds to shut down the machine. Then push the Power button again to restart.

2   Immediately upon hearing the startup sound, hold down the Shift key and keep it held down. This might take a while, like five minutes or even more. Be patient. Keep that Shift key down. You'll eventually get to to a log in screen that says, in red, "Safe Boot." If not, start over—perhaps you didn't get the Shift key down in time.

3   When you get to the Desktop or to the log in screen, restart immediately (either click the restart button if you see one, or go to the Apple menu and "Restart"). Because a safe boot turns off everything that's not essential to start the operating system, the Mac needs to restart to put everything back and turn everything on. See if things work a little better now.

Repair Permissions

Due to occasional file corruption issues, something called "permissions" can go bad
and cause trouble. Repairing the permissions can solve many mysterious things.

Disk Utility.app

1   Open Disk Utility: Go to the Applications menu and open the Utilities folder.
    In the Utilities folder, find the Disk Utility and open it. You'll see this:

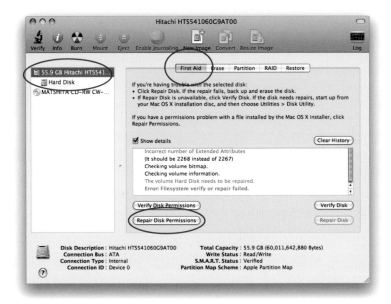

2   Select the hard disk in the left pane. Make sure the "First Aid" tab is selected.

3   Click the button to "Repair Disk Permissions."

    Depending on how much stuff you have on your hard disk, this can take up
    to 20 minutes or so. If the Mac finds any permissions that need to be repaired,
    it will repair them.

    If it finds things it can't repair, as you see above, then you need to go
    to the next step and verify and repair the *disk*. See the following page.

Verify and Repair Disk

First, go through the steps on the previous page to repair permissions, just to clear up any little issues. Don't quit the Disk Utility yet.

If you think the disk might need to be repaired, or if you just want to check to see if the disk has a problem, click the button in Disk Utility (shown on the previous page) to "Verify Disk." This will check the disk to see if it really does have a problem that needs to be repaired.

If the disk needs to be repaired, restart your computer using the original OS X install disk, because *Disk Utility can't repair the same disk it's running on.* If you have an external drive that has been set up as a "Boot" drive (with an operating system on it), you can also use that to start up your computer.

So get the original install disk that came with your Mac. It's a CD or DVD. Then:

1 Insert the original install or upgrade disk. Double-click the "Install" icon as if you were going to install the system again.

2 At the Welcome window, DO NOT INSTALL! Go to the Utilities menu at the top of the screen. Choose "Disk Utility...."

3 You get the window shown on the previous page. *Now* you can click the button to "Repair Disk." Let it run through its process. It might take up to a half hour or more. Be patient.

4 When it's done, it will probably tell you it has repaired the disk. If it can't, it must be a serious problem and you need to take it to a repair shop.

5 Quit Disk Utility and quit the installer.

6 It might ask you to choose a startup disk because if you don't, when you restart your Mac it will boot up from the CD again. If it asks, you will see the disk options; single-click your hard disk, then click the "Restart..." button.

Or restart without choosing a disk and hold the mouse button down until it has restarted. Holding the mouse button down forces the CD to eject so it can't be used to boot the machine. (If you're on a laptop, hold down the bar under the trackpad.)

Check for Software Updates

Make sure you are using the latest versions of all your software. For your Mac OS software, use the Software Update preferences to see if everything is up to date (open it in the System Preferences, as described on the previous pages). It's especially important to check for updated application software when you update your operating system, like when moving from any other OS to Snow Leopard.

TIP —— If your connection to the Internet is a dial-up through a telephone modem, do *not* check the boxes to "Check for updates: Daily/Weekly/Monthly" and "Download important updates automatically" because it will tie up your phone line for hours. Instead, check for updates manually: Click the "Check Now" button.

Create Another User and Test

If you install new software and it just won't work right, or perhaps it won't even open, one good troubleshooting technique is to create another user (see Lesson 18) and install the software in that user's Home folder. See if it works. If it *doesn't* work for the new user, the software itself has a problem—check the package it came in or with the vendor you bought it from to make sure it is the correct version for your operating system.

If the software does work for the other user, that indicates there is something in your system that is conflicting. Try throwing away the preferences, as explained on page 402. If it still doesn't work, you may need to contact the vendor to find out what may be conflicting with that particular software.

If you Forgot your Password

If you forgot the password you entered when you first set up your new Mac or installed your new system (called the Admin password), you'll have to use the original install CD to fix the problem. (I think someone told you that you should have written down your password.)

If you have created more than one user for your Mac, you can use these steps to change the password of any user.

1 Get the original CD. Put it in and double-click the "Install" button. Follow the directions to restart. No, you are not really going to re-install the entire system.

2 All you need to do is wait until the Welcome screen appears. Then go to the Utilities menu at the top of the screen and choose "Reset Password…."

3 Enter your new password—twice. And add a hint. And write that password down where you can find it again. Click OK.

4 Quit the installer from the Installer menu. Your Mac will restart (it might ask you to choose a startup disk—choose your hard disk).

If you did not enter a password when you first set up your Mac, then you can leave the password field empty and just hit the blue "OK" or "Continue" button and it will work just fine (although it's not secure at all). The problem with not having any password is that you will probably forget there is no password and so when it asks you for one, you'll spend hours trying all sorts of possibilities that don't work. Guess how I know this.

Report Crashes

Often when an application crashes, an alert box appears and asks if you want to send a report to Apple. Now, Apple is not going to write you back—this is just an anonymous report you send in so Apple can figure out if there are common issues among many users, enough to warrant looking into. It's good to go ahead and send in the report.

Use Target Disk Mode

It's not unusual to need to move lots of files from one computer to another. If both computers are working fine and you just need to share files, there are lots of ways to do it. Please see Lesson 21, and check the index for "sharing files."

But sometimes one computer is just about defunct or maybe won't wake from sleep and you've got to get the files off quickly. Use **FireWire Target Disk Mode.** You'll need a FireWire cable that can connect to both Macs. A FireWire cable with 6-pin connectors on both ends will probably fit both computers, but check your ports before you buy.

- Unplug all FireWire devices from both computers that you are going to connect to each other.
- If FileVault is enabled on the computer you want to take files from, turn it off (if you can).
- If either machine is a laptop, it's best to plug in its power source.
- The machine you are going to transfer files **to** is the **host** computer. The machine you are going to take files **from** is the **target** computer.

In this process, the *target* computer will appear as a hard disk icon on the Desktop of the *host* computer and you can copy files to and from it.

1   Turn off the *target* computer (the one that's probably going bad). The *host* computer can stay turned on.

2   Connect the two computers with the FireWire cable.

This is the FireWire symbol.

3   Turn on the *target* computer and immediately hold down the T key and keep it down. Keep it held down until you see a FireWire symbol (shown to the left) moving about its screen.

4   On the *host* computer, you will see a hard disk icon representing the *target* computer. You can copy files from the *target* computer and put files onto it.

    If you don't see the *target* computer's hard disk on the host screen, make sure all the cables are securely attached and reboot the *host* computer.

5   When you're finished copying files, eject the *target* hard disk icon from the *host* computer—drag it to the Trash, or select it and choose "Eject" from the File menu.

6   Press and hold the *target* computer's power button until it turns itself off.

7   Unplug the FireWire cable.

Force a CD or DVD to Eject

If a CD or DVD is stuck in the drive and won't come out, this trick almost always works:

1 First make sure you've unmounted the disc: Click the eject icon on the screen, or drag the CD icon to the trash, or Control-click the CD icon and choose "Eject disc."

   But you're probably reading this page because you already did that and there is no icon on the screen but it won't come out. So . . .

2 Restart your Mac. As soon as you hear the restart tone, hold the mouse button down. Hold it down until the disc pops out.

   On a laptop, press the bar beneath the trackpad instead of the mouse (unless you have a mouse attached to your laptop).

If that doesn't work, see if there is a tiny hole next to the CD/DVD drive slot. Not all Macs have a tiny hole here. But if you see one, that hole is specially made for a paper clip (not the kind with the plastic coating). Unfold a metal paper clip and gently but firmly press it into the hole to snap open the mechanism.

One thing that can cause a huge problem in a CD/DVD player is a disc with a paper label glued to the top. If the tiniest little edge peels up, it can get stuck in the drive and ruin not only the disc but the drive itself. So don't buy those CD labels that you can print yourself, and don't put any disc with a paper label into your Mac!

One last warning: Never put one of the mini-discs into a slot-loading optical drive! If your computer has a tray-loading optical drive, you should be able to put a mini-disc in it and eject without a problem. However, the safest thing to do is just use standard discs.

23

GOALS

Learn your
security options

Use passwords
to log on to your Mac

Require a password
to wake computer
and unlock preferences

Securely empty the Trash

Protect information
using Keychain Access

Use FileVault
to secure data

Secure your Mac and its Files

In these days of identity theft and with so much of our personal and financial data being stored on our computers, it's important to take some precautions to make it more difficult for unauthorized trouble-makers to gain access to our Macs.

The tips in this lesson will make your files more secure and you'll discover some useful tricks that help insure your privacy, such as password information, Keychain Access, and securely emptying your Trash.

Know your Security Options

There are a number of **security features** on your Mac. Apple has installed lots of security stuff like Kerberos, Secure Shell, Wired Equivalent Privacy data encryption, Virtual Private Network, firewalls, and other features. It doesn't matter to most of us what those are—they work behind the scenes. Your Software Update software (found in System Preferences) can automatically update security features through the Internet as Apple releases them.

The above features work without you having to do anything. The features that require your participation are explained on the following pages:

- There are a number of **password**-protect options on your Mac that make it difficult to gain casual access.

- You might need security from humans who walk past your desk when you're not there. Your Mac has a number of **low-level security features** to protect your information from the curious. These are good for laptops as well.

- **Keychain Access** stores many of your passwords in locked "keychains." This includes passwords to your MobileMe account, servers, eBay account, PayPal, and more. Keychain Access also lets you store passwords and codes for other things, such as credit card numbers you might like to use while shopping online. Keychain Access does double-duty—it makes things easier for you and harder for thieves. Please see pages 420–421 for details.

- If you have highly personal or valuable stuff on your Mac, you can use **FileVault** for maximum security. If you have a laptop, this is especially important to prevent thieves from accessing your data.

- And don't forget about the feature to **Secure Empty Trash.** This deletes files from your Trash in such a way that no one can retrieve them again. See page 419.

Passwords on your Mac

You have several different passwords on your Macintosh.

■ **Administrator password:** When you first turn on your Mac, you are asked to create a password. Write this down in a safe place! You will need this password whenever you install new software or when you make certain system-wide changes.

You can choose *not* to have a password. Your Mac will still *ask* you to enter a password, however—if you never created one, just leave the password field blank, and click the OK or "Continue" button. But keep in mind that it's not very safe (from a security perspective) to neglect this password.

If you forget your Admin password, you will need to reset it:

1 Insert the original Mac OS X installer CD.

2 Double-click the "Installer" icon to start the process of reinstalling. You are not really going to reinstall!

3 When you get to the Install screen, go to the Utilities menu. Choose "Reset Password...."

4 Enter your new password. Write it down in a safe place!

5 Quit the Installer from the Installer menu.

■ **Login password:** If you have set up multiple users on one Mac, each user has her own password to log in. *An Admin password is also the login password for that Admin user.* By default, your Mac is set to auto-login the Admin so you don't need your password at startup, but you can turn this off to make the computer less accessible (see Lesson 18 for details about multiple users and log in).

—continued

If a standard user forgets his password, the Administrator (or anyone who knows the Admin password) can reset the user password in the Accounts preferences.

- **Keychain Access password:** This is the same as the login password, whether you are a standard user or the Admin (you can change it to create a special keychain password). Keychain Access is the application on your Mac that keeps track of a variety of passwords (and other info, if you choose) for you. If you can remember your login password, then Keychain Access can show you the rest of your passwords. See pages 420–421.

- **Master password:** An Administrator can set up a computer-wide password in case he forgets the login password. Master passwords are usually used in conjunction with FileVault; see pages 422–423. The Admin's Master password can override a standard user's FileVault password.

What to do if you forget the Master password? Well, you can scream. It won't help, but you can scream.

Password tips

- A password should be difficult for others to guess, but easy for you to remember.

- Don't use a word that can be found in a dictionary. Some hackers use software that tries every word in the dictionary in a matter of minutes.

- Combine caps and lowercase and numbers.

- Most passwords are case-specific, meaning a lowercase "r" is completely different from an uppercase "R." Take advantage of this and put capital letters where someone wouldn't expect them.

Security System Preferences

Apple makes it easy for you to turn on a number of the low-level security features in one place, the Security system preferences.

1 Go to the Apple menu and choose "System Preferences…."

2 Click the "Security" icon.

3 Click the "General" tab, as shown below.

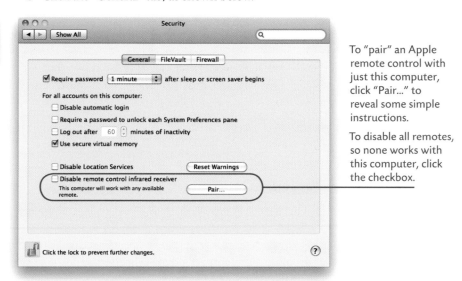

To "pair" an Apple remote control with just this computer, click "Pair…" to reveal some simple instructions.

To disable all remotes, so none works with this computer, click the checkbox.

Require password __ after sleep or screen saver begins: See page 418.

Disable automatic login: See page 417.

Require a password to unlock each System Preferences pane: This would prevent any user from changing any of the preferences without a password.

Log out after __ minutes of inactivity: Self-explanatory. Combine this with "Disable automatic login," so when the Mac logs you out after this amount of time, no one can get in without a password.

Use secure virtual memory: In the Mac's process of swapping data between RAM (random access memory) and virtual memory, it's possible that sensitive information that you assumed was deleted from RAM was actually written to the hard disk through virtual memory. Using secure virtual memory ensures that the sections of the hard disk that were used in the memory-swap process get overwritten, thus protecting your privacy. This is turned on by default.

The **Firewall** pane of the Security preferences is not something you will mess with very often, if at all. The most important thing to understand is that as you use Sharing features (turned on and off in the Sharing preferences), the Mac lets down the firewall (a protective barrier) for the features you have turned on so others can

access your machine to share. This means you are at a little more risk than if that feature was not turned on. So if you're not using a sharing feature, turn it off so the firewall goes back up.

To disable various sharing features (Screen Sharing, File Sharing, Bluetooth Sharing, etc.), go to the Sharing preferences pane and uncheck them.

Click "Stop" button (shown above) to toggle between "Stop" (Off) and "Start" (On). When the Firewall is "On," your Mac determines which programs are allowed incoming connections based on your "Sharing" preferences. If you want to override any of those settings and allow or block specific applications or services, click the "Advanced…" button in the lower-right corner. A dialog sheet drops down, as shown below. To add items to the list, click the Add (**+**) button. To block a service or application, select it, then click the (**–**) button.

After you've customized your settings, click "OK."

This option permits "trusted" sites to make an incoming connection and provide services accessed from the Internet. "Trusted" sites have been verified as authentic and secure.

This option provides an extra level of security and privacy.

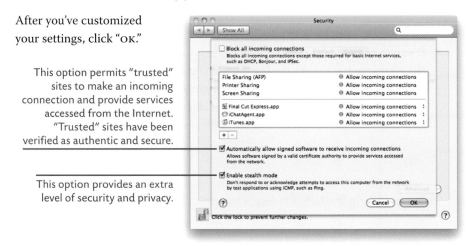

Low-Level Security Features

Here are some simple and quick features to take advantage of if you have any worry at all about casual access to your computer.

Auto login

■ **Turn off auto-login:** Auto-login lets your Mac start up without a password —it automatically logs in the person who has "auto-login" turned on in the Accounts preferences "Login Options."

So turn off auto-login and then be sure to **log out** before you leave your computer for a while. This ensures that people walking by will need a password to log in to your account, even if they restart your Mac. Laptops should always require a login password (because they're too easy to steal).

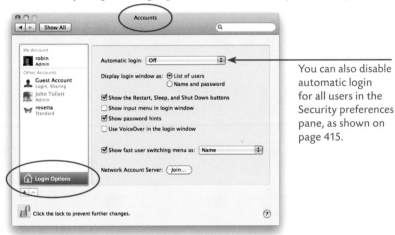

You can also disable automatic login for all users in the Security preferences pane, as shown on page 415.

■ **If you don't want to turn off auto-login,** you might want to at least take the extra step to *un*check the box to "Show the Restart, Sleep, and Shut Down buttons." Because if auto-login is on and you log out and leave your Mac, the login screen appears and you think you're safe. But someone can just click the Restart or Shut Down button and the computer starts back up again and auto-matically logs in to your account. By unchecking this box, no one can restart your computer so easily.

This precaution isn't going to help much if your laptop is stolen because someone can just reboot the computer.

—continued

■ Mac OS X lets you have multiple users on one computer, and each user has a separate, private Home area (see Lesson 18 for details). Even if you are the only one using this Mac, you can **create another user,** a standard user who has no administrative privileges, and regularly log in as the standard user. This is a simple step that just makes it one level more difficult for someone to get into your main account and make system-wide changes. It won't protect any data that you create as that user, but it will make it more difficult to get into your Mac as the Administrator with privileges.

Require a password to wake your Mac

To prevent access to anyone walking by your computer, you can use these simple, yet effective, features. Open the System Preferences from the Apple menu, and then:

1   Use the "Security" preferences to **require a password to wake up the Mac** from sleep or from the screen saver. You can add a delay of five seconds to four hours before the password is required.

2   Go to the "Desktop & Screen Saver" preferences to choose a screen saver and tell it when to start.

3   Then go to the "Energy Saver" preferences to tell your Mac to put either the computer and/or the display (the screen) to sleep after a certain amount of time. Now when the screen saver comes on or your Mac goes to sleep, you'll have to enter your password to get back in to it.

An alternative technique is to set up your Mac so you can **lock it with a mouse click,** not just when the screen saver comes on or when it goes to sleep.

1   Open Keychain Access (first open the Applications folder, then open the Utilities folder; Keychain Access is in the Utilities folder).

2   From the Keychain Access menu in the menu bar across the top of the screen, choose "Preferences...."

3   Check the box to "Show Status in Menu Bar." A padlock icon appears on the right side of your menu bar, as shown on the next page.

4   Quit Keychain Access.

5   Click the padlock icon that now appears in your menu bar to get the menu shown to the right.

6   Choose "Lock Screen." The screen saver will start and no one can access your Mac unless they know your login password.

Higher-Level Security Features

■ **Secure Empty Trash:** You might think that after you empty the Trash, it's gone. But it's possible to recover many deleted files using special data-recovery software. If you are selling or giving away your Mac, you might want to make sure no one can recover your old, trashed files. To completely overwrite files so no one can ever get to them, go to the Finder menu and choose **Secure Empty Trash.** This might take several minutes, depending on how much stuff you've thrown away since you last emptied the Trash!

■ **Encrypt a disk image:** Using the Disk Utility, you can make a password-protected "disk image" of a hard disk, a folder, a CD or a DVD (not an individual file, unless it's in a folder). The disk image can then be stored or transferred via email or any other method without any security concerns. A disk image acts just like any other hard disk—you can move files in it, copy files to it, and delete files from it.

To create a disk image:

1   Open Disk Utility (it's in the Utilities folder, which is inside the Applications folder).

2   From the File menu, select "New," then select "New Disk Image from Folder."

3   Navigate to the folder you want to make a disk image of.

   A prompt lets you choose a name and location for your disk image.

   You also have the options of compressing the data (for smaller file sizes) and adding password protection. The 128-bit encryption is extremely secure; the 256-bit encryption is even more secure, but takes longer to create.

4   Click Save. If you chose one of the encryption options, a password pop-up lets you add a password.

After the disc image is created, no one will be able to open it without the password. Apple estimates that it would take many lifetimes for a password-guessing computer to crack the 128-bit encryption—and even longer to crack the 256-bit encryption.

Use Keychain Access for Protection

Keychain Access provides a secure place to store information that can only be accessed with a user name and password. Keychain automatically and safely stores the passwords you create on your Mac, like those for web sites you go to, servers you connect to, email accounts, etc. Every time you see one of those messages that asks if you want your Mac to remember this password in your keychain, it gets stored here in Keychain Access.

You can also add your own secure collections of Keychains to store your credit card numbers, PINs, bank card information, private notes, passwords, and other things that you want easy access to, but you want them to be secure. They won't be entered automatically anywhere—it's just a safer place to store them than on a sticky note.

Keychain Access sets up your initial Keychain file, the one based on your user name and password, as the default Keychain. This default Keychain automatically opens when you log in. To make other Keychains more secure, such as your list of credit card numbers or banking passwords, be sure to make *new* Keychain files for them instead of *adding* them to your default file.

To open Keychain Access, first open your Applications window. Inside you'll find the Utilities folder. Keychain Access is inside the Utilities folder.

Click this button to show the list of Keychains, now showing at the top of the sidebar. Any new keychain you create will appear in that area.

To access any password Keychain has been storing for you:

1 Find the item in the list of "Passwords," circled on the opposite page.

2 Double-click that item in the list displayed in the large pane on the right side of the window. You will be asked for your Keychain password, which is the same as your login password. If you are the only user of the Mac, it's the password you assigned yourself when you first set up your Mac, the Admin password. A window like the one below appears.

3 Click in the box to "Show password." Your password appears!

You can create a new Keychain: Go to the File menu and choose "New Keychain...." Give it a descriptive name *and a password you will remember.* This Keychain will appear in the top portion of the sidebar, shown on the opposite page. You will need to know that Keychain's password if you want to access things in it!

With that Keychain selected, go back to the File menu and choose to create a new password item or a new secure note to store in it.

Oh, Keychain is a very powerful and fairly complex application! To use it wisely and well, please study the Keychain Help files.

Consider FileVault for Heavy-Duty Protection

FileVault encrypts, or scrambles, the data in your Home folder so unauthorized people or software cannot read it. While you are working on your Mac with FileVault turned on, you won't notice anything. But everything in your Home folder will be safely protected from prying eyes, both in your office and from remote connections. **Don't ever forget the Master password,** though, or you will never again see anything in your Home folder!

To turn on FileVault:

1 Before you begin, make sure you have the Admin name and password, as well as the password for this user (if it's separate from the Admin user).

2 Also before you begin, make sure all other users are logged out.

3 Check to make sure you have enough hard disk space available for the process—you'll need as much free hard disk space as there is data in your Home folder.

   a To check the file size of your Home folder, single-click the Home icon in the Sidebar of any Finder window.

   b Press Command Option I to display the Info window.

   c Check the "Size" of the Home folder (it may take a while to calculate).

   d Now check to see how much free hard disk space you have: Single-click the hard disk icon in the Sidebar. In the Info window (which has now switched to show you the info for the hard disk), find the amount "Available." If you don't have enough free hard disk space, a message will alert you.

4 You must first set a Master password. Keep in mind that once you set a Master password, you can never get rid of it. *If you forget your login password and you also forget the Master password, everything in your Home folder is lost forever.*

   To set a Master password:

   a From the Apple menu, choose "System Preferences...."

   b Single-click the "Security" icon to get the Security pane shown on the opposite page. Click the "FileVault" tab.

   c Read the warning! Then click "Set Master Password...," enter your password and hint, and click OK.

5   Now click the button "Turn On FileVault…."

6   Read the warning! If this is what you really want, click the OK button.
    It may take a few minutes. Your Mac will log itself back into this account
    and FileVault will be on. Close the Security preferences window.

Laptop Precautions

One out of ten laptops in this country gets stolen, which means about 600,000 a
year. They get stolen not only for the hardware, but more and more often for the
valuable personal data that is stored on them. So it's particularly imperative that if
your laptop does happen to get stolen or lost, that the data inside of it is as safe as
possible. Here are a few features (most from this chapter) to take advantage of.

- Use a password to log in. Do not set auto-login for your laptop.

- Set a firmware password; see page 428. It prevents someone from booting
  your computer with another disk.

- Password-protect the screen saver and sleep so if the screen saver turns on
  or the Mac goes to sleep, you need a password to get back in.

- Turn on FileVault (but never forget its password!). When your machine is off
  or sleeping, all of your data in the Home folder is encrypted until you enter
  the password to start working again. This is the strongest protection you can
  have for the data itself on your laptop (but be careful using FileVault!).

- There are devices you can buy that can alert you to when your Mac is moving
  away from you. And services you can subscribe to that can track the stolen
  computer as soon as a person logs on to the Internet with it. Search the web
  for laptop security devices and services.

24

GOALS

Understand whether
to upgrade, archive,
or clean install

Become familiar with the
utilities available from
the startup disk

Use Migration Assistant
to move user accounts
and files to a new Mac

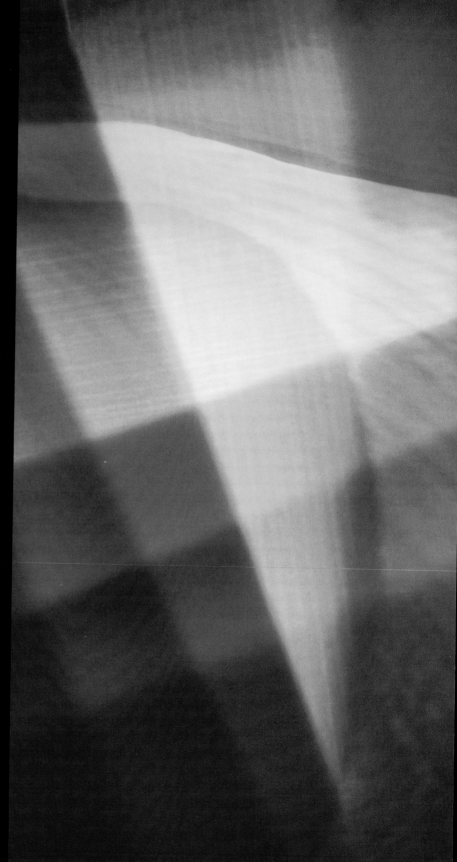

Upgrade your Mac and Migrate your Files

You may have just gotten a brand-new Mac with Snow Leopard already installed, in which case you can skip this chapter altogether, unless you need to learn about transferring your files from an old machine to your new one.

If you upgrade using a Snow Leopard installation disc, Mac OS X version 10.6, the installer presents you with a few choices to make before you upgrade. This chapter explains the choices you will need to make along the way, and provides some tips for migrating user accounts and files from one Mac to another.

Remember, before you do anything serious like upgrade your operating system, first back up your important files. The easiest thing to do is drag your entire hard disk onto an external hard disk. Always create at least two backups and store them in different places—it won't do any good if all your important backups are in the same office that gets burglarized or flooded!

> *Remember, ALWAYS before upgrading or installing, make BACKUPS of your important files. If you don't have the install disks for certain applications or fonts, back them up to disks before you upgrade or install!*

Upgrade to Snow Leopard

To install Snow Leopard, your Mac must have an Intel processor.

If Leopard, Mac OS X 10.5, is already installed on your Mac, you can use the $29 upgrade disc to upgrade to Snow Leopard. Just insert the disc, double-click the "Install Mac OS X.app" icon (shown below) and follow the directions. If you have a MacBook Air (with no optical drive for an install disc), see "Remote Install" on page 433.

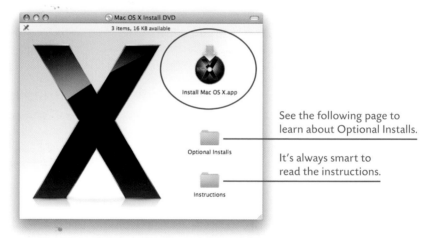

See the following page to learn about Optional Installs.

It's always smart to read the instructions.

Optional clean install

To ensure a pristine computer environment, some people like to completely erase the hard disk before installing Snow Leopard. This is called a **clean install.** It ensures that you don't inherit any little corruptions and problems that might have been occurring in your previous operating system. Of course, in the case of a clean install, first make sure all important information, applications, and files are backed up to another disk. Once everything is backed up, follow these steps:

1   Click the "Install" icon (circled above).

2   Click the "Utilities…" button that appears in the bottom-left corner of the next window that opens.

3   When the Snow Leopard "Welcome" window appears, a menu bar across the
    top of the screen also appears. From the "Utilities" menu in the menu bar,
    choose "Disk Utility."

4   Select your hard disk, listed in the left sidebar of the Disk Utility window,
    then click the "Erase" tab to show the Erase options.

5   Click the "Erase…" button. After the disk has been erased, the installation
    process continues.

Optional installs

When you open the install disk (shown on the previous page), notice the folder
named **Optional Installs.** It contains an installer that lets you select individual
applications, fonts, languages, etc., that need to be reinstalled, or installed for the
first time. In general, everything you need will be installed automatically when you
install Snow Leopard: you may never need to open this folder, but it's here in case
you need it.

For instance, Snow Leopard automatically installs QuickTime Player X. Even though
QuickTime Player X is better than ever, you might still want to use some feature that
was included with QuickTime 7.

To custom install QuickTime 7, or any of the other custom install items:

1   Double-click the "Optional Installs" folder (shown on the previous page) to
    open the window shown below, then double-click the "Optional Installs.mpkg"
    icon (circled below).

2   In the Welcome window that opens, click "Continue."

3   In the license agreement window that opens, click "Agree."

4   Select a destination for the installed item.

5   In the Custom Install window that opens, check the QuickTime 7 item in
    the custom installs list, then click "Continue."

6   Click the "Install" button.

Take Advantage of the Utilities in the Installer

When you run the upgrade or installer and get to the first screen, you'll see a menu item called "Utilities." This menu gives you access to a number of troubleshooting features on your Mac. If you like, you can stop here before installing Snow Leopard and use the Disk Utility to partition your Mac (divide it into several drives; only do this if you know why you are doing it).

All of the utilities mentioned below, except "Reset Password," are in your Utilities folder, which is in your Applications folder. You don't need to use the Install disk to access them. **But if your Mac has totally crashed** and you can't get anywhere at all, insert the original Snow Leopard install or upgrade DVD, then restart your Mac. Immediately hold down the C key to make sure it boots from the DVD. *Do not click any of the installation buttons,* but use the tools that are available here.

From the Utilities menu, choose the appropriate tool:

- **Startup Disk:** Choose which disk you want your Mac to check first when starting up. Only disks that contain operating systems can be used as startup disks.

- **Reset Password:** Here you can reset not only the Administrator password, but the passwords for every user on the Mac. You do not need to know the original passwords to set new ones.

- **Firmware Password Utility:** This option prevents others from starting your computer with a different disk. If someone stole your laptop, this won't get it back for you, but setting this password does make it much more difficult for anyone to log in and get your data. Write down the password!

- **Disk Utility:** Select your hard disk and use the "First Aid" pane to see if anything's wrong with the hard disk. The "Repair Disk Permissions" feature has solved some odd problems for our Macs. This is where you can partition the hard disk before you install.

- **Terminal:** The Terminal lets you use UNIX commands to do all sorts of things. If you don't know anything about UNIX or how to use the Terminal, skip this altogether.

- **System Profiler:** The System Profiler tells you all the gory details about your Mac, the CPU type, the audio, what kinds of devices are attached to your Mac, the speed of everything you can think of, and oh so much more. It will even tell you the serial number of the computer. This information also available at your Desktop: Go to the Apple menu, choose "About This Mac," and click the button labeled "More Info...."

■ **Network Utility:** This utility has a number of great tools. If you know what it means to finger someone, ping your modem, run a lookup or a port scan, or when to use whois, then you'll have fun with this utility. It's also in your Utilities folder (which is in the Applications folder) in case you need it.

■ **Restore System From Backup:** This utility uses Time Machine, which is a big clue that it can't restore the system from a backup until you've first put it all on Time Machine (see Lesson 20). But once you've done that, you can use this option.

Do you Now Own Two Macs? Migrate!

If you have important information on another Mac (a different computer from the one you're installing Snow Leopard onto) or a partition or volume on the new Mac, you can transfer the information from the older machine, partition, or volume to this new Mac. You'll use a feature called **migrating** and the **Target Disk Mode.**

You can either use the Setup Assistant during the Snow Leopard installation, or at any time in the future—use the **Migration Assistant** (it's in the Utilities folder, which is in the Applications folder)t; the instructions on screen are easy to follow. You can migrate the files from the Administrator (main user), from any individual user, or from both. The information on the old Mac or partition is not affected at all.

Migration Assistant

The migration process can automatically transfer:

■ Network and computer settings.

■ User accounts, preferences, and email.

■ Documents and other files.

■ Applications.

Some applications, however, will need to be reinstalled from their original disks because they install necessary files in different system folders. All you can do is transfer them, then open them and see if they work. The more expensive and complex an application, the less likely it will transfer perfectly.

—continued

Requirements for the Migration Assistant

The old Mac must:

- Be running Mac OS X version 10.1 or above.
- Have a built-in FireWire port.
- Support "Target Disk Mode." Apple says that "most do."

You'll also need:

- A standard FireWire cable long enough to reach between the two computers. Or temporarily move the computers closer so they can connect via the cable.
- An Administrator name and password (unless you're doing this during the Snow Leopard installation).

Be aware that:

- This process will tie up both your Macs for hours!
- This process will *not* automatically migrate songs that you bought from the **iTunes Store.** If you want to migrate *all* of your songs, including those you bought at the iTunes Store, you must first deauthorize the old Mac before you migrate files:

    1   Open iTunes on your old Mac.

    2   From the Store menu, choose "Deauthorize Computer...."

    3   Enter your account and password. Click the button to "Deauthorize," then click OK.

    4   To deauthorize any Audible content (books) so you can migrate them over to the new machine, go to the "Advanced" menu and choose "Deauthorize Audible Account...." You'll need your Audible.com name and password.

    Be careful with your **iPod**—if iTunes on your new Mac has no music in it when you plug in your iPod, everything on your iPod could be erased to match your empty iTunes!

Migrate additional users

At any time you can migrate additional users and their files from other computers. Just follow the directions on the previous pages.

You can also use **FireWire Target Disk Mode** at any time to transfer files from one Mac to another; see page 408. This technique is especially useful if one Mac is dying, because in Target Disk Mode, the target computer does not use its operating system—it acts like a plain ol' hard disk that shows up as a disk icon on the Desktop of your healthy computer.

What to do after migrating

It's a good idea to do a quick check of the files on your new Mac after migrating. Open every application to make sure it works okay—make a quick file and try to save it. If an application doesn't work, you will just have to reinstall it from the original disks.

Open sample files by double-clicking them to make sure they can open in the correct application and that their fonts appear correctly.

Connect to the Internet, check your mail, and take a peek at your System Preferences to make sure things are really how you like them.

TIP —— Do not unplug the FireWire cable before you unmount the icon of your old Mac from your new Mac running Snow Leopard! Even though it's "hot swappable," which means you don't have to shut down before you unplug, it's still possible to lose data if you unplug it while the icon is still visible on the screen.

Find the hard disk icon of your old Mac on the Desktop of the Snow Leopard computer. Drag it to the Trash before you unplug the FireWire cable.

Other Ways to Transfer Files from Mac to Mac

The migration process can take quite a long time because it gathers up thousands of files. If you want to transfer just selected files, you might want to consider these other options. Some you can do before you install Snow Leopard; others are new techniques that can only be accomplished in Snow Leopard (or Leopard).

Use an external disk

Use an external hard disk with a USB or FireWire connection. It's worth it to buy one just for this process. Copy the files onto the disk as you usually would from your old machine (drag them from the hard disk of your old Mac onto the disk icon). Then connect the drive to the new machine and copy them onto your hard disk.

If you have a *very* old Mac (one without a FireWire or USB port), the trouble, of course, is finding drives that work with both the old Mac and the new one, or finding software on that old Mac that will still run on the new computer.

Burn a CD or DVD

If your old machine can burn a CD or a DVD, you can transfer quite a few files by burning disks and moving them to the new machine. Plus you'll have ready-made backups (always the smart thing to do).

Send attachments in email

If you don't have huge files, send them as attachments through email. It's kind of funny to send your files around the world to get to the machine sitting two feet away.

Use your MobileMe account

If you have a MobileMe account, put the files from your old Mac onto your iDisk (see www.MobileMe.com). On your new Mac, download them from your iDisk. Also take advantage of syncing your Macs through MobileMe—a terrific option.

Send files through the network

If both machines are on the same network, connect the two computers and copy files directly from one to the other through a variety of methods, including the Bonjour buddy list in iChat. See Lesson 21 for all the details. It's really easy and you'll love knowing how to do it.

Use a FireWire cable

Connect a FireWire cable between two Macs. The other Mac will appear in the "Shared" group in the sidebar of a Finder window. You will probably be able to screen share (see pages 392–396). Or at least you can connect to each other and easily move files back and forth (see Lesson 21). Also look at the FireWire Target Disk Mode option; see page 408.

Remote Install

If you have a MacBook Air, there's no optical drive in which to insert a Snow Leopard install disc. But, there's still a way to do it. One solution is to buy an external USB optical drive from Apple and connect it to your MacBook Air. This is an easy solution, and the drive is barely larger than a DVD disc.

Another solution is to use the optical drive on another computer and install Snow Leopard over a local wireless network.

To install Snow Leopard on an Intel Mac that doesn't have an optical drive, go to an Intel Mac that has an optical drive, open the Utilities folder (inside the Applications folder), and double-click "Remote Install Mac OS X.app." Follow the on-screen directions.

You can also use Remote Install Mac OS X to use Disk Utility (for computer repairs) or some other utility DVD designed for repairs and troubleshooting.

The End **Matters**

Mini-Glossary ❧ *Most words are defined as we use them. Please see the index!*

active window

The *active window* is the one that is in front of everything else and is selected. You can tell if a window is active because the three little buttons in the top-left corner are in color, and the title bar icon is not dimmed. It's important to become aware at all times of which window is active because that is the window that will accept any command. For instance, if you press Command Shift N to create a new folder, that new folder will appear in the *active* Finder window (or on the Desktop, if the Desktop is active). If you press Command W in just about any application or in the Finder, it will close the active window. **To make any window active** (or the Desktop), single-click on it.

alias

An *alias* is a "go-fer"—it goes for things and gets them for you. It's nothing all by itself; it's merely a representative icon (only 2K or 3K in file size) that is *linked* to the original. You double-click the alias and it goes and gets the real thing and opens the real thing for you. The advantage of this is that you can put aliases in multiple places for easy access; in fact, you can have as many aliases of an item as you

Methinks I scent the
morning air

want. Some applications cannot open properly if you move them out of their folders, but if you make an alias of that application, you can put it anywhere.

An alias icon has a visual clue, a tiny arrow in the bottom-left corner of the icon (shown below-left) so you know it's a go-fer.

You can throw away an alias and it does not affect the original at all. You can move an original or rename the original or the alias and everything still works fine.

To make an alias, select a file; press Command L. *Or* hold down the Command and Options keys and drag the file into another folder or onto the Desktop. As you drag, you'll see the tiny alias arrow that tells you that you are indeed dragging to create an alias.

colored labels

To *color-code* a file, Control-click on it and choose a "Color Label" from the menu that pops up. Once a file is color-coded, you can search for it by its label, organize your files, etc.

To change the names of the labels, use the Finder preferences: Go to the Finder menu and choose "Preferences...." Click the "Labels" menu and change the names. For more details, please see page 268, and check the index for "color labels." This is a great organizational tool.

default

A default is something the Mac has chosen for you, until you make your own choice. For instance, TextEdit must have a font chosen to type in, so your Mac chooses one for you. A default window view is chosen for you. But you can at any time change just about anything to something of your own choice.

extension

A *file extension* refers to the short code at the end of a file name. It might be from two to six letters. This extension tells the Mac what to do with that file.

ApplePro Tip of the Week.webloc

The extension, .webloc, tells the Mac this is a web page location.

You might not see the extensions. If you like to have them visible all the time, go to the Finder preferences (from the Finder menu, choose "Preferences…"). Click on the "Advanced" tab. Put a check in the box to "Show all filename extensions."

To show the extensions temporarily or to check to see what the extension is for a particular file, use the Info window (explained in the next column). You'll see an option to see "Name & Extension" information that tells you what kind of file it is, and lets you hide or show the extension for that selected file.

Do not add or change the extensions yourself! The Mac has become very fussy about these extensions and you run the risk that the file will not open if you change its extension without knowing what you are doing.

Info window

The *Info window,* as shown on pages 335 and 353, has a secret **Inspector** mode: If you select a file and press Command I, the Info window appears *for that one particular file.*

But if you select a file and press Command Option I, you get the *Inspector* window, which looks exactly like the Info window *except* the Inspector window changes depending on what you click. That is, if you display the info for one file, then select another file (single-click on another file), the content of the Inspector changes to display info for that next file. Try it.

You can also open the Inspector with a contextual menu: Control-click on a file, then hold the Option key down and you'll see "Get Info" change to "Show Inspector."

screenshots

To make different kinds of *screenshots* (pictures of the screen), use these shortcuts:

Full screen: Command Shift 3

Selection: Command Shift 4, then let go. Use the target cursor that appears to select the area you want to capture as an image: just press in one spot and drag to another spot, to capture the image inside of this invisible box.

Window: Command Shift 4, then let go. Tap the Spacebar and a camera icon appears. As you move the camera icon over different windows, even those that are hidden, you'll see that window highlight. Click on the one you want an image of.

> *The above screenshots land on your Desktop labeled "Picture 1," "Picture 2," etc. They are in the PNG file format.*

Selection you can paste: Press Command Shift 4 and the target cursor appears. Hold down the Control key and drag to select the area, which *copies* that screenshot image. Now you can paste the screenshot somewhere else.

string

A *string* is simply a line of characters that you type. If someone tells you to "enter a search string," all it means is to enter the words you want to search for.

Symbols

Each key has a **symbol** by which it is known. These are the keyboard symbols you will see in menus and charts:

⇧	**Shift**	↻	**Escape (esc)**
⌘	**Command**	⇞ ⇟	**Page Up or Page Down**
⌥	**Option**	⌫	**Delete**
^	**Control**	↑↓←→	**Arrow keys**
↩	**Return**	⌤	**Enter**
⏏	**Eject**		

Index

A

W

Colophon

We wrote and designed and indexed and produced
this book directly in Adobe InDesign on a Mac. The
fonts used are Warnock Pro for body copy (9.5/14)
and Today for the heads, subheads, and captions.